Christianity and Culture

by T. S. Eliot

T. S. Eliot was born in St. Louis in 1888 and educated at Harvard, the Sorbonne, and at Merton College, Oxford. Although his first poems were published as early as 1909, it was not until the appearance of *Prufrock and Other Observations* in 1917 that his verse began to receive general recognition. Harvard, Princeton, and Yale are among the many universities which have conferred honorary degrees upon him, and in 1948 he received the Nobel Prize, as well as one of the British Empire's highest awards, the Order of Merit.

Christianity and Culture

The Idea of a Christian Society
AND
Notes towards the Definition of Culture

BY T. S. Eliot

A Harvest/HBJ Book
Harcourt Brace Jovanovich, Publishers
San Diego   New York   London

Contents

Christianity and
Culture

Preface

THE three lectures which, with some revision and division, are here printed, were delivered in March 1939 at the invitation of the Master and Fellows of Corpus Christi College, Cambridge, on the Boutwood Foundation. I wish to express my thanks to the Master and Fellows for this honour and privilege. The notes I have added while preparing the lectures for press.

My point of departure has been the suspicion that the current terms in which we discuss international affairs and political theory may only tend to conceal from us the real issues of contemporary civilisation. As I have chosen to consider such a large problem, it should be obvious that the following pages can have but little importance by themselves, and that they can only be of use if taken as an individual contribution to a discussion which must occupy many minds for a long time to come. To aim at originality would be an impertinence: at most, this essay can be only an original arrangement of ideas which did not belong to me before and which must become the property of whoever can use them. I owe a great deal to conversations with certain friends whose minds are engrossed by these and similar problems: to make specific acknowledgement might have the effect of imputing to these friends an inconvenient responsibility for my own faults of reasoning. But I owe a great deal also to a number of recent books: for instance, to Mr. Christopher Dawson's *Beyond Politics*, to Mr. Middleton Murry's *The Price of Leadership,* and to writings of the Revd. V. A. Demant (whose *Religious Prospect*

has appeared too recently for me to have made use of it). And
I am deeply indebted to the works of Jacques Maritain, especially his *Humanisme intégral.*

I trust that the reader will understand from the beginning
that this book does not make any plea for a "religious revival"
in a sense with which we are already familiar. That is a task
for which I am incompetent, and the term seems to me to
imply a possible separation of religious feeling from religious
thinking which I do not accept—or which I do not find acceptable for our present difficulties. An anonymous writer has
recently observed in *The New English Weekly* (July 13, 1939)
that

> "men have lived by spiritual institutions (of some kind) in every
> society, and also by political institutions and, indubitably, by eco-
> nomic activities. Admittedly, they have, at different periods, tended
> to put their trust mainly in one of the three as the real cement of
> society, but at no time have they wholly excluded the others, because
> it is impossible to do so."

This is an important, and in its context valuable, distinction; but it should be clear that what I am concerned with
here is not spiritual institutions in their separated aspect, but
the organisation of values, and a direction of religious thought
which must inevitably proceed to a criticism of political and
economic systems.

T HE fact that a problem will certainly take a long time to solve, and that it will demand the attention of many minds for several generations, is no justification for postponing the study. And, in times of emergency, it may prove in the long run that the problems we have postponed or ignored, rather than those we have failed to attack successfully, will return to plague us. Our difficulties of the moment must always be dealt with somehow: but our permanent difficulties are difficulties of every moment. The subject with which I am concerned in the following pages is one to which I am convinced we ought to turn our attention now, if we hope ever to be relieved of the immediate perplexities that fill our minds. It is urgent because it is fundamental; and its urgency is the reason for a person like myself attempting to address, on a subject beyond his usual scope, that public which is likely to read what he writes on other subjects. This is a subject which I could, no doubt, handle much better were I a profound scholar in any of several fields. But I am not writing for scholars, but for people like myself; some defects may be compensated by some advantages; and what one must be judged by, scholar or no, is not particularised knowledge but one's total harvest of thinking, feeling, living and observing human beings.

While the practice of poetry need not in itself confer wisdom or accumulate knowledge, it ought at least to train the mind in one habit of universal value: that of analysing the meanings of words: of those that one employs oneself, as well as the words of others. In using the term "Idea" of a Christian Society I do not mean primarily a concept derived from the study of any societies which we may choose to call Christian; I mean something that can only be found in an understanding of the end to which a Christian Society, to deserve the name, must be directed. I do not limit the application of the term to a perfected Christian Society on earth; and I do not comprehend in it societies merely because some profession of Christian faith, or some vestige of Christian practice, is retained. My concern with contemporary society, accordingly, will not be primarily with specific defects, abuses or injustices but with the question, what—if any—is the "idea" of the society in which we live? to what end is it arranged?

The Idea of a Christian Society is one which we can accept or reject; but if we are to accept it, we must treat Christianity with a great deal more *intellectual* respect than is our wont; we must treat it as being for the individual a matter primarily of thought and not of feeling. The consequences of such an attitude are too serious to be acceptable to everybody: for when the Christian faith is not only felt, but thought, it has practical results which may be inconvenient. For to see the Christian faith in this way—and to see it in this way is not necessarily to accept it, but only to understand the real issues —is to see that the difference between the Idea of a Neutral Society (which is that of the society in which we live at present) and the Idea of a Pagan Society (such as the upholders of democracy abominate) is, in the long run, of minor importance. I am not at this moment concerned with the means for bringing a Christian Society into existence; I am not even primarily concerned with making it appear desirable; but I am very much concerned with making clear its difference from the kind of society in which we are now living. Now, to understand the society in which he lives, must be to the interest of every conscious thinking person. The current terms in which we describe our society, the contrasts with other societies by which we—of the "Western Democracies"—eulogise it, only operate to deceive and stupefy us. To speak of ourselves as a Christian Society, in contrast to that of Germany or Russia, is an abuse of terms. We mean only that we have a society in which no one is penalised for the *formal profession* of Christianity; but we conceal from ourselves the unpleasant knowledge of the real values by which we live. We conceal from ourselves, moreover, the similarity of our society to those which we execrate: for we should have to admit, if we recognised the similarity, that the foreigners do better. I suspect that in our loathing of totalitarianism, there is infused a good deal of admiration for its efficiency.

The political philosopher of the present time, even when he is a Christian himself, is not usually concerned with the possible structure of a Christian state. He is occupied with the possibility of a just State in general, and when he is not an adherent of one or another secular system, is inclined to accept our present system as one to be improved, but not fundamentally altered. Theological writers have more to say that is relevant to my subject. I am not alluding to those writers who endeavour to infuse a vague, and sometimes debased, Christian spirit into the ordinary conduct of affairs; or to those who endeavour, at moments of emergency, to apply Christian principles to particular political situations. Relevant to my subject are the writings of the Christian sociologists—those writers who criticise our economic system in the light of Christian ethics. Their work consists in proclaiming in general, and demonstrating in particular, the incompatibility of Christian principle and a great deal of our social practice. They appeal to the spirit of justice and humanity with which most of us profess to be inspired; they appeal also to the practical reason, by demonstrating that much in our system is not only iniquitous, but in the long run unworkable and conducive to disaster. Many of the changes which such writers advocate, while deducible from Christian principles, can recommend themselves to any intelligent and disinterested person, and do not require a Christian society to carry them into effect, or Christian belief to render them acceptable: though they are changes which would make it more possible for the individual Christian to live out his Christianity. I am here concerned only secondarily with the changes in economic organisation, and only secondarily with the life of the devout Christian: my primary interest is a change in our social attitude, such a change only as could bring about anything worthy to be called a Christian Society. That such a change would compel changes in our organisation of industry and commerce and financial credit, that it would facilitate, where it now impedes, the life of devotion for those who are capable of it, I feel certain. But my point of departure is different from that of the sociologists and economists; though I depend upon them for enlightenment, and a test of my Christian Society would be that it should bring about such reforms as they propose; and though the kind of "change of spirit" which can testify for itself by nothing better than a new revivalistic vocabulary, is a danger against which we must be always on guard.

My subject touches also upon that of another class of Christian writer: that of the ecclesiastical controversialists. The subject of Church and State is, again, not my primary concern. It is not, except at moments which lend themselves to newspaper exploitation, a subject in which the general public takes much interest; and at the moments when the public's interest is aroused, the public is never well enough informed to have the right to an opinion. My subject is a preliminary to the problem of Church and State: it involves that problem in its widest terms and in its most general interest. A usual attitude is to take for granted the existing State, and ask "What Church?" But before we consider what should be the relation of Church and State, we should first ask: "What State?" Is there any sense in which we can speak of a "Christian State," any sense in which the State can be regarded as Christian? for even if the nature of the State be such, that we cannot speak of it in its Idea as either Christian or non-Christian, yet is it obvious that actual States may vary to such an extent that the relation of the Church to the State may be anything from overt hostility to a more or less harmonious co-operation of different institutions in the same society. What I mean by the Christian State is not any particular political form, but whatever State is suitable to a Christian Society, whatever State a particular Christian Society develops for itself. Many Christians there are, I know, who do not believe that a Church in relation to the State is necessary for a Christian Society; and I shall have to give reasons, in later pages, for believing that it is. The point to be made at this stage is that neither the classical English treaties on Church and State, nor contemporary discussion of the subject, give me the assistance that I need. For the earlier treatises, and indeed all up to the present time, assume the existence of a Christian Society; modern writers sometimes assume that what we have is a pagan society: and it is just these assumptions that I wish to question.

Your opinion of what can be done for this country in the future, and incidentally your opinion of what ought to be the relations of Church and State, will depend upon the view you take of the contemporary situation. We can abstract three positive historical points: that at which Christians are a new minority in a society of positive pagan traditions—a position which cannot recur within any future with which we are concerned; the point at which the whole society can be called Christian, whether in one body or in a prior or subsequent stage of division into sects; and finally the point at which practising Christians must be recognised as a minority (whether static or diminishing) in a society which has ceased to be Christian. Have we reached the third point? Different observers will give different reports; but I would remark that there are two points of view for two contexts. The first is that a society has ceased to be Christian when religious practices have been abandoned, when behaviour ceases to be regulated by reference to Christian principle, and when in effect prosperity in this world for the individual or for the group has become the sole conscious aim. The other point of view, which is less readily apprehended, is that a society has not ceased to be Christian until it has become positively something else. It is my contention that we have today a culture which is mainly negative, but which, so far as it is positive, is still Christian. I do not think that it can remain negative, because a negative culture has ceased to be efficient in a world where economic as well as spiritual forces are proving the efficiency of cultures which, even when pagan, are positive; and I believe that the choice before us is between the formation of a new Christian culture, and the acceptance of a pagan one. Both involve radical changes; but I believe that the majority of us, if we could be faced immediately with all the changes which will only be accomplished in several generations, would prefer Christianity.

I do not expect everyone to agree that our present organisation and temper of society—which proved, in its way, highly successful during the nineteenth century—is "negative": many will maintain that British, French and American civilisation still stands integrally for something positive. And there are others who will insist, that if our culture is negative, then a negative culture is the right thing to have. There are two distinct arguments to be employed in rebuttal: one, an argument of principle, that such a culture is undesirable; the other, a judgment of fact, that it must disappear anyway. The defenders of the present order fail to perceive either how far it is vestigial of a positive Christianity, or how far it has already advanced towards something else.

There is one class of persons to which one speaks with difficulty, and another to which one speaks in vain. The second, more numerous and obstinate than may at first appear, because it represents a state of mind into which we are all prone through natural sloth to relapse, consists of those people who cannot believe that things will ever be very different from what they are at the moment. From time to time, under the influence perhaps of some persuasive writer or speaker, they may have an instant of disquiet or hope; but an invincible sluggishness of imagination makes them go on behaving as if nothing would ever change. Those to whom one speaks with difficulty, but not perhaps in vain, are the persons who believe that great changes must come, but are not sure either of what is inevitable, or of what is probable, or of what is desirable.

What the Western world has stood for—and by that I mean the terms to which it has attributed sanctity—is "Liberalism" and "Democracy." The two terms are not identical or inseparable. The term "Liberalism" is the more obviously ambiguous, and is now less in favour; but the term "Democracy" is at the height of its popularity. When a term has become so universally sanctified as "democracy" now is, I begin to wonder whether it means anything, in meaning too many things: it has arrived perhaps at the position of a Merovingian Emperor, and wherever it is invoked, one begins to look for the Major of the Palace. Some persons have gone so far as to affirm, as something self-evident, that democracy is the only régime compatible with Christianity; on the other hand, the word is not abandoned by sympathisers with the government of Germany. If anybody ever attacked democracy, I might discover what the word meant. Certainly there is a sense in which Britain and America are more democratic than Germany; but on the other hand, defenders of the totalitarian system can make out a plausible case for maintaining that what we have is not democracy, but financial oligarchy.

Mr. Christopher Dawson considers that "what the non-dictatorial States stand for today is not Liberalism but Democracy," and goes on to foretell the advent in these States of a kind of totalitarian democracy. I agree with his prediction, but if one is considering, not merely the non-dictatorial States, but the societies to which they belong, his statement does less than justice to the extent to which Liberalism still permeates our minds and affects our attitude towards much of life. That Liberalism may be a tendency towards something very different from itself, is a possibility in its nature. For it is something which tends to release energy rather than accumulate it, to relax, rather than to fortify. It is a movement not so much defined by its end, as by its starting point; away from, rather than towards, something definite. Our point of departure is more real to us than our destination; and the destination is likely to present a very different picture when arrived at, from the vaguer image formed in imagination. By destroying traditional social habits of the people, by dissolving their natural collective consciousness into individual constituents, by licensing the opinions of the most foolish, by substituting instruction for education, by encouraging cleverness rather than wisdom, the upstart rather than the qualified, by fostering a notion of *getting on* to which the alternative is a hopeless apathy, Liberalism can prepare the way for that which is its own negation: the artificial, mechanised or brutalised control which is a desperate remedy for its chaos.

It must be evident that I am speaking of Liberalism in a sense much wider than any which can be fully exemplified by the history of any political party, and equally in a wider sense than any in which it has been used in ecclesiastical controversy. True, the tendency of Liberalism can be more clearly illustrated in religious history than in politics, where principle is more diluted by necessity, where observation is more confused by detail and distracted by reforms each valid within its own limited reference. In religion, Liberalism may be characterised as a progressive discarding of elements in historical Christianity which appear superfluous or obsolete, confounded with practices and abuses which are legitimate objects of attack. But as its movement is controlled rather by its origin than by any goal, it loses force after a series of rejections, and with nothing to destroy is left with nothing to uphold and with nowhere to go. With religious Liberalism, however, I am no more specifically concerned than with political Liberalism: I am concerned with a state of mind which, in certain circumstances, can become universal and infect opponents as well as defenders. And I shall have expressed myself very ill if I give the impression that I think of Liberalism as something simply to be rejected and extirpated, as an evil for which there is a simple alternative. It is a necessary negative element; when I have said the worst of it, that worst comes only to this, that a negative element made to serve the purpose of a positive is objectionable. In the sense in which Liberalism is contrasted with Conservatism, both can be equally repellant: if the former can mean chaos, the latter can mean petrifaction. We are always faced both with the question "what must be destroyed?" and with the question "what must be preserved?" and neither Liberalism nor Conservatism, which are not philosophies and may be merely habits, is enough to guide us.

In the nineteenth century the Liberal Party had its own conservatism, and the Conservative Party had its own liberalism; neither had a political philosophy. To hold a political philosophy is in fact not the function of a political, that is, a Parliamentary party: a party with a political philosophy is a revolutionary party. The politics of political parties is not my concern. Nor am I concerned with the politics of a revolutionary party. If a revolutionary party attains its true end, its political philosophy will, by a process of growth, become that of a whole culture; if it attains its more facile end, its political philosophy will be that of a dominant class or group, in a society in which the majority will be passive, and the minority oppressed. But a political philosophy is not merely a formalised system set forth by a theorist. The permanent value of such treaties as Aristotle's *Politics* and *Poetics* is found at the opposite extreme to anything that we can call *doctrinaire*. Just as his views on dramatic poetry were derived from a study of the existing works of Attic drama, so his political theory was founded on a perception of the unconscious aims implicit in Athenian democracy at its best. His limitations are the condition of his universality; and instead of ingenious theories spun out of his head, he wrote studies full of universal wisdom. Thus, what I mean by a political philosophy is not merely even the conscious formulation of the ideal aims of a people, but the substratum of collective temperament, ways of behaviour and unconscious values which provides the material for the formulation. What we are seeking is not a programme for a party, but a way of life for a people: it is this which totalitarianism has sought partly to revive, and partly to impose by force upon its peoples. Our choice now is not between one abstract form and another, but between a pagan, and necessarily stunted culture, and a religious, and necessarily imperfect culture.

The attitudes and beliefs of Liberalism are destined to disappear, are already disappearing. They belong to an age of free exploitation which has passed; and our danger now is, that the term may come to signify for us only the disorder the fruits of which we inherit, and not the permanent value of the negative element. Out of Liberalism itself come philosophies which deny it. We do not proceed, from Liberalism to its apparent end of authoritarian democracy, at a uniform pace in every respect. There are so many centres of it—Britain, France, America and the Dominions—that the development of Western society must proceed more slowly than that of a compact body like Germany, and its tendencies are less apparent. Furthermore, those who are the most convinced of the necessity of *étatisme* as a control of some activities of life, can be the loudest professors of libertarianism in others, and insist upon the preserves of "private life" in which each man may obey his own convictions or follow his own whim: while imperceptibly this domain of "private life" becomes smaller and smaller, and may eventually disappear altogether. It is possible that a wave of terror of the consequences of depopulation might lead to legislation having the effect of compulsory breeding.

If, then, Liberalism disappears from the philosophy of life of a people, what positive is left? We are left only with the term "democracy," a term which, for the present generation, still has a Liberal connotation of "freedom." But totalitarianism can retain the terms "freedom" and "democracy" and give them its own meaning: and its right to them is not so easily disproved as minds inflamed by passion suppose. We are in danger of finding ourselves with nothing to stand for except a *dislike* of everything maintained by Germany and/or Russia: a dislike which, being a compost of newspaper sensations and prejudice, can have two results, at the same time, which appear at first incompatible. It may lead us to reject possible improvements, because we should owe them to the example of one or both of these countries; and it may equally well lead us to be mere imitators *à rebours,* in making us adopt uncritically almost any attitude which a foreign nation rejects.

We are living at present in a kind of doldrums between opposing winds of doctrine, in a period in which one political philosophy has lost its cogency for behaviour, though it is still the only one in which public speech can be framed. This is very bad for the English language: it is this disorder (for which we are all to blame) and not individual insincerity, which is responsible for the hollowness of many political and ecclesiastical utterances. You have only to examine the mass of newspaper leading articles, the mass of political exhortation, to appreciate the fact that good prose cannot be written by a people without convictions. The fundamental objection to fascist doctrine, the one which we conceal from ourselves because it might condemn ourselves as well, is that it is pagan.

There are other objections too, in the political and economic sphere, but they are not objections that we can make with dignity until we set our own affairs in order. There are still other objections, to oppression and violence and cruelty, but however strongly we feel, these are objections to means and not to ends. It is true that we sometimes use the word "pagan," and in the same context refer to ourselves as "Christian." But we always dodge the real issue. Our newspapers have done all they could with the red herring of the "German national religion," an eccentricity which is after all no odder than some cults held in Anglo-Saxon countries: this "German national religion" is comforting in that it persuades us that *we* have a Christian civilisation; it helps to disguise the fact that our aims, like Germany's, are materialistic. And the last thing we should like to do would be to examine the "Christianity" which, in such contexts as this, we say we keep.

If we have got so far as accepting the belief that the only alternative to a progressive and insidious adaptation to totalitarian worldliness for which the pace is already set, is to aim at a Christian society, we need to consider both what kind of a society we have at this time, and what a Christian society would be like. We should also be quite sure of what we want: if your real ideals are those of materialistic efficiency, then the sooner you know your own mind, and face the consequences, the better. Those who, either complacently or despairingly, suppose that the aim of Christianisation is chimerical, I am not here attempting to convert. To those who realise what a well-organised pagan society would mean for us, there is nothing to say. But it is as well to remember that the imposition of a pagan theory of the State does not necessarily mean a wholly pagan society. A compromise between the theory of the State and the tradition of society exists in Italy, a country which is still mainly agricultural and Catholic. The more highly industrialised the country, the more easily a materialistic philosophy will flourish in it, and the more deadly that philosophy will be. Britain has been highly industrialised longer than any other country. And the tendency of un-limited industrialism is to create bodies of men and women—of all classes—detached from tradition, alienated from re-ligion and susceptible to mass suggestion: in other words, a mob. And a mob will be no less a mob if it is well fed, well clothed, well housed, and well disciplined.

The Liberal notion that religion was a matter of pri-vate belief and of conduct in private life, and that there is no reason why Christians should not be able to accommodate themselves to any world which treats them good-naturedly, is becoming less and less tenable. This notion would seem to have become accepted gradually, as a false inference from the subdivision of English Christianity into sects, and the happy results of universal toleration. The reason why members of different communions have been able to rub along together, is that in the greater part of the ordinary business of life they have shared the same assumptions about behaviour. When they have been wrong, they have been wrong together. We have less excuse than our ancestors for un-Christian con-duct, because the growth of an un-Christian society about us, its more obvious intrusion upon our lives, has been breaking down the comfortable distinction between public and private morality. The problem of leading a Christian life in a non-Christian society is now very present to us, and it is a very different problem from that of the accommodation between an Established Church and dissenters. It is not merely the problem of a minority in a society of *individuals* holding an alien belief. It is the problem constituted by our implication in a network of institutions from which we cannot dissociate ourselves: institutions the operation of which appears no longer neutral, but non-Christian. And as for the Christian who is not conscious of his dilemma—and he is in the ma-

jority—he is becoming more and more de-Christianised by all
sorts of unconscious pressure: paganism holds all the most
valuable advertising space. Anything like Christian traditions
transmitted from generation to generation within the family
must disappear, and the small body of Christians will consist
entirely of adult recruits. I am saying nothing at this point
that has not been said before by others, but it is relevant. I
am not concerned with the problem of Christians as a perse-
cuted minority. When the Christian is treated as an enemy of
the State, his course is very much harder, but it is simpler. I
am concerned with the dangers to the tolerated minority; and
in the modern world, it may turn out that the most tolerable
thing for Christians is to be tolerated.

To attempt to make the prospect of a Christian society im
mediately attractive to those who see no prospect of deriving
direct personal benefit from it, would be idle; even the ma
jority of professing Christians may shrink from it. No scheme
for a change of society can be made to appear immediately
palatable, except by falsehood, until society has become so
desperate that it will accept any change. A Christian society
only becomes acceptable after you have fairly examined the
alternatives. We might, of course, merely sink into an apa-
thetic decline: without faith, and therefore without faith in
ourselves; without a philosophy of life, either Christian or
pagan; and without art. Or we might get a "totalitarian democracy," different but having much in common with other
pagan societies, because we shall have changed step by step
in order to keep pace with them: a state of affairs in which
we shall have regimentation and conformity, without respect
for the needs of the individual soul; the puritanism of a hygienic morality in the interest of efficiency; uniformity of opinion through propaganda, and art only encouraged when it
flatters the official doctrines of the time. To those who can
imagine, and are therefore repelled by, such a prospect, one

can assert that the only possibility of control and balance is a religious control and balance; that the only hopeful course for a society which would thrive and continue its creative activity in the arts of civilisation, is to become Christian. That prospect involves, at least, discipline, inconvenience and discomfort: but here as hereafter the alternative to hell is purgatory.

MY thesis has been, simply, that a liberalised or negative condition of society must either proceed into a gradual decline of which we can see no end, or (whether as a result of catastrophe or not) reform itself into a positive shape which is likely to be effectively secular. We need not assume that this secularism will approximate closely to any system in the past or to any that can now be observed in order to be apprehensive about it: the Anglo-Saxons display a capacity for *diluting* their religion, probably in excess of that of any other race. But unless we are content with the prospect of one or the other of these issues, the only possibility left is that of a positive Christian society. The third will only commend itself to those who agree in their view of the present situation, and who can see that a thoroughgoing secularism would be objectionable, in its consequences, even to those who attach no positive importance to the survival of Christianity for its own sake.

I am not investigating the possible lines of action by which such a Christian society could be brought into being. I shall confine myself to a slight outline of what I conceive to be essential features of this society, bearing in mind that it can neither be mediaeval in form, nor be modelled on the seventeenth century or any previous age. In what sense, if any, can we speak of a "Christian State"? I would ask to be allowed to use the following working distinctions: the Christian State, the Christian Community, and the Community of Christians, as elements of the Christian Society.

I conceive then of the Christian State as of the Christian Society under the aspect of legislation, public administration, legal tradition, and form. Observe that at this point I am not approaching the problem of Church and State except with the question: with what kind of State can the Church have a relation? By this I mean a relation of the kind which has hitherto obtained in England; which is neither merely reciprocal tolerance, nor a Concordat. The latter seems to me merely a kind of compromise, of doubtful durability, resting on a dubious division of authority, and often a popular division of loyalty; a compromise which implies perhaps a hope on the part of the rulers of the State that their rule will outlast Christianity, and a faith on the part of the Church that it will survive any particular form of secular organisation. A relation between Church and State such as is, I think, implied in our use of the term, implies that the State is in some sense Christian. It must be clear that I do not mean by a Christian State one in which the rulers are chosen because of their qualifications, still less their eminence, as Christians. A regiment of Saints is apt to be too uncomfortable to last. I do not deny that some advantages may accrue from persons in authority, in a Christian State, being Christians. Even in the present conditions, that sometimes happens; but even if, in the present conditions, *all* persons in positions of the highest authority were devout and orthodox Christians, we should not expect to see very much difference in the conduct of affairs. The Christian and the unbeliever do not, and cannot, behave very differently in the exercise of office; for it is the general ethos of the people they have to govern, not their own piety, that determines the behaviour of politicians. One may even accept F. S. Oliver's affirmation—following Buelow, following Disraeli—that real statesmen are inspired by nothing else than their instinct for power and their love of country. It is not primarily the Christianity of the statesmen that matters, but their being confined, by the temper and traditions of the people which they rule, to a Christian framework within which to realise their ambitions and advance the prosperity and prestige of their country. They may frequently perform un-Christian acts; they must never attempt to defend their actions on un-Christian principles.

The rulers and would-be rulers of modern states may be divided into three kinds, in a classification which cuts across the division of fascism, communism and democracy. There are such as have taken over or adapted some philosophy, as of Marx or Aquinas. There are those who, combining invention with eclecticism, have devised their own philosophy—not usually distinguished by either the profundity or the consistency one expects of a philosophy of life—and there are those who pursue their tasks without appearing to have any philosophy at all. I should not expect the rulers of a Christian State to be philosophers, or to be able to keep before their minds at every moment of decision the maxim that the life of virtue is the purpose of human society—*virtuosa . . . vita est congregationis humanae finis;* but they would neither be self-educated, nor have been submitted in their youth merely to that system of miscellaneous or specialised instruction which passes for education: they would have received a Christian education. The purpose of a Christian education would not be merely to make men and women pious Christians: a system which aimed too rigidly at this end alone would become only obscurantist. A Christian education would primarily train people to be able to think in Christian categories, though it could not compel belief and would not impose the necessity for insincere profession of belief. What the rulers believed, would be less important than the beliefs to which they would be obliged to conform. And a skeptical or indifferent statesman, working within a Christian frame, might be more effective than a devout Christian statesman obliged to conform to a secular frame. For he would be required to design his policy for the government of a Christian Society.

The relation of the Christian State, the Christian Community, and the Community of Christians, may be looked at in connexion with the problem of *belief*. Among the men of state, you would have as a minimum, conscious conformity of behaviour. In the Christian Community that they ruled, the Christian faith would be ingrained, but it requires, as a minimum, only a largely unconscious behaviour; and it is only from the much smaller number of conscious human beings, the Community of Christians, that one would expect a conscious Christian life on its highest social level.

For the great mass of humanity whose attention is occupied mostly by their direct relation to the soil, or the sea, or the machine, and to a small number of persons, pleasures and duties, two conditions are required. The first is that, as their capacity for *thinking* about the objects of faith is small, their Christianity may be almost wholly realised in behaviour: both in their customary and periodic religious observances, and in a traditional code of behaviour towards their neighbours. The second is that, while they should have some perception of how far their lives fall short of Christian ideals, their religious and social life should form for them a natural whole, so that the difficulty of behaving as Christians should not impose an intolerable strain. These two conditions are really the same differently stated; they are far from being realised today.

The traditional unit of the Christian Community in England is the parish. I am not here concerned with the problem of how radically this system must be modified to suit a future state of things. The parish is certainly in decay, from several causes of which the least cogent is the division into sects: a much more important reason is urbanisation—in which I am including also *sub*-urbanisation, and all the causes and effects of urbanisation. How far the parish must be superseded will depend largely upon our view of the necessity of accepting the causes which tend to destroy it. In any case, the parish will serve my purpose as an example of community unit. For this unit must not be solely religious, and not solely social; nor should the individual be a member of two separate, or even overlapping units, one religious and the other social. The unitary community should be religious-social, and it must be one in which all classes, if you have classes, have their centre of interest. That is a state of affairs which is no longer wholly realised except in very primitive tribes indeed.

It is a matter of concern not only in this country, but has been mentioned with concern by the late Supreme Pontiff, speaking not of one country but of all civilised countries, that the masses of the people have become increasingly alienated from Christianity. In an industrialised society like that of England, I am surprised that the people retains as much Christianity as it does. For the great majority of the people—and I am not here thinking of social classes, but of intellectual strata—religion must be primarily a matter of behaviour and habit, must be integrated with its social life, with its business and its pleasures; and the specifically religious emotions must be a kind of extension and sanctification of the domestic and social emotions. Even for the most highly developed and conscious individual, living in the world, a consciously Christian direction of thought and feeling can only occur at particular moments during the day and during the week, and these moments themselves recur in consequence of formed habits; to be conscious, without remission, of a Christian and a non-Christian alternative at moments of choice, imposes a very great strain. The mass of the population, in a Christian society, should not be exposed to a way of life in which there is too sharp and frequent a conflict between what is easy for them or what their circumstances dictate and what is Christian. The compulsion to live in such a way that Christian behaviour is only possible in a restricted number of situations, is a very powerful force against Christianity; for behaviour is as potent to affect belief, as belief to affect behaviour.

I am not presenting any idyllic picture of the rural parish, either present or past, in taking as a norm, the idea of a small and mostly self-contained group attached to the soil and having its interests centred in a particular place, with a kind of unity which may be designed, but which also has to grow through generations. It is the idea, or ideal, of a community small enough to consist of a nexus of direct personal relationships, in which all iniquities and turpitudes will take the simple and easily appreciable form of wrong relations between one person and another. But at present not even the smallest community, unless so primitive as to present objectionable features of another kind, is so simplified as this; and I am not advocating any complete reversion to any earlier state of things, real or idealised. The example appears to offer no solution to the problem of industrial, urban and suburban life which is that of the majority of the population. In its religious organisation, we may say that Christendom has remained fixed at the stage of development suitable to a simple agricultural and piscatorial society, and that modern material organisation —or if "organisation" sounds too complimentary, we will say "complication"—has produced a world for which Christian social forms are imperfectly adapted. Even if we agree on this point, there are two simplifications of the problem which are suspect. One is to insist that the only salvation for society is to return to a simpler mode of life, scrapping all the constructions of the modern world that we can bring ourselves to dispense with. This is an extreme statement of the neo-Ruskinian view, which was put forward with much vigour by the late A. J. Penty. When one considers the large amount of determination in social structure, this policy appears Utopian: if such a way of life ever comes to pass, it will be—as may well happen in the long run—from natural causes, and not from the moral will of men. The other alternative is to accept the modern world as it is and simply try to adapt Christian social ideals to it. The latter resolves itself into a mere doctrine of expediency; and is a surrender of the faith that Christianity itself can play any part in shaping social forms. And it does not require a Christian attitude to perceive that the modern system of society has a great deal in it that is inherently bad.

We now reach a point from which there is a course that I do not propose to take; and as it is an obvious course, and to some may appear to be the main thoroughfare, I ought to explain as briefly as I can why I do not propose to take it. We are accustomed to make the distinction (though in practice we are frequently confused) between the evil which is present in human nature at all times and in all circumstances, and the evil in particular institutions at particular times and places, and which, though attributable to some individuals rather than others, or traceable to the cumulative deflection of the wills of many individuals throughout several generations, cannot at any moment be fastened upon particular persons. If we make the mistake of assuming that this kind of evil results from causes wholly beyond the human will, then we are liable to believe that only other non-human causes can change it. But we are equally likely to take another line, and to place all our hopes in the replacement of our machinery. Nevertheless, the lines of thought, which I am doing no more than indicate, for the realisation of a Christian society, must lead us inevitably to face such problems as the hypertrophy of the motive of Profit into a social ideal, the distinction between the *use* of natural resources and their exploitation, the use of labour and its exploitation, the advantages unfairly accruing to the trader in contrast to the primary producer, the misdirection of the financial machine, the iniquity of usury, and other features of a commercialised society which must be scrutinised on Christian principles. In ignoring these problems, I am not taking refuge in a mere admission of incompetence, though the suspicion that I am incompetent might operate against the acceptance of any observations that I made; nor am I simply resigning them to the supposed technical authorities, for that would be a surrender of the primacy of ethics. My point is that, while there is a considerable measure of agreement that certain things are wrong, the question of how they should be put right is so extremely controversial, that any proposal is immediately countered by a dozen others; and in this context, attention would be concentrated on the imperfections of my proposals, and away from my main concern, the end to be attained. I confine myself therefore to the assertion, which I think few will dispute, that a great deal of the machinery of modern life is merely a sanction for un-Christian aims, that it is not only hostile to the conscious pursuit of the Christian life in the world by the few, but to the maintenance of any Christian society *of* the world. We must abandon the notion that the Christian should be content with freedom of cultus, and with suffering no worldly disabilities on account of his faith. However bigoted the announcement may sound, the Christian can be satisfied with nothing less than a Christian organisation of society—which is not the same thing as a society consisting exclusively of devout Christians. It would be a society in which the natural end of man—virtue and well-being in community—is acknowledged for all, and the supernatural end—beatitude—for those who have the eyes to see it.

I do not wish, however, to abandon my previous point, that a Christian community is one in which there is a unified religious-social code of behaviour. It should not be necessary for the ordinary individual to be wholly conscious of what elements are distinctly religious and Christian, and what are merely social and identified with his religion by no logical implication. I am not requiring that the community should contain more "good Christians" than one would expect to find under favourable conditions. The religious life of the people would be largely a matter of behaviour and conformity; social customs would take on religious sanctions; there would no doubt be many irrelevant accretions and local emphases and observances—which, if they went too far in eccentricity or superstition, it would be the business of the Church to correct, but which otherwise could make for social tenacity and coherence. The traditional way of life of the community would not be imposed by law, would have no sense of outward constraint, and would not be the result merely of the sum of individual belief and understanding.

The rulers, I have said, will, *qua* rulers, accept Christianity not simply as their own faith to guide their actions, but as the system under which they are to govern. The people will accept it as a matter of behaviour and habit. In the abstraction which I have erected, it is obvious that the tendency of the State is toward expediency that may become cynical manipulation, the tendency of the people toward intellectual lethargy and superstition. We need therefore what I have called "the Community of Christians," by which I mean, not local groups, and not the Church in any one of its senses, unless we call it "the Church within the Church." These will be the consciously and thoughtfully practising Christians, especially those of intellectual and spiritual superiority. It will be remarked at once that this category bears some resemblance to what Coleridge has called "the clerisy"—a term recently revived, and given a somewhat different application, by Mr. Middleton Murry. I think that my "Community of Christians" is somewhat different from either use of the term "clerisy." The content which Coleridge gave to the term, certainly, has been somewhat voided by time. You will remember that Coleridge included in the extension of meaning three classes: the universities and great schools of learning, the parochial pastorate, and the local schoolmasters. Coleridge's conception of the clerical function, and of its relation to education, was formed in a world that has since been strangely altered: his insistence that clergy should be "in the rule married men and heads of families" and his dark references to a foreign ecclesiastical power, now sound merely quaint; and he quite failed to recognise the enormous value which monastic orders can and should have in the community. The term which I use is meant to be at once wider and more restricted. In the field of education it is obvious that the conformity to Christian belief and the possession of Christian knowledge, can no longer be taken for granted; nor can the supremacy of the theologian be either expected or imposed in the same way. In any future Christian society that I can conceive, the educational system will be formed according to Christian presuppositions of what education—as distinct from mere instruction—is for; but the personnel will inevitably be mixed: one may even hope that the mixture may be a benefit to its intellectual vitality. The mixture will include persons of exceptional ability who may be indifferent or disbelieving; there will be room for a proportion of other persons professing other faiths than Christianity. The limitations imposed upon such persons would be similar to those imposed by social necessity upon the politician who, without being able to believe the Christian faith, yet has abilities to offer in the public service, with which his country could ill dispense.

It would be still more rash of me to embark upon a criticism of the contemporary ideals of education, than it is for me to venture to criticise politics; but it is not impertinent to remark upon the close relationship of educational theory and political theory. One would indeed be surprised to find the educational system and the political system of any country in complete disaccord; and what I have said about the negative character of our political philosophy should suggest a parallel criticism of our education, not as it is found in practice here or there, but in the assumptions about the nature and purpose of education which tend to affect practice throughout the country. And I do not need to remind you that a pagan totalitarian government is hardly likely to leave education to look after itself, or to refrain from interfering with the traditional methods of the oldest institutions: of some of the results abroad of such interference on the most irrelevant grounds we are quite well aware. There is likely to be, everywhere, more and more pressure of circumstance towards adapting educational ideals to political ideals, and in the one as in the other sphere, we have only to choose between a higher and a lower rationalisation. In a Christian Society education must be religious, not in the sense that it will be administered by ecclesiastics, still less in the sense that it will exercise pressure, or attempt to instruct everyone in theology, but in the sense that its aims will be directed by a Christian philosophy of life. It will no longer be merely a term comprehending a variety of unrelated subjects undertaken for special purposes or for none at all.

My Community of Christians, then, in contrast to Coleridge's clerisy, could hardly include the whole of the teaching body. On the other hand, it would include, besides many of the laity engaged in various occupations, many, but not all, of the clergy. A national clergy must of course include individual priests of different intellectual types and levels; and, as I suggested before, belief has a vertical as well as a horizontal measurement: to answer fully the question "What does *A* believe?" one must know enough about *A* to have some notion of the level on which he is capable of believing anything. The Community of Christians—a body of very nebulous outline— would contain both clergy and laity of superior intellectual and/or spiritual gifts. And it would include some of those who are ordinarily spoken of, not always with flattering intention, as "intellectuals."

That culture and the cultivation of philosophy and the arts should be confined to the cloister would be a decline into a Dark Age that I shudder to contemplate; on the other hand, the segregation of lay "intellectuals" into a world of their own, which very few ecclesiastics or politicians either penetrate or have any curiosity about, is not a progressive situation either. A good deal of waste seems to me to occur through pure ignorance; a great deal of ingenuity is expended on half-baked philosophies, in the absence of any common background of knowledge. We write for our friends—most of whom are also writers—or for our pupils—most of whom are going to be writers; or we aim at a hypothetical popular audience which we do not know and which perhaps does not exist. The result, in any case, is apt to be a refined provincial crudity. What are the most fruitful social conditions for the production of works of the first order, philosophical, literary or in the other arts, is perhaps one of those topics of controversy more suitable for conversation than for writing about. There may perhaps be no one set of conditions most suitable for the efflorescence of all these activities; it is equally possible that the necessary conditions may vary from one country and civilisation to another. The régime of Louis XIV or of the Tudors and Stuarts could hardly be called libertarian; on the other hand, the rule of authoritarian governments in our time does not appear conducive to a renascence of the arts. Whether the arts flourish best in a period of growth and expansion, or in one of decay, is a question that I cannot answer. A strong and even tyrannous government may do no harm, so long as the sphere of its control is strictly limited; so long as it limits itself to restricting the liberties, without attempting to influence the minds, of its subjects; but a régime of unlimited demagogy appears to be stultifying. I must restrict my consideration to the position of the arts in our present society, and to what it should be in such a future society as I envisage.

It may be that the conditions unfavourable to the arts today lie too deep and are too extensive to depend upon the differences between one form of government and another; so that the prospect before us is either of slow continuous decay or of sudden extinction. You cannot, in any scheme for the reformation of society, aim directly at a condition in which the arts will flourish: these activities are probably by-products for which we cannot deliberately arrange the conditions. On the other hand, their decay may always be taken as a symptom of some social ailment to be investigated. The future of art and

thought in a democratic society does not appear any brighter
than any other, unless democracy is to mean something very
different from anything actual. It is not that I would defend
a moral censorship: I have always expressed strong objections
to the suppression of books possessing, or even laying claim to
literary merit. But what is more insidious than any censorship, is the steady influence which operates silently in any
mass society organised for profit, for the depression of standards of art and culture. The increasing organisation of advertisement and propaganda—or the influencing of masses of
men by any means except through their intelligence—is all
against them. The economic system is against them; the chaos
of ideals and confusion of thought in our large scale mass
education is against them; and against them also is the disappearance of any class of people who recognise public and
private responsibility of patronage of the best that is made and
written. At a period in which each nation has less and less
"culture" for its own consumption, all are making furious
efforts to export their culture, to impress upon each other their
achievements in arts which they are ceasing to cultivate or
understand. And just as those who should be the intellectuals
regard theology as a special study, like numismatics or her-
aldry, with which they need not concern themselves, and theologians observe the same indifference to literature and art,
as special studies which do not concern *them,* so our political
classes regard both fields as territories of which they have no
reason to be ashamed of remaining in complete ignorance.
Accordingly the more serious authors have a limited, and even
provincial audience, and the more popular write for an il-
literate and uncritical mob.

You cannot expect continuity and coherence in politics, you
cannot expect reliable behaviour on fixed principles persisting
through changed situations, unless there is an underlying political philosophy: not of a party, but of the nation. You cannot expect continuity and coherence in literature and the arts,

unless you have a certain uniformity of culture, expressed in education by a settled, though not rigid agreement as to what everyone should know to some degree, and a positive distinction—however undemocratic it may sound—between the educated and the uneducated. I observed in America, that with a very high level of intelligence among undergraduates, progress was impeded by the fact that one could never assume that any two, unless they had been at the same school under the influence of the same masters at the same moment, had studied the same subjects or read the same books, though the number of subjects in which they had been instructed was surprising. Even with a smaller amount of total information, it might have been better if they had read fewer, but the same books. In a negative liberal society you have no agreement as to there being any body of knowledge which any educated person should have acquired at any particular stage: the idea of wisdom disappears, and you get sporadic and unrelated experimentation. A nation's system of education is much more important than its system of government; only a proper system of education can unify the active and the contemplative life, action and speculation, politics and the arts. But "education," said Coleridge, "is to be reformed, and defined as synonymous with instruction." This revolution has been effected: to the populace education *means* instruction. The next step to be taken by the clericalism of secularism, is the inculcation of the political principles approved by the party in power.

I may seem to have wandered from my course, but it seemed necessary to mention the capital responsibility of education in the condition which we find or anticipate: a state secularised, a community turned into a mob, and a clerisy disintegrated. The obvious secularist solution for muddle is to subordinate everything to political power: and in so far as this involves the subordination of the money-making interests to those of the nation as a whole, it offers some immediate, though perhaps illusory relief: a people feels at least more dignified if its hero is the statesman however unscrupulous, or the warrior however brutal, rather than the financier. But it also means the confinement of the clergy to a more and more restricted field of activity, the subduing of free intellectual speculation, and the debauching of the arts by political criteria. It is only in a society with a religious basis—which is not the same thing as an ecclesiastical despotism—that you can get the proper harmony and tension, for the individual or for the community.

In any Christian society which can be imagined for the future—in what M. Maritain calls a *pluralist* society—my "Community of Christians" cannot be a body of the definite vocational outline of the "clerisy" of Coleridge: which, viewed in a hundred years' perspective, appears to approximate to the rigidity of a caste. The Community of Christians is not an organisation, but a body of indefinite outline; composed of both clergy and laity, of the more conscious, more spiritually and intellectually developed of both. It will be their identity of belief and aspiration, their background of a common system of education and a common culture, which will enable them to influence and be influenced by each other, and collectively to form the conscious mind and the conscience of the nation.

The Spirit descends in different ways, and I cannot foresee any future society in which we could classify Christians and non-Christians simply by their professions of belief, or even, by any rigid code, by their behaviour. In the present ubiquity of ignorance, one cannot but suspect that many who call themselves Christians do not understand what the word means, and that some who would vigorously repudiate Christianity are more Christian than many who maintain it. And perhaps there will always be individuals who, with great creative gifts of value to mankind, and the sensibility which such gifts imply, will yet remain blind, indifferent, or even hostile. That must not disqualify them from exercising the talents they have been given.

The foregoing sketch of a Christian society, from which are omitted many details that will be considered essential, could not stand even as a rough sketch—an *ébauche*—without some treatment, according to the same economy, of the relation of Church and State in such a society. So far, nothing has suggested the existence of an organised Church at all. But the State would remain under the necessity of respecting Christian principles, only so far as the habits and feelings of the people were not too suddenly affronted or too violently outraged, or so far as it was deterred by any univocal protest of the most influential of the Community of Christians. The State is Christian only negatively; its Christianity is a reflection of the Christianity of the society which it governs. We have no safeguard against its proceeding, from un-Christian acts, to action on implicitly un-Christian principles, and thence to action on avowedly un-Christian principles. We have no safeguard for the purity of our Christianity; for, as the State may pass from expediency to lack of principle, and as the Christian Community may sink into torpor, so the Community of Christians may be debilitated by group or individual eccentricity and error. So far, we have only a society such that it can have a significant relation to a Church; a relationship which is not of hostility or even of accommodation. And this relation is so important that without discussing it we have not even shown the assembled skeleton of a Christian Society, we have only exposed the unarticulated bones.

I HAVE spoken of this essay as being, in one aspect, a kind of preface to the problem of Church and State; it is as well, at this point, to indicate its prefatorial limitations The problem is one of concern to every Christian country— that is, to every possible form of Christian society. It will take a different form according to the traditions of that society— Roman, Orthodox, or Lutheran. It will take still another form in those countries, obviously the United States of America and the Dominions, where the variety of races and religious communions represented appears to render the problem insoluble. Indeed, for these latter countries the problem might not appear even to exist: these countries might appear to be committed from their origin to a neutral form of society. I am not ignoring the possibility of a neutral society, under such conditions, persisting indefinitely. But I believe that if these countries are to develop a positive culture of their own, and not remain merely derivatives of Europe, they can only proceed either in the direction of a pagan or of a Christian society. I am not suggesting that the latter alternative must lead to the forcible suppression, or to the complete disappearance of dissident sects; still less, I hope, to a superficial union of Churches under an official exterior, a union in which theological differences would be so belittled that its Christianity might become wholly bogus. But a positive culture must have a positive set of values, and the dissentients must remain marginal, tending to make only marginal contributions.

However dissimilar the local conditions, therefore, this ques-

tion of Church and State is of importance everywhere. Its
actuality in Europe may make it appear all the more remote
in America, just as its actuality in England raises a number of
considerations remote to the rest of Europe. But if what I say
in the following pages has its direct application only in England, it is not because I am thinking of local matters without
relation to Christendom as a whole. It is partly that I can
only discuss profitably the situations with which I am most
familiar, and partly that a more generalised consideration
would appear to deal only with figments and fancies. I have
therefore limited my field to the possibility of a Christian society in England, and in speaking of Church and State it is
the Anglican Church that I have in mind. But it must be
remembered that such terms as "Establishment" and "Established Church" can have a wider meaning than we ordinarily
give them. On the other hand, I only mean such a Church as
can claim to represent the traditional form of Christian belief
and worship of the great mass of people of a particular
country.

If my outline of a Christian society has commanded the
assent of the reader, he will agree that such a society can only
be realised when the great majority of the sheep belong to
one fold. To those who maintain that unity is a matter of indifference, to those who maintain even that a diversity of theological views is a good thing to an indefinite degree, I can
make no appeal. But if the desirability of unity be admitted,
if the idea of a Christian society be grasped and accepted, then
it can only be realised, in England, through the Church of
England. This is not the place for discussing the theological
position of that Church: if in any points it is wrong, inconsistent, or evasive, these are matters for reform within the
Church. And I am not overlooking the possibility and hope of
eventual reunion or reintegration, on one side and another;
I am only affirming that it is this Church which, by reason of
its tradition, its organisation, and its relation in the past to

the religious-social life of the people, is the one for our purpose—and that no Christianisation of England can take place
without it.

The Church of a Christian society, then, should have some
relation to the three elements in a Christian society that I
have named. It must have a hierarchical organisation in direct
and official relation to the State: in which relation it is always
in danger of sinking into a mere department of State. It must
have an organisation, such as the parochial system, in direct
contact with the smallest units of the community and their
individual members. And finally, it must have, in the persons
of its more intellectual, scholarly and devout officers, its masters of ascetic theology and its men of wider interests, a relation to the Community of Christians. In matters of dogma,
matters of faith and morals, it will speak as the final authority
within the nation; in more mixed questions it will speak
through individuals. At times, it can and should be in conflict
with the State, in rebuking derelictions in policy, or in defending itself against encroachments of the temporal power,
or in shielding the community against tyranny and asserting
its neglected rights, or in contesting heretical opinion or im-
moral legislation and administration. At times, the hierarchy
of the Church may be under attack from the Community of
Christians, or from groups within it: for any organisation is
always in danger of corruption and in need of reform from
within.

Although I am not here concerned with the means by which
a Christian society could be brought about, it is necessary always to consider the idea in relation to particular existing
societies; because one does not expect or desire that its constitution would be identical in all Christian countries. I do not
assume that the relation of Church and State in England,
either as it is or as it might be, is a model for all other communities. Whether an "Establishment" is the best relation in
the abstract, is nowhere my question. Were there no Estab-

lishment in England, we should have to examine its desirability. But as we have the Establishment, we must take the situation as we find it, and consider for a moment the merits of the problem of Disestablishment. The advocates of this course, within the Church, have many cogent reasons to expose: the abuses and scandals which such a change might remedy, the inconsistencies which might be removed, and the advantages which might accrue, are too patent to require mention. That abuses and defects of another kind might make their appearance in a disestablished Church, is a possibility which has not perhaps received enough attention. But what is much more to my point is the gravity of the abdication which the Church—whether voluntarily or under pressure— would be making. Setting aside the anomalies which might be corrected without going to that length, I will admit that an Established Church is exposed to peculiar temptations and compulsions: it has greater advantages and greater difficulties. But we must pause to reflect that a Church, once disestablished, cannot easily be re-established, and that the very act of disestablishment separates it more definitely and irrevocably from the life of the nation than if it had never been established. The effect on the mind of the people of the visible and dramatic withdrawal of the Church from the affairs of the nation, of the deliberate recognition of two standards and ways of life, of the Church's abandonment of all those who are not by their wholehearted profession within the fold—this is incalculable; the risks are so great that such an act can be nothing but a desperate measure. It appears to assume something which I am not yet ready to take for granted: that the division between Christians and non-Christians in this country is already, or is determined to become, so clear that it can be reduced to statistics. But if one believes, as I do, that the great majority of people are neither one thing nor the other, but are living in a no man's land, then the situation looks very different; and disestablishment instead of being the *recogni-*

tion of a condition at which we have arrived, would be the *creation* of a condition the results of which we cannot foresee.

With the reform of the Establishment I am not here concerned: the discussion of that requires a familiarity with constitutional, canon, and civil law. But I do not think that the argument from the prosperity of the disestablished Church of Wales, sometimes brought forward by advocates of disestablishment, is to the point. Apart from the differences of racial temperament which must be taken into account, the full effect of disestablishment cannot be seen from the illustration of a small part of the island; and, if disestablishment were made general, the full effect would not appear at once. And I think that the tendency of the time is opposed to the view that the religious and the secular life of the individual and the community can form two separate and autonomous domains. I know that a theology of the absolute separation of the life of the Spirit and the life of the World has spread from Germany. Such a doctrine appears more plausible, when the Church's position is wholly defensive, when it is subject to daily persecution, when its spiritual claims are questioned and when its immediate necessity is to keep itself alive and to keep its doctrine pure. But this theology is incompatible with the assumptions underlying everything that I have been saying. The increasing complexity of modern life renders it unacceptable, for, as I have already said, we are faced with vital problems arising not merely out of the necessity of cooperating with non-Christians, but out of our unescapable implication in non-Christian institutions and systems. And finally, the totalitarian tendency is against it, for the tendency of totalitarianism is to re-affirm, on a lower level, the religious-social nature of society. And I am convinced that you cannot have a national Christian society, a religious-social community, a society with a political philosophy founded upon the Christian faith, if it is constituted as a mere congeries of private and independent sects. The national faith must have an official recognition by the

State, as well as an accepted status in the community and a basis of conviction in the heart of the individual.

Heresy is often defined as an insistence upon one half of the truth; it can also be an attempt to simplify the truth, by reducing it to the limits of our ordinary understanding, instead of enlarging our reason to the apprehension of truth. Monotheism or tritheism is easier to grasp than trinitarianism. We have observed the lamentable results of the attempt to isolate the Church from the World; there are also instances of the failure of the attempt to integrate the World in the Church; we must also be on guard against the attempt to integrate the Church in the World. A permanent danger of an established Church is Erastianism: we do not need to refer to the eighteenth century, or to prewar Russia, to remind ourselves of that. Deplorable as such a situation is, it is not so much the immediate and manifest scandals but the ultimate consequences of Erastianism that are the most serious offences. By alienating the mass of the people from orthodox Christianity, by leading them to identify the Church with the actual hierarchy and to suspect it of being an instrument of oligarchy or class, it leaves men's minds exposed to varieties of irresponsible and irreflective enthusiasm followed by a second crop of paganism.

The danger of a National Church becoming a class Church, is not one that concerns us immediately today; for now that it is possible to be respectable without being a member of the Church of England, or a Christian of any kind, it is also possible to be a member of the Church of England without being —in that sense—respectable. The danger that a National Church might become also a nationalistic Church is one to which our predecessors theorising about Church and State could hardly have been expected to devote attention, since the danger of nationalism itself, and the danger of the supersession of every form of Christianity, could not have been very present to their minds. Yet the danger was always there:

and, for some persons still, Rome is associated with the Armada and Kingsley's *Westward Ho!* For a National Church tends to reflect only the religious-social habits of the nation; and its members, in so far as they are isolated from the Christian communities of other nations, may tend to lose all criteria by which to distinguish, in their own religious-social complex, between what is universal and what is local, accidental, and erratic. Within limits, the cultus of the universal Church may quite properly vary according to the racial temperaments and cultural traditions of each nation. Roman Catholicism is not quite the same thing (to the eye of the sociologist, if not to that of the theologian) in Spain, France, Ireland and the United States of America, and but for central authority it would differ much more widely. The tendency to differ may be as strong among bodies of the same communion in different countries, as among various sects within the same country; and, indeed, the sects within one country may be expected to show traits in common, which none of them will share with the same communion abroad.

The evils of nationalistic Christianity have, in the past, been mitigated by the relative weakness of national consciousness and the strength of Christian tradition. They have not been wholly absent: missionaries have sometimes been accused of propagating (through ignorance, not through cunning) the customs and attitudes of the social groups to which they have belonged, rather than giving the natives the essentials of the Christian faith in such a way that they might harmonise their own culture with it. On the other hand, I think that some events during the last twenty-five years have led to an increasing recognition of the supra-national Christian society: for if that is not marked by such conferences as those of Lausanne, Stockholm, Oxford, Edinburgh—and also Malines—then I do not know of what use these conferences have been. The purpose of the labours involved in arranging intercommunion between the official Churches of certain countries is not merely to provide reciprocal sacramental advantages for travellers, but to affirm the Universal Church on earth. Certainly, no one today can defend the idea of a National Church, without balancing it with the idea of the Universal Church, and without keeping in mind that truth is one and that theology has no frontiers.

I think that the dangers to which a National Church is exposed, when the Universal Church is no more than a pious ideal, are so obvious that only to mention them is to command assent. Completely identified with a particular people, the National Church may at all times, but especially at moments of excitement, become no more than the voice of that people's prejudice, passion or interest. But there is another danger, not quite so easily identified. I have maintained that the idea of a Christian society implies, for me, the existence of one Church which shall *aim at* comprehending the whole nation. Unless it has this aim, we relapse into that conflict between citizenship and church-membership, between public and private morality, which today makes moral life so difficult for everyone, and which in turn provokes that craving for a simplified, monistic solution of statism or racism which the National Church can only combat if it recognises its position as a part of the Universal Church. But if we allowed ourselves to entertain for Europe (to confine our attention to that continent) the ideal merely of a kind of society of Christian societies, we might tend unconsciously to treat the idea of the Universal Church as only the idea of a supernatural League of Nations. The direct allegiance of the individual would be to his National Church alone, and the Universal Church would remain an abstraction or become a cockpit for conflicting national interests. But the difference between the Universal Church and a perfected League of Nations is this, that the allegiance of the individual to his own Church is secondary to his allegiance to the Universal Church. Unless the National Church is a part of the whole, it has no claim upon me: but a League

of Nations which could have a claim upon the devotion of the
individual, prior to the claim of his country, is a chimaera
which very few persons can even have endeavoured to picture
to themselves. I have spoken more than once of the intolerable
position of those who try to lead a Christian life in a non-
Christian world. But it must be kept in mind that even in
a Christian society as well organised as we can conceive possible in this world, the limit would be that our temporal and
spiritual life should be harmonised: the temporal and spiritual
would never be identified. There would always remain a dual
allegiance, to the State and to the Church, to one's country-
men and to one's fellow-Christians everywhere, and the latter
would always have the primacy. There would always be a
tension; and this tension is essential to the idea of a Christian
society, and is a distinguishing mark between a Christian and
a pagan society.

IT SHOULD be obvious that the form of political organisation of a Christian State does not come within the scope of this discussion. To identify any particular form of government with Christianity is a dangerous error: for it confounds the permanent with the transitory, the absolute with the contingent. Forms of government, and of social organisation, are in constant process of change, and their operation may be very different from the theory which they are supposed to exemplify. A theory of the State may be, explicitly or implicitly, anti-Christian: it may arrogate rights which only the Church is entitled to claim, or pretend to decide moral questions on which only the Church is qualified to pronounce. On the other hand, a régime may in practice claim either more or less than it professes, and we have to examine its working as well as its constitution. We have no assurance that a democratic régime might not be as inimical to Christianity in practice, as another might be in theory: and the best government must be relative to the character and the stage of intelligence and education of a particular people in a particular place at a particular time. Those who consider that a discussion of the nature of a Christian society should conclude by supporting a particular form of political organisation, should ask themselves whether they really believe our form of government to be more important than our Christianity; and those who are convinced that the present form of government of Britain is the one most suitable for any Christian people, should ask themselves whether they are confusing a Christian society with a society in which individual Christianity is tolerated.

This essay is not intended to be either an anti-communist or an anti-fascist manifesto; the reader may by this time have forgotten what I said at the beginning, to the effect that I was less concerned with the more superficial, though important differences between the regimens of different nations, than with the more profound differences between pagan and Christian society. Our preoccupation with foreign politics during the last few years has induced a surface complacency rather than a consistent attempt at self-examination of conscience. Sometimes we are almost persuaded that we are getting on very nicely, with a reform here and a reform there, and would have been getting on still better, if only foreign governments did not insist upon breaking all the rules and playing what is really a different game. What is more depressing still is the thought that only fear or jealousy of foreign success can alarm us about the health of our own nation; that only through this anxiety can we see such things as depopulation, malnutrition, moral deterioration, the decay of agriculture, as evils at all. And what is worst of all is to advocate Christianity, not because it is true, but because it might be beneficial. Towards the end of 1938 we experienced a wave of revivalism which should teach us that folly is not the prerogative of any one political party or any one religious communion, and that hysteria is not the privilege of the uneducated. The Christianity expressed has been vague, the religious fervour has been a fervour for democracy. It may engender nothing better than a disguised and peculiarly sanctimonious nationalism, accelerating our progress towards the paganism which we say we abhor. To justify Christianity because it provides a foundation of morality, instead of showing the necessity of Christian morality from the truth of Christianity, is a very dangerous inversion; and we may reflect, that a good deal of the attention of totalitarian states has been devoted, with a steadiness of purpose not always found in democracies, to providing their national life with a foundation of morality—the wrong kind perhaps, but a good deal more of it. It is not enthusiasm, but dogma, that differentiates a Christian from a pagan society.

I have tried to restrict my ambition of a Christian society to a social minimum: to picture, not a society of saints, but of ordinary men, of men whose Christianity is communal before being individual. It is very easy for speculation on a possible Christian order in the future to tend to come to rest in a kind of apocalyptic vision of a golden age of virtue. But we have to remember that the Kingdom of Christ on earth will never be realised, and also that it is always being realised; we must remember that whatever reform or revolution we carry out, the result will always be a sordid travesty of what human society should be—though the world is never left wholly without glory. In such a society as I imagine, as in any that is not petrified, there will be innumerable seeds of decay. Any human scheme for society is realised only when the great mass of humanity has become adapted to it; but this adaptation becomes also, insensibly, an adaptation of the scheme itself to the mass on which it operates: the overwhelming pressure of mediocrity, sluggish and indomitable as a glacier, will mitigate the most violent, and depress the most exalted revolution, and what is realised is so unlike the end that enthusiasm conceived, that foresight would weaken the effort. A wholly Christian society might be a society for the most part on a low level; it would engage the cooperation of many whose Christianity was spectral or superstitious or feigned, and of many whose motives were primarily worldly and selfish. It would require constant reform.

I should not like it to be thought, however, that I considered the presence of the higher forms of devotional life to be a matter of minor importance for such a society. I have, it is true, insisted upon the communal, rather than the individual aspect: a community of men and women, not individually better than they are now, except for the capital difference of holding the Christian faith. But their holding the Christian faith would give them something else which they lack: a *respect* for the religious life, for the life of prayer and contemplation, and for those who attempt to practise it. In this I am asking no more of the British Christian, than is characteristic of the ordinary Moslem or Hindu. But the ordinary man would need the opportunity to know that the religious life existed, that it was given its due place, would need to recognise the profession of those who have abandoned the world, as he recognises the professions practised in it. I cannot conceive a Christian society without religious orders, even purely contemplative orders, even enclosed orders. And, incidentally, I should not like the "Community of Christians" of which I have spoken, to be thought of as merely the nicest, most intelligent and public-spirited of the upper middle class —it is not to be conceived on that analogy.

We may say that religion, as distinguished from modern paganism, implies a life in conformity with nature. It may be observed that the natural life and the supernatural life have a conformity to each other which neither has with the mechanistic life: but so far has our notion of what is natural become distorted, that people who consider it "unnatural" and therefore repugnant, that a person of either sex should elect a life of celibacy, consider it perfectly "natural" that families should be limited to one or two children. It would perhaps be more natural, as well as in better conformity with the Will of God, if there were more celibates and if those who were married had larger families. But I am thinking of "conformity to nature" in a wider sense than this. We are being made aware that the organisation of society on the principle of private profit, as well as public destruction, is leading both to the deformation of humanity by unregulated industrialism, and to the exhaustion of natural resources, and that a good deal of our material progress is a progress for which succeeding generations may have to pay dearly. I need only mention, as an instance now very much before the public eye, the results of "soil-erosion"—the exploitation of the earth, on a vast scale for two generations, for commercial profit: immediate benefits leading to dearth and desert. I would not have it thought that I condemn a society because of its material ruin, for that would be to make its material success a sufficient test of its excellence; I mean only that a wrong attitude towards nature implies, somewhere, a wrong attitude towards God, and that the consequence is an inevitable doom. For a long enough time we have believed in nothing but the values arising in a mechanised, commercialised, urbanised way of life: it would be as well for us to face the permanent conditions upon which God allows us to live upon this planet. And without sentimentalising the life of the savage, we might practise the humility to observe, in some of the societies upon which we look down as primitive or backward, the operation of a social-religious-artistic complex which we should emulate upon a higher plane. We have been accustomed to regard "progress" as always integral; and have yet to learn that it is only by an effort and a discipline, greater than society has yet seen the need of imposing upon itself, that material knowledge and power is gained without loss of spiritual knowledge and power. The struggle to recover the sense of relation to nature and to God, the recognition that even the most primitive feelings should be part of our heritage, seems to me to be the explanation and justification of the life of D. H. Lawrence, and the excuse for his aberrations. But we need not only to learn how to look at the world with the eyes of a Mexican Indian—and I hardly think that Lawrence succeeded—and we certainly cannot afford to stop there. We need to know how to see the world as the Christian Fathers saw it; and the purpose of re-ascending to origins is that we should be able to return, with greater spiritual knowledge, to our own situation. We need to recover the sense of religious fear, so that it may be overcome by religious hope.

I should not like to leave the reader supposing that I have attempted to contribute one more amateur sketch of an abstract and impracticable future: the blue-print from which the doctrinaire criticises the piecemeal day to day efforts of political men. These latter efforts have to go on; but unless we can find a pattern into which all problems of life can have their place, we are only likely to go on complicating chaos. So long, for instance, as we consider finance, industry, trade, agriculture merely as competing interests to be reconciled from time to time as best they may, so long as we consider "education" as a good in itself of which everyone has a right to the utmost, without any ideal of the good life for society or for the individual, we shall move from one uneasy compromise to another. To the quick and simple organisation of society for ends which, being only material and worldly, must be as ephemeral as worldly success, there is only one alternative. As political philosophy derives its sanction from ethics, and ethics from the truth of religion, it is only by returning to the eternal source of truth that we can hope for any social organisation which will not, to its ultimate destruction, ignore some essential aspect of reality. The term "democracy," as I have said again and again, does not contain enough positive content to stand alone against the forces that you dislike—it can easily be transformed by them. If you will not have God (and He is a jealous God) you should pay your respects to Hitler or Stalin.

I believe that there must be many persons who, like myself, were deeply shaken by the events of September 1938, in a way from which one does not recover; persons to whom that month brought a profounder realisation of a general plight. It was not a disturbance of the understanding: the events themselves were not surprising. Nor, as became increasingly evident, was our distress due merely to disagreement with the policy and behaviour of the moment. The feeling which was new and unexpected was a feeling of humiliation, which seemed to demand an act of personal contrition, of humility, repentance and amendment; what had happened was something in which one was deeply implicated and responsible. It was not, I repeat, a criticism of the government, but a doubt of the validity of a civilisation. We could not match conviction with conviction, we had no ideas with which we could either meet or oppose the ideas opposed to us. Was our society, which had always been so assured of its superiority and rectitude, so confident of its unexamined premises, assembled round anything more permanent than a congeries of banks, insurance companies and industries, and had it any beliefs more essential than a belief in compound interest and the maintenance of dividends? Such thoughts as these formed the starting point, and must remain the excuse, for saying what I have to say.

September 6th, 1939. The whole of this book, with Preface and Notes, was completed before it was known that we should be at war. But the possibility of war, which has now been realised, was always present to my mind, and the only additional observations which I feel called upon to make are these: first, that the alignment of forces which has now revealed itself should bring more clearly to our consciousness the alternative of Christianity or paganism; and, second, that we cannot afford to defer our constructive thinking to the conclusion of hostilities—a moment when, as we should know from experience, good counsel is liable to be obscured.

Notes

Page 6. In using the term "Idea" I have of course had in mind the definition given by Coleridge, when he lays down at the beginning of his *Church and State* that: "By an idea I mean (in this instance) that conception of a thing, which is not abstracted from any particular state, form or mode, in which the thing may happen to exist at this or that time; nor yet generalised from any number or succession of such forms or modes; but which is given by the knowledge of its ultimate aim."

P. 7. Christian sociologists. I am deeply indebted to several Christian economists and sociologists, both in England and elsewhere, and notably to R. H. Tawney. My difference of approach in these pages need not be further elaborated, but it is interesting to compare the treatment of the problem of Church and State by V. A. Demant in his very valuable *Christian Polity*, p. 120 ff. and p. 135 ff. Fr. Demant observes that the authority of the Church "cannot now be claimed on the ground that it represents all citizens." But while the Church does not represent all citizens in the sense in which a Member of Parliament may be said to "represent" his constituents, even those who vote consistently against him, yet its function seems to me wider than only to "safeguard the individual in his right to pursue certain purposes which are not political purposes"; what I am primarily concerned with throughout is not the responsibility of the Church towards the individual but towards the community. The relation of the Church with the State may be one of checks and balances, but the background and justification of this relation is the Church's relation to *Society*. Fr. Demant gives a very good account of the forces tending towards acceptance of the absolutist State, and remarks truly that: "This fact of the secularisation of human life does not arise mainly from the extension of the State's powers. This is rather the effort of the State to recover significance in the life of a people which has become disintegrated through the confusion of social means and ends which is its secularisation."

One of the causes of the totalitarian State is an effort of the State to supply a function which the Church has ceased to serve; to enter into a relation to the community which the Church has failed to maintain; which leads to the recognition as full citizens only of those who are prepared to accept it in this relation.

I agree cordially with Fr. Demant's observation that: "The fact which renders most of our theories of Church and State irrelevant is the domination of politics by economics and finance; and this is most true in democratic states. The subservience of politics to plutocracy is the main fact about the State confronting the Church today."

Fr. Demant is concerned with the reform of this situation, in a secular society; and with the right position of the Church in a secular society. But unless I have misunderstood him, he appears to me to take this secularisation for granted. Assuming that our present society is neutral rather than non-Christian, I am concerned with enquiring what it might be like if it took the Christian direction.

P. 15. "Totalitarianism can retain the terms 'freedom' and 'democracy' and give them its own meaning." A letter appeared in *The Times* (April 24, 1939) from General J. F. C. Fuller, who, as *The Times* had previously stated, was one of the two British visitors invited to Herr Hitler's birthday cele-

brations. General Fuller states that he is "a firm believer in
the democracy of Mazzini, because he places duty to the nation before individual rights." General Fuller calls himself a
"British Fascist," and believes that Britain "must swim with
the out-flowing tide of this great political change" (i.e. to a
fascist system of government).

From my point of view, General Fuller has as good a title
to call himself a "believer in democracy" as anyone else.

P. 15. Imitation *à rebours.* A column in the *Evening Standard* of May 10, 1939, headed *"Back to the Kitchen Creed De-
nounced,"* reported the annual conference of the Civil Service
Clerical Association.

"Miss Bower of the Ministry of Transport, who moved that
the association should take steps to obtain the removal of the
ban (i.e. against married women Civil Servants) said it was
wise to abolish an institution which embodied one of the
main tenets of the Nazi creed—the relegation of women to the
sphere of the kitchen, the children and the church."

The report, by its abbreviation, may do less than justice to
Miss Bower, but I do not think that I am unfair to the report, in finding the implication that what is Nazi is wrong,
and need not be discussed on its own merits. Incidentally, the
term "relegation of women" prejudices the issue. Might one
suggest that the kitchen, the children and the church could be
considered to have a claim upon the attention of married
women? or that no normal married woman would prefer to
be a wage-earner if she could help it? What is miserable is a
system that makes the dual wage necessary.

P. 15. Fascist doctrine. I mean only such doctrine as asserts
the absolute authority of the state, or the infallibility of a
ruler. "The corporative state," recommended by *Quadrigesimo
Anno,* is not in question. The economic organisation of to-

talitarian states is not in question. The ordinary person does not object to fascism because it is pagan, but because he is fearful of authority, even when it is pagan.

P. 16. The red herring of the German national religion. I cannot hold such a low opinion of German intelligence as to accept any stories of the revival of pre-Christian cults. I can, however, believe that the kind of religion expounded by Professor Wilhelm Hauer is really in existence—and I am very sorry to believe it. I rely upon the essay contributed by Dr. Hauer to a very interesting volume, *Germany's New Religion* (Allen and Unwin, 1937), in which orthodox Lutheranism is defended by Karl Heim, and Catholicism by Karl Adam.

The religion of Hauer is deistic, claiming to "worship a more than human God." He believes it to be "an eruption from the biological and spiritual depths of the German nation," and unless one is prepared to deny that the German nation has such depths, I do not see that the statement can be ridiculed. He believes that "each new age must mold its own religious forms"—alas, many persons in Anglo-Saxon countries hold the same belief. He professes himself to be particularly a disciple of Eckhart; and whether or not one believes that the doctrines condemned by the Church were what Eckhart strove to propagate, it is certainly the condemned doctrine that Hauer holds. He considers that the "revolt of the German from Christianity reached its culmination in Nietzsche": many people would not limit that revolt to the German. He advocates tolerance. He objects to Christianity because "it claims to possess the absolute truth, and with this claim is bound up the idea that men can only achieve salvation in one way, through Christ, and that it must send to the stake those whose faith and life do not conform, or pray for them till they quit the error of their ways for the kingdom of God." Thousands of people in Western countries would agree with this attitude

He objects to sacramental religion, because "everyone has an immediate relation to God, is, in fact, in the depths of his heart one with the eternal Ground of the world." Faith comes not from revelation but from "personal experience." He is not interested in "the mass of intellectuals," but in the "multitudes of ordinary people" who are looking for "Life." "We believe," he says, "that God has laid a great task on our nation, and that he has therefore revealed himself specially in its history and will continue to do so." To my ear, such phrases have a not altogether unfamiliar ring. Hauer believes also in something very popular in this country, the religion of the blue sky, the grass and flowers. He believes that Jesus (even if he was wholly Semitic on both sides) is one of the "great figures who soar above the centuries."

I have quoted so much, in order to let Professor Hauer declare himself for what he is: the end product of German Liberal Protestantism, a nationalistic Unitarian. Translated into English terms, he might be made to appear as simply a patriotic Modernist. The German National Religion, as Hauer expounds it, turns out to be something with which we are already familiar. So, if the German Religion is also your religion, the sooner you realise the fact the better.

P. 18. "Hygienic morality." M. Denis de Rougemont, in his remarkable book *L'Amour et l'occident,* has this sentence (p. 269) which is to the point: "L'anarchie des moeurs et l'hygiène autoritaire agissent à peu près dans le même sens: elles déçoivent le besoin de passion, héréditaire ou acquis par la culture; elles détendent ses ressorts intimes et personnels."

P. 18. It may be opportune at this point to say a word about the attitude of a Christian Society towards Pacifism. I am not concerned with rationalistic pacifism, or with humanitarian pacifism, but with Christian pacifism—that which asserts that all warfare is categorically forbidden to followers of Our Lord. This absolute Christian pacifism should be distinguished again from another: that which would assert that only a *Christian* society is worth fighting for, and that a particular society may fall so far short, or may be so positively anti-Christian, that no Christian will be justified or excused for fighting for it. With this relative Christian pacifism I cannot be concerned, because my hypothesis is that of a Christian Society. In such a society, what will be the place of the Christian pacifist?

Such a person would continue to exist, as sects and individual vagaries would probably continue to exist; and it would be the duty of the Christian who was not a pacifist to treat the pacifist with consideration and respect. It would also be the duty of the State to treat him with consideration and respect, having assured itself of his sincerity. The man who believes that a particular war in which his country proposes to engage is an aggressive war, who believes that his country could refuse to take part in it without its legitimate interests being imperilled, and without failing in its duty to God and its neighbours, would be wrong to remain silent (the attitude of the late Charles Eliot Norton in regard to the Spanish-American War of 1898 is to the point). But I cannot but believe that the man who maintains that war is in all circumstances wrong, is in some way repudiating an obligation towards society; and in so far as the society is a Christian society the obligation is so much the more serious. Even if each particular war proves in turn to have been unjustified, yet the idea of a Christian society seems incompatible with the idea of absolute pacifism; for pacifism can only continue to flourish so long as the majority of persons forming a society are not pacifists; just as sectarianism can only flourish against the background of orthodoxy. The notion of communal responsibility, of the responsibility of every individual for the sins of the society to which he belongs, is one that needs to be more firmly apprehended; and if I share the guilt of my society in time of "peace," I do not see how I can absolve myself from it in time of war, by abstaining from the common action.

P. 20. The Community of Christians. This term is perhaps open to objection. I did not wish to employ Coleridge's term "clerisy" while altering its meaning, but I assume that the reader is familiar with "clerisy" in his *Church and State,* and with Mr. Middleton Murry's use of the same word. Perhaps the term "Community of Christians" may connote to some a kind of esoteric *chapelle* or fraternity of the self-appointed, but I hope that what is said later in this chapter may prevent that inference. I wished to avoid excessive emphasis on nominal function, as it seemed to me that Coleridge's "clerisy" might tend to become merely a brahminical *caste.*

I should add, as a note on the use of the phrase "superior intellectual and/or spiritual gifts" (p. 30), that the possession of intellectual or spiritual gifts does not necessarily confer that intellectual understanding of spiritual issues which is the qualification for exerting the kind of influence here required. Nor is the person who possesses this qualification necessarily a "better Christian" in his private life than the man whose insight is less profound; nor is he necessarily exempt from doctrinal error. I prefer that the definition should be, provisionally, too comprehensive rather than too narrow.

P. 29. Christian Education. This note, as well as that on "The Community of Christians," is elicited by a searching comment by Bro. George Every, S.S.M., who has been so kind as to read this book in proof. Those who have read a paper called "Modern Education and the Classics," written in a different context, and published in a volume entitled *Essays Ancient and Modern,* may assume that what I have in mind is simply the "classical education" of earlier times. The problem of Education is too large to be considered in a brief book like this, and the question of the best curriculum is not here raised. I limit myself to the assertion that the miscellaneous curriculum will not do, and that education must be something more than the acquisition of information, technical competence, or superficial culture. Furthermore, I am not here concerned with what must occupy the mind of anyone approaching the subject of Education directly, that is the question of what should be done *now*. The point upon which all who are dissatisfied with contemporary Education can agree, is the necessity for criteria and values. But one must start by expelling from one's mind any mere prejudice or sentiment in favour of any previous system of education, and recognising the differences between the society for which we have to legislate, and any form of society which we have known in the past.

P. 33. Uniformity of culture. In an important passage in *Beyond Politics* (pp. 23-31) Mr. Christopher Dawson discusses the possibility of an "organisation of culture." He recognises that it is impossible to do this "by any kind of philosophic or scientific dictatorship," or by a return "to the old humanist discipline of letters, for that is inseparable from the aristocratic ideal of a privileged caste of scholars." He asserts that "a democratic society must find a correspondingly democratic organisation of culture"; and finds that "the form of organisation appropriate to our society in the field of culture as well as in that of politics is the party—that is to say a voluntary organisation for common ends based on a common 'ideology.' "

I think that I am in close sympathy with Mr. Dawson's aims, and yet I find it difficult to apprehend the meaning of this "culture" which will have no philosophy (for philosophy, he reminds us, has lost its ancient prestige) and which will not be specifically religious. What, in the kind of society to which we are approximating, will be a "democratic organisation of culture"? To substitute for "democratic" a term which for me has greater concreteness, I should say that the society which is coming into existence, and which is advancing in every country whether "democratic" or "totalitarian," is a lower middle class society: I should expect the culture of the twentieth century to belong to the lower middle class as that of the Victorian age belonged to the upper middle class or commercial aristocracy. If then for Mr. Dawson's phrase we substitute the words "a lower middle class society must find a correspondingly lower middle class organisation of culture" we have something which seems to me to possess more meaning, though it leaves us in greater perplexity. And if Mr. Dawson's Culture Party—about which, however, our information is still meagre—is to be representative of this future society, is it likely to provide anything more important than, for example, a lower middle class Royal Academy instead of one supplying portrait painters for aldermen?

It may be that I have wholly failed to understand what Mr. Dawson is after: if so, I can only hope that he will let us have a fuller exposition of his ideas. Unless some useful analogy can be given from the past, I cannot understand the "organisation of culture," which appears to be without precedent; and in isolating culture from religion, politics and philosophy we seem to be left with something no more apprehensible than the scent of last year's roses. When we speak of culture, I suppose that we have in mind the existence of two classes of people: the producers and the consumers of culture—the existence of men who can create new thought and new art (with middlemen who can teach the consumers to like it) and the existence of a cultivated society to enjoy and patronise it. The former you can only encourage, the latter you can only educate.

I would not belittle the importance, in a period of transition, of the rearguard action; of such institutions, in their various special ways, as the National Trust, the Society for the Preservation of Ancient Buildings, even the National Society. We ought not to cut down old trees until we have learned to plant new ones. But Mr. Dawson is concerned with something more important than the preservation of relics of former culture. My provisional view can only be that "culture" is a by-product, and that those who sympathise with Mr. Dawson in resenting the tyranny of politics, must direct their attention to the problem of Education, and of how, in the lower middle class society of the future, to provide for the training of an élite of thought, conduct and taste.

When I speak of a probable "lower middle class society" I do not anticipate—short of some at present unpredictable revolution—the rise in Britain of a lower middle class political hierarchy, though our ruling class will have to cultivate, in its dealings with foreign countries, an understanding of that mentality. Britain will presumably continue to be governed by the same mercantile and financial class which, with a continual change of personnel, has been increasingly important since the fifteenth century. I mean by a "lower middle class society" one in which the standard man legislated for and catered for, the man whose passions must be manipulated, whose prejudices must be humoured, whose tastes must be gratified, will be the lower middle class man. He is the most numerous, the one most necessary to flatter. I am not necessarily implying that this is either a good or a bad thing: that depends upon what lower middle class Man does to himself, and what is done to him.

P. 40. Advocates of Disestablishment. It is interesting to compare Bishop Hensley Henson's vigorous defence of the Establishment, *Cui Bono?,* published more than forty years ago, with his more recent *Disestablishment,* in which he took a contrary view, but too great importance could be attached, by one side or the other, to this recantation. The argument for Establishment in the early essay, and the argument against it in the later, are both well presented, and both deserve study. What has happened seems to me to be simply that Bishop Hensley Henson has come to take a different view of the tendencies of modern society; and the changes since the end of the last century are great enough to excuse such a change of opinion. His early argument is not invalidated; he might say that the situation is now such that it cannot be applied.

I must take this occasion for calling attention to the great excellence of Bishop Hensley Henson's prose, whether it is employed in a volume prepared at leisure, or in an occasional letter to *The Times*. For vigour and purity of controversial English, he has no superior today, and his writings should long continue to be studied by those who aspire to write well.

P. 41. The dangers of a nationalistic Church. Doubts about the doctrinal security of a national Church must come to the mind of any reader of Mr. Middleton Murry's *The Price of Leadership*. The first part of this book I read with the warmest admiration, and I can support all that Mr. Murry says in favour of a National Church against sectarianism and private Christianity. But at the point at which Mr. Murry allies himself with Dr. Thomas Arnold I begin to hesitate. I have no firsthand acquaintance with the doctrines of Dr. Arnold, and must rely upon Mr. Murry's exposition of them. But Mr. Murry does not engage my complete confidence in Arnold; nor do the citations of Arnold reassure me about the orthodoxy of Mr. Murry. Mr. Murry holds that "the real conflict that is preparing is the conflict between Christianity and anti-Christian nationalism": but surely a nationalism which is overtly antagonistic to Christianity is a less dangerous menace for us than a nationalism which professes a Christianity from which all Christian content has been evacuated. That the Church in England should be identical with the nation—a view which Mr. Murry believes he has found in Arnold and before him in Coleridge, and which Mr. Murry himself accepts—is a laudable aim so long as we keep in mind that we are speaking of one aspect of the Church; but unless this is balanced by the idea of the relation of the Church in England to the Universal Church, I see no safeguard for the purity or the catholicity of its doctrine. I am not even sure that Mr. Murry desires such a safeguard. He quotes, with apparent approval, this sentence by Matthew Arnold: "Will there never arise among Catholics some great soul, to perceive that the eternity and universality, which is vainly claimed for Catholic dogma and the ultramontane system, might really be possible for Catholic worship?"

Well! if eternity and universality is to be found, not in dogma, but in worship—that means, in a common form of worship which will mean to the worshippers anything that they like to fancy, then the result seems to me to be likely to be the most corrupt form of ritualism. What does Mr. Murry mean by Christianity in his National Church, except whatever the nation as such may decide to call Christianity, and what is to prevent the Christianity from being degraded to the nationalism, rather than the nationalism being raised to Christianity?

Mr. Murry holds that Dr. Arnold introduced a new Christian spirit into the public schools. I would not deny to Dr. Arnold the honour of having reformed and improved the moral standards inculcated by public schools, or dispute the assertion that to him and to his son "we owe the tradition of disinterested public service." But at what price? Mr. Murry believes that the ideals of Dr. Arnold have been degraded and adulterated by a subsequent generation: I would like to be sure that the results were not implicit in the principles. To me there appear to be further possible results. Mr. Murry says: "The main organ of this new national and Christian society is the state; the state is, indeed, the organ indispensable to its manifestation. For this reason it is inevitable that in the new national society, if it is to be in some real sense a Christian society, the Church and the state should draw together. On the nature of this drawing together of Church and state, everything depends."

This paragraph, especially in conjunction with Mr. Murry's

suggestion that the public schools should be taken over by the State, makes me suspect that Mr. Murry is ready to go a long way towards totalitarianism; and without any explicit statement on his part about the Christian beliefs which are necessary for salvation, or about the supernatural reality of the Church, we might even conclude that he would go some way in the direction of an English National Religion, the formulation of which would be taken in hand by the moral re-armament manufacturers.

Mr. Murry appears (p. 111) to follow Dr. Arnold in attaching little importance to the apostolical succession. With regard to the position of Matthew Arnold, he says (p. 125), "in this situation no mere revival of Christian piety could possibly avail: not even a rebirth of Christian saintliness (such as he admired in Newman) could be efficacious against it." It is only a short step from employing the adjective *mere* to ignoring Christian piety. He continues, "What was required was a renovation of Christian understanding, an enlarged conception of the spiritual life itself."

How such an enlargement of the conception of the spiritual life is to take place without spiritual masters, without the rebirth of saintliness, I cannot conceive.

P. 46. Wave of revivalism. "Moral re-armament" has been competently and authoritatively analysed from the theological point of view by Fr. Hilary Carpenter, O.P., in the April 1939 issue of *Blackfriars,* and by Professor H. A. Hodges in the May issue of *Theology.* But I feel that everything that remains of clear thinking in this country should be summoned to protest against this abuse of Christianity and of English. A reading of Mr. H. W. Austin's compilation *Moral Re-Armament* suggests several lines of thought. Our immediate reflection is upon the extraordinary facility with which men of the greatest eminence will lend their names to any public appeal, however obscure or ambiguous. Another thought is that the kind of mental activity exposed by these letters must have a very demoralising effect upon the language. Coleridge remarked that "in a language like ours, where so many words are derived from other languages, there are few modes of instruction more useful or more amusing than that of accustoming young people to seek for the etymology, or primary meaning, of the words they use. There are cases, in which more knowledge of more value may be conveyed by the history of a word, than by the history of a campaign." For instance, in a letter to *The Times* reprinted in Mr. Austin's pamphlet, it is said that "national security at home and abroad can only be gained through moral regeneration." Even allowing that "*moral* regeneration" is intended to represent some milder form of parturition than *regeneration,* it is a very striking adaptation of the words of the Gospel to declare that unless a nation be born again it cannot achieve national security. The word *regeneration* appears to have degenerated. In the next paragraph "regeneration" has been replaced by "re-armament." I do not doubt that the term "moral and spiritual re-armament" was originally coined merely as a striking reminder that we need something more than material equipment, but it has quickly shrunk to imply another kind of equipment *on the same plane:* that is, for ends which need be no better than worldly.

In spite of the fervour which tinges the whole correspondence, I cannot find anything to suggest that *Christianity* is needed. Some of the signers, at least, I know to be Christians, but the movement in itself, to judge by this pamphlet, is no more essentially Christian than the German National Religion of Professor Hauer. I have no first-hand experience of the Buchmanite Movement, by which this pamphlet appears to be inspired, but I have never seen any evidence that to be a Buchmanite it was necessary to hold the Christian Faith according to the Creeds, and until I have seen a statement to that effect, I shall continue to doubt whether there is any reason to call Buchmanism a Christian movement.

I am alarmed, by what are not necessary implications, but are certainly possibilities, and to my mind probabilities, of further development of this kind. It is the possibility of gradually adapting our religion to fit our secular aims—*some* of which may be worthy aims, but none of which will be criticised by a supernatural measure. Moral re-armament in my opinion may easily lead to a progressive Germanisation of our society. We observe the efficiency of the German machine, and we perceive that we cannot emulate it without a kind of religious enthusiasm. Moral re-armament will provide the enthusiasm, and be the most useful kind of political drug—that is to say, having the potency at once of a stimulant and a narcotic: but it will supply this function to the detriment of our religion.

"There is a tendency, especially among the English-speaking Protestant peoples, to treat religion as a kind of social tonic that can be used in times of national emergency in order to extract a further degree of moral effort from the people. But apart from the Pelagian conception of religion that this view implies, it is not wholly sound from the psychological point of view, since it merely heightens the amount of moral tension without increasing the sources of spiritual vitality or resolving the psychological conflicts from which the society suffers."

Christopher Dawson: *Beyond Politics*, p. 21.

"While the humanistic religious sentiment which expresses itself by the catch in the throat at the last Evensong in the old School Chapel, the community singing of *Abide with me* at a torchlight tattoo, and the standing to attention during the Two Minutes' Silence, can be utilised by totalitarianism, a religion which speaks of redemption by the incarnate Son of God, which offers mankind the sacramental means of union with the eternal life of the God-Man Jesus Christ, and which makes the perpetual representation of His atoning Sacrifice its essential act of worship must be the declared enemy of all who see in the state the be-all and end-all of man's life."

Humphrey Beevor: *Peace and Pacifism*, p. 207.

P. 51. I have permission to reprint, from *The Times* of October 5, 1938, the following letter, which might serve either as prologue or epilogue to all that I have said, and which provided the immediate stimulus for the lectures which form this book.

3rd October, 1938.

Sir,

The lessons which are being drawn from the unforgettable experiences through which we have lived during the past few days do not for the most part seem to me to go deep enough. The period of grace that has been given us may be no more than a postponement of the day of reckoning unless we make up our minds to seek a radical cure. Our civilisation can recover only if we are determined to root out the cancerous growths which have brought it to the verge of complete collapse. Whether truth and justice or caprice and violence are to prevail in human affairs is a question on which the fate of mankind depends. But to equate the conflict between these opposing forces with the contrast between democracies and dictatorships, real and profound as is this difference, is a dangerous simplification of the problem. To focus our attention on evil in others is a way of escape from the painful struggle of eradicating it from our own hearts and lives and an evasion of our real responsibilities.

The basal truth is that the spiritual foundations of western civilisation have been undermined. The systems which are in the ascendant on the continent may be regarded from one point of view as convulsive attempts to arrest the process of disintegration. What clear alternative have we in this country? The mind of England is confused and uncertain. Is it possible that a simple question, an affirmative answer to which is for many a matter of course and for many others an idle dream or sheer lunacy, might in these circumstances become a live and serious issue? May our salvation lie in an attempt to recover our Christian heritage, not in the sense of going back to the past but of discovering in the central affirmations and insights of the Christian faith new spiritual energies to regenerate and vitalise our sick society? Does not the public repudiation of the whole Christian scheme of life in a large part of what was once known as Christendom force to the front the question whether the path of wisdom is not rather to attempt to work out a Christian doctrine of modern society and to order our national life in accordance with it?

Those who would give a quick, easy or confident answer to this question have failed to understand it. It cannot even be seriously considered without a profound awareness of the extent to which Christian ideas have lost their hold over, or faded from the consciousness of, large sections of the population; of the far-reaching changes that would be called for in the structure, institutions and activities of existing society, which is in many of its features a complete denial of the Christian understanding of the meaning and end of man's existence; and of the stupendous and costly spiritual, moral and intellectual effort that any genuine attempt to order the national life in accordance with the Christian understanding of life would demand. Realistically viewed the task is so far beyond the present capacity of our British Christianity that I write as a fool. But if the will were there, I believe that the first steps to be taken are fairly clear. The presupposition of all else, however, is the recognition that nothing short of a really heroic effort will avail to save mankind from its present evils and the destruction which must follow in their train.

I am, Sir,

Yours etc.

(Signed) J. H. OLDHAM

Postscript

A distinguished theologian, who has been so kind as to read the proofs of this book, has made criticisms of which I should have liked to avail myself by a thorough revision of the text. He has allowed me to quote the following passage from his criticism, which the reader may find helpful in correcting some of the defects of my presentation:

"The main theses of this book seem to me so important, and their application so urgently necessary, that I want to call attention to two points which I think need further emphasis, lest the point of the argument should be missed.

"A main part of the problem, as regards the actual Church and its existing members, is the defective realisation among us of the fundamental fact that Christianity is primarily a Gospel-message, a dogma, a belief about God and the world and man, which demands of man a response of faith and repentance. The common failure lies in putting the human response first, and so thinking of Christianity as primarily a *religion*. Consequently there is among us a tendency to view the problems of the day in the light of what is practically possible, rather than in the light of what is imposed by the principles of that truth to which the Church is set to bear witness.

"Secondly, there is a general vagueness about 'the Community of Christians.' I fear the phrase will be interpreted to mean nice Christianly-minded people of the upper middle class (p. 48). But the Community of Christians ought to mean those who are gathered into unity in the sacramental life of the visible Church: and this community in the life of faith ought to be producing something of a common mind about the questions of the day. It cannot indeed be assumed that the mind of the Community of Christians is truly reflected in the ecclesiastical pronouncements which from time to time appear: that mind does not form itself quickly, in these matters in which it is so hard to see the way. There ought however to be, and to some real extent there is now, in the minds of Christian people a sense of the proportion of things and a spirit of discipline, which are direct fruits of the life of faith: and it is these that need to be brought to bear if the questions are to be answered in the light of Christian principles."

Appendix

The following broadcast talk, delivered in February 1937 in a series on "Church, Community and State," and printed in "The Listener," has some relevance to the matter of the preceding pages of this book.

THAT there is an antithesis between the Church and the World is a belief we derive from the highest authority. We know also from our reading of history, that a certain tension between Church and State is desirable. When Church and State fall out completely, it is ill with the commonwealth; and when Church and State get on too well together, there is something wrong with the Church. But the distinction between the Church and the World is not so easy to draw as that between Church and State. Here we mean not any one communion or ecclesiastical organisation but the whole number of Christians as Christians; and we mean not any particular State, but the whole of society, the world over, in its secular aspect. The antithesis is not simply between two opposed groups of individuals: every individual is himself a field in which the forces of the Church and the world struggle.

By "the Church's message to the World" you might think that what was meant was only the business of the Church to go on talking. I should like to make it more urgent by expanding the title to "the Church's business to interfere with the World." What is often assumed, and it is a principle that I wish to oppose, is the principle of live-and-let-live. It is assumed that if the State leaves the Church alone, and to some

71

extent protects it from molestation, then the Church has no right to interfere with the organisation of society, or with the conduct of those who deny its beliefs. It is assumed that any such interference would be the oppression of the majority by a minority. Christians must take a very different view of their duty. But before suggesting *how* the Church should interfere with the World, we must try to answer the question: *why* should it interfere with the World?

It must be said bluntly that between the Church and the World there is no permanent *modus-vivendi* possible. We may unconsciously draw a false analogy between the position of the Church in a secular society and the position of a dissenting sect in a Christian society. The situation is very different. A dissenting minority in a Christian society can persist because of the fundamental beliefs it has in common with that society, because of a common morality and of common grounds of Christian action. Where there is a different morality there is conflict. I do not mean that the Church exists primarily for the propagation of Christian morality: morality is a means and not an end. The Church exists for the glory of God and the sanctification of souls: Christian morality is part of the means by which these ends are to be attained. But because Christian morals are based on fixed beliefs which cannot change they also are essentially unchanging: while the beliefs and in consequence the morality of the secular world can change from individual to individual, or from generation to generation, or from nation to nation. To accept two ways of life in the same society, one for the Christian and another for the rest, would be for the Church to abandon its task of evangelising the world. For the more alien the non-Christian world becomes, the more difficult becomes its conversion.

The Church is not merely for the elect—in other words, those whose temperament brings them to that belief and that behaviour. Nor does it allow us to be Christian in some social relations and non-Christian in others. It wants everybody, and it wants each individual as a whole. It therefore must struggle for a condition of society which will give the maximum of opportunity for us to lead wholly Christian lives, and the maximum of opportunity for others to become Christians. It maintains the paradox that while we are each responsible for our own souls, we are all responsible for all other souls, who are, like us, on their way to a future state of heaven or hell. And—another paradox—as the Christian attitude towards peace, happiness and well-being of peoples is that they are a means and not an end in themselves, Christians are more deeply committed to realising these ideals than are those who regard them as ends in themselves.

Now, *how* is the Church to interfere in the World? I do not propose to take up the rest of my time by denouncing Fascism and Communism. This task has been more ably performed by others, and the conclusions may be taken for granted. By pursuing this charge, I might obtain from you a kind of approval that I do not want. I suspect that a good deal of the dislike of these philosophies in this country is due to the wrong reasons as well as the right, and is coloured with complacency and sanctimony. It is easy, safe and pleasant to criticise foreigners; and it has the advantage of distracting attention from the evils of our own society. We must distinguish also between our opposition to *ideas* and our disapproval of *practices*. Both Fascism and Communism have fundamental ideas which are incompatible with Christianity. But in practice, a Fascist or a Communist State might realise its idea more or less, and it might be more or less tolerable. And on the other hand, the practices, or others equally objectionable, might easily intrude themselves into a society nominally attached to quite different principles. We need not assume that our form of constitutional democracy is the only one suitable for a Christian people, or that it is in itself a guarantee against an anti-Christian world. Instead of merely condemning Fascism and Communism, therefore, we might do well to consider that we also live in a mass-civilisation following many wrong ambitions and wrong desires, and that if our society renounces completely its obedience to God, it will become no better, and possibly worse, than some of those abroad which are popularly execrated.

By "the World," then, I mean for my present purpose particularly the world in this island. The influence of the Church can be exerted in several ways. It may oppose, or it may support, particular actions at particular times. It is acclaimed when it supports any cause that is already assured of a good deal of secular support: it is attacked, quite naturally, when it opposes anything that people think they want. Whether people say that the Church ought to interfere, or whether they say it ought to mind its own business, depends mostly on whether they agree or disagree with its attitude upon the issue of the moment. A very difficult problem arises whenever there is occasion for the Church to resist any innovation—either in legislation or in social practice—which is contrary to Christian principles. To those who deny, or do not fully accept, Christian doctrine, or who wish to interpret it according to their private lights such resistance often appears oppressive. To the unreasoning mind the Church can often be made to appear to be the enemy of progress and enlightenment. The Church may not always be strong enough to resist successfully: but I do not see how it can ever accept as a permanent settlement one law for itself and another for the world.

I do not wish, however, to pursue the question of the kinds of issue which may arise from time to time. I want to suggest that a task for the Church in our age is a more profound scrutiny of our society, which shall start from the question: to what depth is the foundation of our society not merely neutral but positively anti-Christian?

It ought not to be necessary for me to insist that the final aims of the churchman, and the aims of the secular reformer, are very different. So far as the aims of the latter are for true social justice, they ought to be comprehended in those of the former. But one reason why the lot of the secular reformer or revolutionist seems to me to be the easier is this: that for the most part he conceives of the evils of the world as something external to himself. They are thought of either as completely impersonal, so that there is nothing to alter but machinery; or if there is evil *incarnate,* it is always incarnate in the *other people*—a class, a race, the politicians, the bankers, the armament makers, and so forth—never in oneself. There are individual exceptions: but so far as a man sees the need for converting *himself* as well as the World, he is approximating to the religious point of view. But for most people, to be able to simplify issues so as to see only the definite external enemy, is extremely exhilarating, and brings about the bright eye and the springy step that go so well with the political uniform. This is an exhilaration that the Christian must deny himself. It comes from an artificial stimulant bound to have bad after-effects. It causes pride, either individual or collective, and pride brings its own doom. For only in humility, charity and purity—and most of all perhaps humility—can we be prepared to receive the grace of God without which human operations are vain.

It is not enough simply to see the evil and injustice and suffering of this world, and precipitate oneself into action. We must know, what only theology can tell us, why these things are wrong. Otherwise, we may right some wrongs at the cost of creating new ones. If this is a world in which I, and the majority of my fellow-beings, live in that perpetual distraction from God which exposes us to the one great peril, that of final and complete alienation from God after death, there is some wrong that I must try to help to put right. If there is any profound immorality to which we are all committed as a condition of living in society at all, that is a matter of the gravest

concern to the Church. I am neither a sociologist nor an econo-
mist, and in any case it would be inappropriate, in this context, to produce any formula for setting the world right. It is
much more the business of the Church to say what is wrong,
that is, what is inconsistent with Christian doctrine, than to
propose particular schemes of improvement. What is right
enters the realm of the *expedient* and is contingent upon place
and time, the degree of culture, the temperament of a people.
But the Church can say what is always and everywhere *wrong*.
And without this firm assurance of first principles which it
is the business of the Church to repeat in and out of season,
the World will constantly confuse the *right* with the expedient. In a society based on the use of slave labour men tried
to prove from the Bible that slavery was something ordained
by God. For most people, the actual constitution of Society,
or that which their more generous passions wish to bring
about, is right, and Christianity must be adapted to it. But the
Church cannot be, in any political sense, either conservative,
or liberal, or revolutionary. Conservatism is too often con-
servation of the wrong things: liberalism a relaxation of discipline; revolution a denial of the permanent things.

Perhaps the dominant vice of our time, from the point of
view of the Church, will be proved to be Avarice. Surely there
is something wrong in our attitude towards money. The ac-
quisitive, rather than the creative and spiritual instincts, are
encouraged. The fact that money is always forthcoming for the
purpose of making more money, whilst it is so difficult to obtain for purposes of exchange, and for the needs of the most
needy, is disturbing to those who are not economists. I am by
no means sure that it is right for me to improve my income
by investing in the shares of a company, making I know not
what, operating perhaps thousands of miles away, and in the
control of which I have no effective voice—but which is recommended as a sound investment. I am still less sure of the
morality of my being a money-lender: that is, of investing in

bonds and debentures. I know that it is wrong for me to speculate: but where the line is to be drawn between speculation and what is called legitimate investment is by no means clear. I seem to be a petty usurer in a world manipulated largely by big usurers. And I know that the Church once condemned these things. And I believe that modern war is chiefly caused by some immorality of competition which is always with us in times of "peace"; and that until this evil is cured, no leagues or disarmaments or collective security or conferences or conventions or treaties will suffice to prevent it.

Any machinery, however beautiful to look at and however wonderful a product of brains and skill, can be used for bad purposes as well as good: and this is as true of social machinery as of constructions of steel. I think that, more important than the invention of a new machine, is the creation of a temper of mind in people such that they can learn to use a new machine rightly. More important still at the moment would be the diffusion of knowledge of what is wrong—*morally* wrong —and of *why* it is wrong. We are all dissatisfied with the way in which the world is conducted: some believe that it is a misconduct in which we all have some complicity; some believe that if we trust ourselves entirely to politics, sociology or economics we shall only shuffle from one makeshift to another. And here is the perpetual message of the Church: to affirm, to teach and to apply, true theology. We cannot be satisfied to be Christians at our devotions and merely secular reformers all the rest of the week, for there is one question that we need to ask ourselves every day and about whatever business. The Church has perpetually to answer this question: to what purpose were we born? What is the end of Man?

Notes towards
the Definition of Culture

DEFINITION: 1. The setting of bounds;
limitation (rare)—1483
—*Oxford English Dictionary*

To
PHILIP MAIRET
in gratitude and admiration

Preface

THIS essay was begun four or five years ago. A preliminary sketch, under the same title, was published in three successive numbers of *The New English Weekly*. From this sketch took shape a paper called "Cultural Forces in the Human Order," which appeared in the volume *Prospect for Christendom*, edited by Mr. Maurice B. Reckitt (Faber, 1945): a revision of this paper forms the first chapter of the present book. The second chapter is a revision of a paper published in *The New English Review* in October, 1945.

I have added as an appendix the English text of three broadcast talks to Germany which have appeared under the title of "Die Einheit der Europaeischen Kultur" (Carl Habel Verlagsbuchhandlung, Berlin, 1946).

Throughout this study, I recognise a particular debt to the writings of Canon V. A. Demant, Mr. Christopher Dawson, and the late Professor Karl Mannheim. It is the more necessary to acknowledge this debt in general, since I have not in my text referred to the first two of these writers, and since my debt to the third is much greater than appears from the one context in which I discuss his theory.

I have also profited by reading an article by Mr. Dwight Macdonald in *Politics* (New York) for February 1944, entitled "A Theory of 'Popular Culture' "; and an anonymous critique ot this article in the issue of the same periodical for November 1946. Mr. Macdonald's theory strikes me as the best *alternative* to my own that I have seen.

T. S. E.

January, 1948.

Introduction

MY purpose in writing the following chapters is not, as might appear from a casual inspection of the table of contents, to outline a social or political philosophy; nor is the book intended to be merely a vehicle for my observations on a variety of topics. My aim is to help to define a word, the word *culture*.

Just as a doctrine only needs to be defined after the appearance of some heresy, so a word does not need to receive this attention until it has come to be misused. I have observed with growing anxiety the career of this word *culture* during the past six or seven years. We may find it natural, and significant, that during a period of unparalleled destructiveness, this word should come to have an important role in the journalistic vocabulary. Its part is of course doubled by the word *civilisation*. I have made no attempt in this essay to determine the frontier between the meanings of these two words: for I came to the conclusion that any such attempt could only produce an artificial distinction, peculiar to the book, which the reader would have difficulty in retaining; and which, after closing the book, he would abandon with a sense of relief. We do use one word, frequently enough, in a context where the other would do as well; there are other contexts where one word obviously fits and the other does not; and I do not think that this need cause embarrassment. There are enough inevitable obstacles, in this discussion, without erecting unnecessary ones.

In August, 1945, there was published the text of a draft constitution for a "United Nations Educational Scientific and Cultural Organisation." The purpose of this organisation was, in Article I, defined as follows:

1. To develop and maintain mutual understanding and appreciation of the life and culture, the arts, the humanities, and the sciences of the peoples of the world, as a basis for effective international organisation and world peace.

2. To co-operate in extending and in making available to all peoples for the service of common human needs the world's full body of knowledge and culture, and in assuring its contribution to the economic stability, political security, and general well-being of the peoples of the world.

I am not at the moment concerned to extract a meaning from these sentences: I only quote them to call attention to the word *culture*, and to suggest that before acting on such resolutions we should try to find out what this one word means. This is only one of innumerable instances which might be cited, of the use of a word which nobody bothers to examine. In general, the word is used in two ways: by a kind of synecdoche, when the speaker has in mind one of the elements or evidences of culture—such as "art"; or, as in the passage just quoted, as a kind of emotional stimulant—or anaesthetic.[1]

[1] The use of the word *culture*, by those who have not, as it seems to me, pondered deeply on the meaning of the word before employing it, might be illustrated by countless examples. Another instance may suffice. I quote from the *Times Educational Supplement* of November 3, 1945 (p. 522):

" 'Why should we bring into our scheme for international collaboration machinery concerning education and culture?' Such was the question asked by the Prime Minister when, in addressing the delegates of nearly 40 nations attending the United Nations Conference to establish an Educational and Cultural Organisation in London on Thursday afternoon, he extended to them the greetings of His Majesty's Government. . . . Mr. Attlee concluded with a plea that if we were to know our neighbours we must understand their culture, through their books, newspapers, radio and films."

The Minister of Education committed herself to the following:
"Now we are met together: workers in education, in scientific re-

At the beginning of my first chapter I have endeavoured to distinguish and relate the three principal uses of the word: and to make the point, that when we use the term in one of these three ways we should do so in awareness of the others. I then try to expose the essential relation of culture to religion, and to make clear the limitations of the word *relation* as an ex· pression of this "relation." The first important assertion is that no culture has appeared or developed except together with a religion: according to the point of view of the observer, the culture will appear to be the product of the religion, or the religion the product of the culture.

In the next three chapters I discuss what seem to me to be three important conditions for culture. The first of these is organic (not merely planned, but growing) structure, such as will foster the hereditary transmission of culture within a culture: and this requires the persistence of social classes. The second is the necessity that a culture should be analysable, geographically, into local cultures: this raises the problem of "regionalism." The third is the balance of unity and diversity in religion—that is, universality of doctrine with particularity

search, and in the varied fields of culture. We represent those who teach, those who discover, those who write, those who express their inspiration in music or in art. . . . Lastly we have culture. Some may argue that the artist, the musician, the writer, all the creative workers in the humanities and the arts, cannot be organised either nationally or internationally. The artist, it has been said, works to please himself. That might have been a tenable argument before the war. But those of us who remember the struggle in the Far East and in Europe in the days preceding the open war know how much the fight against Fascism depended upon the determination of writers and artists to keep their international contacts that they might reach across the rapidly rising frontier barriers."

It is only fair to add, that when it comes to talking nonsense about culture, there is nothing to choose between politicians of one stripe or another. Had the election of 1945 brought the alternative party into power, we should have heard much the same pronouncements in the same circumstances. The pursuit of politics is incompatible with a strict attention to exact meanings on all occasions. The reader should therefore abstain from deriding either Mr. Attlee or the late regretted Miss Wilkinson.

of cult and devotion. The reader must keep in mind that I
am not pretending to account for all the necessary conditions
for a flourishing culture; I discuss three which have especially
struck my attention.[1] He must also remember that what I
offer is not a set of directions for fabricating a culture. I do
not say that by setting about to produce these, and any other
additional conditions, we can confidently expect to improve
our civilisation. I say only that, so far as my observation goes,
you are unlikely to have a high civilisation where these conditions are absent.

The remaining two chapters of the book make some slight
attempt to disentangle culture from politics and education.

I dare say that some readers will draw political inferences
from this discussion: what is more likely is that particular
minds will read into my text a confirmation or repudiation
of their own political convictions and prejudices. The writer
himself is not without political convictions and prejudices;
but the imposition of them is no part of his present intention. What I try to say is this: here are what I believe to be
essential conditions for the growth and for the survival of
culture. If they conflict with any passionate faith of the reader
—if, for instance, he finds it shocking that culture and equal-
itarianism should conflict, if it seems monstrous to him that
anyone should have "advantages of birth"—I do not ask him

---

[1] In an illuminating supplement to the *Christian News-Letter* of
July 24, 1946, Miss Marjorie Reeves has a very suggestive paragraph
on "The Culture of an Industry." If she somewhat enlarged her
meaning, what she says would fit in with my own way of using the
word "culture." She says, of the culture of an industry, which she
believes quite rightly should be presented to the young worker: "it
includes the geography of its raw materials and final markets, its
historical evolution, inventions and scientific background, its economics and so forth." It includes all this, certainly; but an industry,
if it is to engage the interest of more than the conscious mind of the
worker, should also have a way of life somewhat peculiar to its in-
itiates, with its own forms of festivity and observances. I mention
this interesting reminder of the culture of industry, however, as
evidence that I am aware of other nuclei of culture than those discussed in this book.

to change his faith, I merely ask him to stop paying lip-service to culture. If the reader says: "the state of affairs which I wish to bring about is *right* (or is *just*,[1] or is *inevitable*); and if this must lead to a further deterioration of culture, we must accept that deterioration"—then I can have no quarrel with him. I might even, in some circumstances, feel obliged to support him. The effect of such a wave of honesty would be that the word *culture* would cease to be abused, cease to appear in contexts where it does not belong: and to rescue this word is the extreme of my ambition.

As things are, it is normal for anybody who advocates any social change, or any alteration of our political system, or any expansion of public education, or any development of social service, to claim confidently that it will lead to the improvement and increase of culture. Sometimes culture, or civilisation, is set in the forefront, and we are told that what we need, must have, and shall get, is a "new civilisation." In 1944 I read a symposium in *The Sunday Times* (November 31) in which Professor Harold Laski, or his headline writer, affirmed that we were fighting the late war for a "new civilisation." Mr. Laski at least asserted this:

> If it is agreed that these who seek to rebuild what Mr. Churchill likes to call "traditional" Britain have no hope of fulfilling that end, it follows that there must be a new Britain in a new civilisation.

We might murmur "it is not agreed," but that would be to miss my point. Mr. Laski is right to this extent, that *if* we lose

[1] I must introduce a parenthetical protest against the abuse of the current term "social justice." From meaning "justice in relations between groups or classes" it may slip into meaning a particular assumption as to what these relations should be; and a course of action might be supported because it represented the aim of "social justice," which from the point of view of "justice" was not just. The term "social justice" is in danger of losing its rational content—which would be replaced by a powerful emotional charge. I believe that I have used the term myself: it should never be employed unless the user is prepared to define clearly what social justice means to him. and why he thinks it just.

anything finally and irreparably, we must make do without it: but I think he meant to say something more than that.

Mr. Laski is, or was convinced that the particular political and social changes which he desires to bring about, and which he believes to be advantageous for society, will, because they are so radical, result in a new civilisation. That is quite conceivable: what we are not justified in concluding, with regard to his or any other changes in the social framework which anybody advocates, is that the "new civilisation" is itself desirable. For one thing, we can have no notion of what the new civilisation will be like: so many other causes operate than those we may have in mind, and the results of these and the others, operating together, are so incalculable, that we cannot imagine what it would *feel* like to live in that new civilisation. For another thing, the people who live in that new civilisation will, by the fact of belonging to it, be different from ourselves, and they will be just as different from Mr. Laski. Every change we make is tending to bring about a new civilisation of the nature of which we are ignorant, and in which we should all of us be unhappy. A new civilisation is, in fact, coming into being all the time: the civilisation of the present day would seem very new indeed to any civilised man of the eighteenth century, and I cannot imagine the most ardent or radical reformer of that age taking much pleasure in the civilisation that would meet his eye now. All that a concern for civilisation can direct us to do, is to improve such civilisation as we have, for we can imagine no other. On the other hand, there have always been people who have believed in particular changes as good in themselves, without worrying about the future of civilisation, and without finding it necessary to recommend their innovations by the specious glitter of unmeaning promises.

A new civilisation is always being made: the state of affairs that we enjoy today illustrates what happens to the aspirations of each age for a better one. The most important question that we can ask, is whether there is any permanent standard, by which we can compare one civilisation with another, and by which we can make some guess at the improvement or decline of our own. We have to admit, in comparing one civilisation with another, and in comparing the different stages of our own, that no one society and no one age of it realises all the values of civilisation. Not all of these values may be compatible with each other: what is at least as certain is that in realising some we lose the appreciation of others. Nevertheless, we can distinguish between higher and lower cultures; we can distinguish between advance and retrogression. We can assert with some confidence that our own period is one of decline; that the standards of culture are lower than they were fifty years ago; and that the evidences of this decline are visible in every department of human activity.[1] I see no reason why the decay of culture should not proceed much further, and why we may not even anticipate a period, of some duration, of which it is possible to say that it will have *no* culture. Then culture will have to grow again from the soil; and when I say it must grow again from the soil, I do not mean that it will be brought into existence by any activity of political demagogues. The question asked by this essay, is whether there are any permanent conditions, in the absence of which no higher culture can be expected.

If we succeed even partially in answering this question, we must then put ourselves on guard against the delusion of trying to bring about these conditions *for the sake of* the improvement of our culture. For if any definite conclusions emerge from this study, one of them is surely this, that culture is the one thing that we cannot deliberately aim at. It is the product of a variety of more or less harmonious activities, each pursued for its own sake: the artist must concentrate

[1] For confirmation from a point of view very different from that from which this essay is written, see *Our Threatened Values* by Victor Gollancz (1946).

upon his canvas, the poet upon his typewriter, the civil ser-
vant upon the just settlement of particular problems as they
present themselves upon his desk, each according to the situation in which he finds himself. Even if these conditions with
which I am concerned, seem to the reader to represent desirable social aims, he must not leap to the conclusion that
these aims can be fulfilled solely by deliberate organisation.
A class division of society planned by an absolute authority
would be artificial and intolerable; a decentralisation under
central direction would be a contradiction; an ecclesiastical
unity cannot be imposed in the hope that it will bring about
unity of faith, and a religious diversity cultivated for its own
sake would be absurd. The point at which we can arrive, is
the recognition that these conditions of culture are "natural"
to human beings; that although we can do little to encourage
them, we can combat the intellectual errors and the emotional prejudices which stand in their way. For the rest, we
should look for the improvement of society, as we seek our
own individual improvement, in relatively minute particulars.
We cannot say: "I shall make myself into a different person";
we can only say: "I will give up this bad habit, and endeavour
to contract this good one." So of society we can only say: "We
shall try to improve it in this respect or the other, where excess or defect is evident; we must try at the same time to embrace so much in our view, that we may avoid, in putting one
thing right, putting something else wrong." Even this is to express an aspiration greater than we can achieve: for it is as
much, or more, because of what we do piecemeal without
understanding or foreseeing the consequences, that the culture
of one age differs from that of its predecessor.

The Three Senses of "Culture"

THE term *culture* has different associations according to whether we have in mind the development of an *individual*, of a *group* or *class*, or of a *whole society*. It is a part of my thesis that the culture of the individual is dependent upon the culture of a group or class, and that the culture of the group or class is dependent upon the culture of the whole society to which that group or class belongs. Therefore it is the culture of the society that is fundamental, and it is the meaning of the term "culture" in relation to the whole society that should be examined first. When the term "culture" is applied to the manipulation of lower organisms —to the work of the bacteriologist or the *agri*culturalist— the meaning is clear enough, for we can have unanimity in respect of the ends to be attained, and we can agree when we have or have not attained them. When it is applied to the improvement of the human mind and spirit, we are less likely to agree as to what culture is. The term itself, as signifying something to be consciously aimed at in human affairs, has not a long history. As something to be achieved by deliberate effort, "culture" is relatively intelligible when we are concerned with the self-cultivation of the individual, whose culture is seen against the background of the culture of the group and of the society. The culture of the group also has a definite meaning in contrast to the less developed culture of the mass of society. The difference between the three applications of the term can be best apprehended by asking how far, in relation to the individual, the group, and society as a whole the *conscious aim to achieve culture* has any meaning. A good deal of confusion could be avoided, if we refrained from setting before the group, what can be the aim only of the individual; and before society as a whole, what can be the aim only of a group.

The general, or anthropological sense of the word *culture*, as used for instance by E. B. Tylor in the title of his book *Primitive Culture*, has flourished independently of the other senses: but if we are considering highly developed societies, and especially our own contemporary society, we have to consider the relationship of the three senses. At this point anthropology passes over into sociology. Amongst men of letters and moralists, it has been usual to discuss culture in the first two senses, and especially the first, without relation to the third. The most easily remembered example of this selection is Matthew Arnold's *Culture and Anarchy*. Arnold is concerned primarily with the individual and the "perfection" at which he should aim. It is true that in his famous classification of "Barbarians, Philistines, Populace" he concerns himself with a critique of classes; but his criticism is confined to an indictment of these classes for their shortcomings, and does not proceed to consider what should be the proper function or "perfection" of each class. The effect, therefore, is to exhort the individual who would attain the peculiar kind of "perfection" which Arnold calls "culture," to rise superior to the limitations of any class, rather than to realise its highest attainable ideals.

The impression of thinness which Arnold's "culture" conveys to a modern reader is partly due to the absence of social background to his picture. But it is also due, I think, to his failure to take account of another way in which we use the word "culture," besides the three already mentioned. There are several kinds of attainment which we may have in mind in different contexts. We may be thinking of refinement of manners—or *urbanity* and *civility:* if so, we shall think first of a social class, and of the superior individual as representative of the best of that class. We may be thinking of *learning* and a close acquaintance with the accumulated wisdom of the past: if so, our man of culture is the scholar. We may be thinking of *philosophy* in the widest sense—an interest in, and some ability to manipulate, abstract ideas: if so, we may mean the intellectual (recognising the fact that this term is now used very loosely, to comprehend many persons not conspicuous for strength of intellect). Or we may be thinking of *the arts:* if so, we mean the artist and the amateur or dilettante. But what we seldom have in mind is all of these things at the same time. We do not find, for instance, that an understanding of music or painting figures explicitly in Arnold's description of the cultured man: yet no one will deny that these attainments play a part in culture.

If we look at the several activities of culture listed in the preceding paragraph, we must conclude that no perfection in any one of them, to the exclusion of the others, can confer culture on anybody. We know that good manners, without education, intellect or sensibility to the arts, tends towards mere automatism; that learning without good manners or sensibility is pedantry; that intellectual ability without the more human attributes is admirable only in the same way as the brilliance of a child chess prodigy; and that the arts without intellectual context are vanity. And if we do not find culture in any one of these perfections alone, so we must not expect any one person to be accomplished in all of them; we shall come to infer that the wholly cultured individual is a phantasm; and we shall look for culture, not in any individual or in any one group of individuals, but more and more widely; and we are driven in the end to find it in the pattern of the society as a whole. This seems to me a very obvious reflection: but it is frequently overlooked. People are always ready to consider themselves persons of culture, on the strength of one proficiency, when they are not only lacking in others, but blind to those they lack. An artist of any kind, even a very great artist, is not for this reason alone a man of culture: artists are not only often insensitive to other arts than those which they practise, but sometimes have very bad manners or meagre intellectual gifts. The person who contributes to culture, however important his contribution may be, is not always a "cultured person."

It does not follow from this that there is no meaning in speaking of the culture of an individual, or of a group or class. We only mean that the culture of the individual cannot be isolated from that of the group, and that the culture of the group cannot be abstracted from that of the whole society; and that our notion of "perfection" must take all three senses of "culture" into account at once. Nor does it follow that in a society, of whatever grade of culture, the groups concerned with each activity of culture will be distinct and exclusive: on the contrary, it is only by an overlapping and sharing of interests, by participation and mutual appreciation, that the cohesion necessary for culture can obtain. A religion requires not only a body of priests who know what they are doing, but a body of worshippers who know what is being done.

It is obvious that among the more primitive communities the several activities of culture are inextricably interwoven. The Dyak who spends the better part of a season in shaping, carving and painting his barque of the peculiar design required for the annual ritual of head-hunting, is exercising several cultural activities at once—of art and religion, as well as of amphibious warfare. As civilisation becomes more complex, greater occupational specialisation evinces itself: in the "stone age" New Hebrides, Mr. John Layard says, certain islands specialise in particular arts and crafts, exchanging their wares and displaying their accomplishments to the reciprocal satisfaction of the members of the archipelago. But while the individuals of a tribe, or of a group of islands or villages, may have separate functions—of which the most peculiar are those of the king and the witch-doctor—it is only at a much further stage that religion, science, politics and art become abstractly conceived apart from each other. And just as the functions of individuals become hereditary, and hereditary function hardens into class or caste distinction, and class distinction leads to conflict, so do religion, politics, science and art reach a point at which there is conscious struggle between them for autonomy or dominance. This friction is, at some stages and in some situations, highly creative: how far it is the result, and how far the cause, of increased consciousness need not here be considered. The tension within the society may become also a tension within the mind of the more conscious individual: the clash of duties in *Antigone,* which is not simply a clash between piety and civil obedience, or between religion and politics, but between conflicting laws within what is still a religious-political complex, represents a very advanced stage of civilisation: for the conflict must have meaning in the audience's experience before it can be made articulate by the dramatist and receive from the audience the response which the dramatist's art requires.

As a society develops towards functional complexity and differentiation, we may expect the emergence of several cultural levels: in short, the culture of the class or group will present itself. It will not, I think, be disputed that in any future society, as in every civilised society of the past, there must be these different levels. I do not think that the most ardent champions of social equality dispute this: the difference of opinion turns on whether the transmission of group culture must be by inheritance—whether each cultural level must propagate itself—or whether it can be hoped that some mechanism of selection will be found, so that every individual

shall in due course take his place at the highest cultural level
for which his natural aptitudes qualify him. What is pertinent at this point is that the emergence of more highly cultured groups does not leave the rest of society unaffected: it
is itself part of a process in which the whole society changes.
And it is certain—and especially obvious when we turn our
attention to the arts—that as new values appear, and as
thought, sensibility and expression become more elaborate,
some earlier values vanish. That is only to say that you cannot expect to have all stages of development at once; that a
civilisation cannot simultaneously produce great folk poetry
at one cultural level and *Paradise Lost* at another. Indeed,
the one thing that time is ever sure to bring about is the loss:
gain or compensation is almost always conceivable but never
certain.

While it appears that progress in civilisation will bring
into being more specialised culture groups, we must not
expect this development to be unattended by perils. Cultural
disintegration may ensue upon cultural specialisation: and
it is the most radical disintegration that a society can suffer.
It is not the only kind, or it is not the only aspect, under
which disintegration can be studied; but, whatever be cause
or effect, the disintegration of culture is the most serious and
the most difficult to repair. (Here, of course, we are empha-
sising the culture of the whole society.) It must not be confused with another malady, ossification into caste, as in Hindu
India, of what may have been originally only a hierarchy of
functions: even though it is possible that both maladies have
some hold upon British society today. Cultural disintegration
is present when two or more strata so separate that these
become in effect distinct cultures; and also when culture at
the upper group level breaks into fragments each of which
represents one cultural activity alone. If I am not mistaken,
some disintegration of the classes in which culture is, or
should be, most highly developed, has already taken place in
western society—as well as some cultural separation between

one level of society and another. Religious thought and practice, philosophy and art, all tend to become isolated areas cultivated by groups in no communication with each other. The artistic sensibility is impoverished by its divorce from the religious sensibility, the religious by its separation from the artistic; and the vestige of *manners* may be left to a few survivors of a vanishing class who, their sensibility untrained by either religion or art and their minds unfurnished with the material for witty conversation, will have no context in their lives to give value to their behaviour. And deterioration on the higher levels is a matter of concern, not only to the group which is visibly affected, but to the whole people.

The causes of a total decline of culture are as complex as the evidence of it is various. Some may be found in the accounts given, by various specialists, of the causes of more readily apprehended social ailments for which we must continue to seek specific remedies. Yet we become more and more aware of the extent to which the baffling problem of "culture" underlies the problems of the relation of every part of the world to every other. When we concern ourselves with the relation of the great nations to each other; the relation of the great to the small nations; [1] the relation of intermixed "communities," as in India, to each other; the relation of parent nations to those which have originated as colonies; the relation of the colonist to the native; the relation between peoples of such areas as the West Indies, where compulsion or economic inducement has brought together large

[1] This point is touched upon, though without any discussion of the meaning of "culture," by E. H. Carr: *Conditions of Peace,* Part I, ch. iii. He says: "In a clumsy but convenient terminology which originated in Central Europe, we must distinguish between 'cultural nation' and 'state nation.' The existence of a more or less homogeneous racial or linguistic group bound together by a common tradition and the cultivation of a common culture must cease to provide a *prima facie* case for the setting up or the maintenance of an independent political unit." But Mr. Carr is here concerned with the problem of political unity, rather than with that of the preservation of cultures, or the question whether they are worth preserving, in the political unit.

numbers of different races: behind all these perplexing questions, involving decisions to be made by many men every day, there is the question of what culture is, and the question whether it is anything that we can control or deliberately influence. These questions confront us whenever we devise a theory, or frame a policy, of education. If we take culture seriously, we see that a people does not need merely enough to eat (though even that is more than we seem able to ensure) but a proper and particular *cuisine:* one symptom of the decline of culture in Britain is indifference to the art of preparing food. Culture may even be described simply as that which makes life worth living. And it is what justifies other peoples and other generations in saying, when they contemplate the remains and the influence of an extinct civilisation, that it was *worth while* for that civilisation to have existed.

I have already asserted, in my introduction, that no culture can appear or develop except in relation to a religion. But the use of the term *relation* here may easily lead us into error. The facile assumption of a relationship between culture and religion is perhaps the most fundamental weakness of Arnold's *Culture and Anarchy*. Arnold gives the impression that Culture (as he uses the term) is something more comprehensive than religion; that the latter is no more than a necessary element, supplying ethical formation and some emotional colour, to Culture which is the ultimate value.

It may have struck the reader that what I have said about the development of culture, and about the dangers of disintegration when a culture has reached a highly developed stage, may apply also in the history of religion. The development of culture and the development of religion, in a society uninfluenced from without, cannot be clearly isolated from each other: and it will depend upon the bias of the particular observer, whether a refinement of culture is held to be the cause of progress in religion, or whether a progress in religion is held to be the cause of a refinement of the culture. What perhaps influences us towards treating religion and

culture as two different things is the history of the penetration of Graeco-Roman culture by the Christian Faith—a
penetration which had profound effects both upon that culture and upon the course of development taken by Christian
thought and practice. But the culture with which primitive
Christianity came into contact (as well as that of the environment in which Christianity took its origins) was itself a religious culture in decline. So, while we believe that the same
religion may inform a variety of cultures, we may ask whether
any culture could come into being, or maintain itself, without a religious basis. We may go further and ask whether
what we call the culture, and what we call the religion, of a
people are not different aspects of the same thing: the culture
being, essentially, the incarnation (so to speak) of the religion
of a people. To put the matter in this way may throw light
on my reservations concerning the word *relation.*

As a society develops, a greater number of degrees and kinds
of religious capacity and function—as well as of other capacities and functions—will make their appearance. It is to be
noticed that in some religions the differentiation has been so
wide that there have resulted in effect two religions—one for
the populace and one for the adepts. The evils of "two nations" in religion are obvious. Christianity has resisted this
malady better than Hinduism. The schisms of the sixteenth
century, and the subsequent multiplication of sects, can be
studied either as the history of division of religious thought,
or as a struggle between opposing social groups—as the varia-
tion of doctrine, or as the disintegration of European culture.
Yet, while these wide divergences of belief on the same level
are lamentable, the Faith can, and must, find room for many
degrees of intellectual, imaginative and emotional receptivity
to the same doctrines, just as it can embrace many variations
of order and ritual. The Christian Faith also, psychologically
considered—as systems of beliefs and attitudes in particular
embodied minds—will have a history: though it would be a
gross error to suppose that the sense in which it can be spoken

of as developing and changing, implies the possibility of greater sanctity or divine illumination becoming available to human beings through collective progress. (We do not assume that there is, over a long period, progress even in art, or that "primitive" art is, as art, necessarily inferior to the more sophisticated.) But one of the features of development, whether we are taking the religious or the cultural point of view, is the appearance of *scepticism*—by which, of course, I do not mean infidelity or destructiveness (still less the unbelief which is due to mental sloth) but the habit of examining evidence and the capacity for delayed decision. Scepticism is a highly civilised trait, though, when it declines into pyrrhonism, it is one of which civilisation can die. Where scepticism is strength, pyrrhonism is weakness: for we need not only the strength to defer a decision, but the strength to make one.

The conception of culture and religion as being, when each term is taken in the right context, different aspects of the same thing, is one which requires a good deal of explanation. But I should like to suggest first, that it provides us with the means of combating two complementary errors. The one more widely held is that culture can be preserved, extended and developed in the absence of religion. This error may be held by the Christian in common with the infidel, and its proper refutation would require an historical analysis of considerable refinement, because the truth is not immediately apparent, and may seem even to be contradicted by appearances: a culture may linger on, and indeed produce some of its most brilliant artistic and other successes after the religious faith has fallen into decay. The other error is the belief that the preservation and maintenance of religion need not reckon with the preservation and maintenance of culture: a belief which may even lead to the rejection of the products of culture as frivolous obstructions to the spiritual life To be in a position to reject this error, as with the other, requires us to take a distant view; to refuse to accept the conclusion, when the culture that we see is a culture in decline, that culture is something to which we can afford to remain indifferent. And I must add that to see the unity of culture and religion in this way neither implies that all the products of art can be accepted uncritically, nor provides a criterion by which everybody can immediately distinguish between them. Esthetic sensibility must be extended into spiritual perception, and spiritual perception must be extended into esthetic sensibility and disciplined taste before we are qualified to pass judgment upon decadence or diabolism or nihilism in art. To judge a work of art by artistic or by religious standards, to judge a religion by religious or artistic standards should come in the end to the same thing: though it is an end at which no individual can arrive.

The way of looking at culture and religion which I have been trying to adumbrate is so difficult that I am not sure I grasp it myself except in flashes, or that I comprehend all its implications. It is also one which involves the risk of error at every moment, by some unperceived alteration of the meaning which either term has when the two are coupled in this way, into some meaning which either may have when taken alone. It holds good only in the sense in which people are unconscious of both their culture and their religion. Anyone with even the slightest religious consciousness must be afflicted from time to time by the contrast between his religious faith and his behaviour; anyone with the taste that *individual* or *group* culture confers must be aware of values which he cannot call religious. And both "religion" and "culture," besides meaning different things from each other, should mean for the individual and for the group something towards which they strive, not merely something which they possess. Yet there is an aspect in which we can see a religion as the *whole way of life* of a people, from birth to the grave, from morning to night and even in sleep, and that way of life is also its culture. And at the same time we must recognise that when this identification is complete, it means in actual societies both an inferior culture and an inferior religion. A universal

religion is at least potentially higher than one which any race
or nation claims exclusively for itself; and a culture realising
a religion also realised in other cultures is at least potentially
a higher culture than one which has a religion exclusively to
itself. From one point of view we may identify: from another,
we must separate.

Taking now the point of view of identification, the reader
must remind himself, as the author has constantly to do, of
how much is here embraced by the term *culture*. It includes
all the characteristic activities and interests of a people: Derby
Day, Henley Regatta, Cowes, the twelfth of August, a cup
final, the dog races, the pin table, the dart board, Wensleydale
cheese, boiled cabbage cut into sections, beetroot in vinegar,
nineteenth-century Gothic churches and the music of Elgar.
The reader can make his own list. And then we have to face
the strange idea that what is part of our culture is also a part
of our *lived* religion.

We must not think of our culture as completely unified—
my list above was designed to avoid that suggestion. And
the actual religion of no European people has ever been
purely Christian, or purely anything else. There are always
bits and traces of more primitive faiths, more or less absorbed;
there is always the tendency towards parasitic beliefs; there
are always perversions, as when patriotism, which pertains
to natural religion and is therefore licit and even encouraged
by the Church, becomes exaggerated into a caricature of itself.
And it is only too easy for a people to maintain contradictory
beliefs and to propitiate mutually antagonistic powers.

The reflection that what we believe is not merely what we
formulate and subscribe to, but that behaviour is also belief,
and that even the most conscious and developed of us live also
at the level on which belief and behaviour cannot be distinguished, is one that may, once we allow our imagination
to play upon it, be very disconcerting. It gives an importance
to our most trivial pursuits, to the occupation of our every
minute, which we cannot contemplate long without the horror

of nightmare. When we consider the quality of the integration required for the full cultivation of the spiritual life, we must keep in mind the possibility of grace and the exemplars of sanctity in order not to sink into despair. And when we consider the problem of evangelisation, of the development of a Christian society, we have reason to quail. To believe that *we* are religious people and that other people are without religion is a simplification which approaches distortion. To reflect that from one point of view religion is culture, and from another point of view culture is religion, can be very disturbing. To ask whether the people have not a religion already, in which Derby Day and the dog track play their parts, is embarrassing; so is the suggestion that part of the religion of the higher ecclesiastic is gaiters and the Athenaeum. It is inconvenient for Christians to find that as Christians they do not believe enough, and that on the other hand they, with everybody else, believe in too many things: yet this is a consequence of reflecting, that bishops are a part of English culture, and horses and dogs are a part of English religion.

It is commonly assumed that there is culture, but that it is the property of a small section of society; and from this assumption it is usual to proceed to one of two conclusions: either that culture can only be the concern of a small minority, and that therefore there is no place for it in the society of the future; or that in the society of the future the culture which has been the possession of the few must be put at the disposal of everybody. This assumption and its consequences remind us of the Puritan antipathy to monasticism and the ascetic life: for just as a culture which is only accessible to the few is now deprecated, so was the enclosed and contemplative life condemned by extreme Protestantism, and celibacy regarded with almost as much abhorrence as perversion.

In order to apprehend the theory of religion and culture which I have endeavoured to set forth in this chapter, we have to try to avoid the two alternative errors: that of regarding religion and culture as two separate things between which there is a *relation*, and that of *identifying* religion and culture. I spoke at one point of the culture of a people as an *incarnation* of its religion; and while I am aware of the temerity of employing such an exalted term, I cannot think of any other which would convey so well the intention to avoid *relation* on the one hand and *identification* on the other. The truth, partial truth, or falsity of a religion neither consists in the cultural achievements of the peoples professing that religion, nor submits to being exactly tested by them. For what a people may be said to believe, as shown by its behaviour, is, as I have said, always a great deal more and a great deal less than its professed faith in its purity. Furthermore, a people whose culture has been formed together with a religion of partial truth, may live that religion (at some period in its history, at least) with greater fidelity than another people which has a truer light. It is only when we imagine our culture as it ought to be, if our society were a really Christian society, that we can dare to speak of Christian culture as the highest culture; it is only by referring to all the phases of this culture, which has been the culture of Europe, that we can affirm that it is the highest culture that the world has ever known. In comparing our culture as it is today, with that of non-Christian peoples, we must be prepared to find that ours is in one respect or another inferior. I do not overlook the possibility that Britain, if it consummated its apostasy by reforming itself according to the prescriptions of some inferior or materialistic religion, might blossom into a culture more brilliant than that we can show today. That would not be evidence that the new religion was true, and that Christianity was false. It would merely prove that any religion, while it lasts, and on its own level, gives an apparent meaning to life, provides the framework for a culture, and protects the mass of humanity from boredom and despair.

CHAPTER II

The Class and the Elite

I T would appear, according to the account of levels of
culture put forward in the previous chapter, that among
the more primitive societies, the higher types exhibit
more marked differentiations of function amongst their members than the lower types.[1] At a higher stage still, we find that
some functions are more honoured than others, and this division promotes the development of *classes,* in which higher
honour and higher privilege are accorded, not merely to the
person as functionary but as member of the class. And the
class itself possesses a function, that of maintaining that part
of the total culture of the society which pertains to that class.
We have to try to keep in mind, that in a healthy society this
maintenance of a particular level of culture is to the benefit,
not merely of the class which maintains it, but of the society
as a whole. Awareness of this fact will prevent us from supposing that the culture of a "higher" class is something super-
nuous to society as a whole, or to the majority, and from
supposing that it is something which ought to be shared
equally by all other classes. It should also remind the "higher"

[1] I am anxious to avoid speaking as if the evolution of primitive
culture to higher forms was a process which we knew by observation.
We *observe* the differences, we *infer* that some have developed from
a stage similar to that of the lower stages which we observe: but however legitimate our inference, I am here not concerned with that
development.

class, in so far as any such exists, that the survival of the culture in which it is particularly interested is dependent upon the health of the culture of the people.

It has now become a commonplace of contemporary thinking, that a society thus articulated is not the highest type to which we may aspire; but that it is indeed in the nature of things for a progressive society eventually to overcome these divisions, and that it is also within the power of our conscious direction, and therefore a duty incumbent upon us, to bring about a classless society. But while it is generally supposed that class, in any sense which maintains associations of the past, will disappear, it is now the opinion of some of the most advanced minds that some qualitative differences between individuals must still be recognised, and that the superior individuals must be formed into suitable groups, endowed with appropriate powers, and perhaps with varied emoluments and honours. Those groups, formed of individuals apt for powers of government and administration, will direct the public life of the nation; the individuals composing them will be spoken of as "leaders." There will be groups concerned with art, and groups concerned with science, and groups concerned with philosophy, as well as groups consisting of men of action: and these groups are what we call élites.

It is obvious, that while in the present state of society there is found the voluntary association of like-minded individuals, and association based upon common material interest, or common occupation or profession, the élites of the future will differ in one important respect from any that we know: they will replace the classes of the past, whose positive functions they will assume. This transformation is not always explicitly stated. There are some philosophers who regard class divisions as intolerable, and others who regard them merely as moribund. The latter may simply ignore class, in their design for an élite-governed society, and say that the élites will "be drawn from all sections of society." But it would seem that as we perfect the means for identifying at an early age, educating for their future role, and settling into positions of authority, the individuals who will form the élites, all former class distinctions will become a mere shadow or vestige, and the only social distinction of rank will be between the élites and the rest of the community, unless, as may happen, there is to be an order of precedence and prestige amongst the several élites themselves.

However moderately and unobtrusively the doctrine of élites is put, it implies a radical transformation of society. Superficially, it appears to aim at no more than what we must all desire—that all positions in society should be occupied by those who are best fitted to exercise the functions of the positions. We have all observed individuals occupying situations in life for which neither their character nor their intellect qualified them, and so placed only through nominal education, or birth or consanguinity. No honest man but is vexed by such a spectacle. But the doctrine of élites implies a good deal more than the rectification of such injustice. It posits an *atomic* view of society.

The philosopher whose views on the subject of élites deserve the closest attention, both for their own value and because of the influence they exert, is the late Dr. Karl Mannheim. It is, for that matter, Dr. Mannheim who has founded the fortunes, in this country, of the term élite. I must remark that Dr. Mannheim's description of culture is different from that given in the previous chapter of this essay. He says:

A sociological investigation of culture in liberal society must begin with the life of those who create culture, i.e. the intelligentsia and their position within society as a whole.[1]

According to the account which I have given, a "culture" is conceived as the creation of the society as a whole: being, from another aspect, that which makes it a society. It is not

[1] P. 81, *Man and Society in an Age of Reconstruction,* 1940, New York, Harcourt. Brace.

the creation of any one part of that society. The function of what Dr. Mannheim would call the culture-creating groups, according to my account, would be rather to bring about a further development of the culture in organic complexity: culture at a more conscious level, but still the same culture. This higher level of culture must be thought of both as valuable in itself, and as enriching the lower levels: thus the movement of culture would proceed in a kind of cycle, each class nourishing the others.

This is, already, a difference of some importance. My next observation is that Dr. Mannheim is concerned rather with élites than with an élite.

We may distinguish [he says, in *Man and Society*, p. 82] the following types of élites: the political, the organising, the intellectual, the artistic, the moral and the religious. Whereas the political and organising élites aim at integrating a great number of individual wills, it is the function of the intellectual, aesthetic, and moral-religious élites to sublimate those psychic energies which society, in the daily struggle for existence, does not fully exhaust.

This departmentalisation of élites already exists, to some extent; and to some extent it is a necessary and a good thing. But, so far as it can be observed to exist, it is not *altogether* a good thing. I have suggested elsewhere that a growing weakness of our culture has been the increasing isolation of élites from each other, so that the political, the philosophical, the artistic, the scientific, are separated to the great loss of each of them, not merely through the arrest of any general circulation of ideas, but through the lack of those contacts and mutual influences at a less conscious level, which are perhaps even more important than ideas. The problem of the formation, preservation and development of the élites is therefore also the problem of the formation, preservation and development of *the* élite, a problem upon which Dr. Mannheim does not touch.

As an introduction to this problem, I must draw attention

to another difference between my view and that of Dr. Mannheim. He observes, in a passage which I think contains an important truth (p. 85):

> The crisis of culture in liberal-democratic society is due, in the first place, to the fact that the fundamental social processes, which previously favoured the development of the culturally creative élites, now have the opposite effect, i.e. have become obstacles to the forming of élites because wider sections of the population take an active part in cultural activities.

I cannot, of course, admit the last clause of this sentence as it stands. According to my view of culture, the whole of the population *should* "take an active part in cultural activities" —not all in the same activities or on the same level. What this clause means, in my terms, is that an increasing proportion of the population is concerned with group culture. This comes about, I think Dr. Mannheim would agree, through the gradual alteration of the class-structure. But at this point it seems to me that Dr. Mannheim begins to confuse élite with *class.* For he says (p. 89):

> If one calls to mind the essential forms of selecting élites which up to the present have appeared on the historical scene, three principles can be distinguished: selection on the basis of *blood, property* and *achievement.* Aristocratic society, especially after it had entrenched itself, chose its élites primarily on the blood principle. Bourgeois society gradually introduced, as a supplement, the principle of wealth, a principle which also obtained for the intellectual élite, inasmuch as education was more or less available only to the off-spring of the well-to-do. It is, of course, true that the principle of achievement was combined with the two other principles in earlier periods, but it is the important contribution of modern democracy as long as it is rigorous, that the achievement principle increasingly tends to become the criterion of social success.

I am ready to accept, in a rough and ready way, this account of three historical periods. But I would remark that we are here not concerned with élites but with *classes* or, more precisely with the evolution from a class to a classless society.

It seems to me that at the stage of the sharpest division into classes we can distinguish an élite also. Are we to believe that the artists of the Middle Ages were all men of noble rank, or that the hierarchy and the statesmen were all selected according to their pedigrees?

I do not think that this is what Dr. Mannheim wishes us to believe; but I think that he is confusing the élites with the dominant section of society which the élites served, from which they took their colour, and into which some of their individual members were recruited. The general scheme of the transition of society, in the last five hundred years or so, is usually accepted, and I have no interest in questioning it. I would only propose one qualification. At the stage of dominance of *bourgeois* society (I think it would be more exact to say here, "upper middle class society") there is a difference applying particularly to England. However powerful it was—for its power is now commonly said to be passing—it would not have been what it was, without the existence of a class above it, from which it drew some of its ideals and some of its criteria, and to the condition of which its more ambitious members aspired. This gives it a difference in kind from the aristocratic society which preceded it, and from the mass-society which is expected to follow it.

I now come to another passage in Dr. Mannheim's discussion, which seems to me true. His intellectual integrity prevents him from dissimulating the gloom of our present position; but he succeeds, so far as I can judge, in communicating to most of his readers a feeling of active hopefulness, by infecting them with his own passionate faith in the possibilities of "planning." Yet he says quite clearly:

We have no clear idea how the selection of élites would work in an open mass society in which only the principle of achievement mattered. It is possible that in such a society the succession of the élites would take place much too rapidly, and social continuity which is essentially due to the slow and gradual broadening of the influence of the dominant groups would be lacking in it.[1]

This raises a problem of the first importance to my present discussion, with which I do not think Dr. Mannheim has dealt in any detail: that of the *transmission of culture*.

When we are concerned with the history of certain parts of culture, such as the history of art, or of literature, or of philosophy, we naturally isolate a particular class of phenomena; though there has been a movement, which has produced books of interest and value, to relate these subjects more closely to a general social history. But even such accounts are usually only the history of one class of phenomena interpreted in the light of the history of another class of phenomena and, like that of Dr. Mannheim, tend to take a more limited view of culture than that adopted here. What we have to consider is the parts played by the élite and by the class in the transmission of culture from one generation to the next.

We must remind ourselves of the danger, mentioned in the previous chapter, of identifying culture with the *sum* of distinct cultural activities; and if we avoid this identification we shall also decline to identify our group culture with the sum of the activities of Dr. Mannheim's élites. The anthropologist may study the social system, the economics, the arts, and the religion of a particular tribe, he may even study their psychological peculiarities: but it is not merely by observing in detail all of these manifestations, and grasping them together, that he will approach to an understanding of the culture. For to understand the culture is to understand the people, and this means an imaginative understanding. Such understanding can never be complete: either it is abstract—and the essence escapes—or else it is *lived;* and in so far as it is

---

[1] Dr. Mannheim proceeds to call attention to a tendency in mass-society to renounce even the achievement principle. This passage is important; but as I agree with him that the dangers from this are still more alarming, it is unnecessary to quote it here.

lived, the student will tend to identify himself so completely with the people whom he studies, that he will lose the point of view from which it was worth while and possible to study it. Understanding involves an area more extensive than that of which one can be conscious; one cannot be outside and inside at the same time. What we ordinarily mean by understanding of another people, of course, is an approximation towards understanding which stops short at the point at which the student would begin to lose some essential of his own culture. The man who, in order to understand the inner world of a cannibal tribe, has partaken of the practice of cannibalism, has probably gone too far: he can never quite be one of his own folk again.[1]

I have raised this question, however, solely in support of my contention that culture is not merely the sum of several activities, but a *way of life*. Now the specialist of genius, who may be fully qualified on the ground of his vocational attainment for membership of one of Dr. Mannheim's élites, may very well not be one of the "cultured persons" representative of group culture. As I have said before, he may be only a highly valued contributor to it. Yet group culture, as observable in the past, has never been co-extensive with class, whether an aristocracy or an upper middle class. A very large number of members of these classes always have been conspicuously deficient in "culture." I think that in the past the repository of this culture has been *the* élite, the major part of which was drawn from the dominant class of the time, constituting the primary consumers of the work of thought and art produced by the minority members, who will have originated from various classes, including that class itself. The units of this majority will, some of them, be individuals; others will be families. But the individuals from the dominant class who compose the nucleus of the cultural élite

[1] Joseph Conrad's *Heart of Darkness* gives a hint of something similar.

must not thereby be cut off from the class to which they belong, for without their membership of that class they would not have their part to play. It is their function, in relation to the producers, to transmit the culture which they have inherited; just as it is their function, in relation to the rest of their class, to keep it from ossification. It is the function of the class as a whole to preserve and communicate standards of *manners*—which are a vital element in group culture.[1] It is the function of the superior members and superior families to preserve the group culture, as it is the function of the producers to alter it.

In an élite composed of individuals who find their way into it solely for their individual pre-eminence, the differences of background will be so great, that they will be united only by their common interests, and separated by everything else. An élite must therefore be attached to *some* class, whether higher or lower: but so long as there are classes at all it is likely to be the dominant class that attracts this élite to itself. What would happen in a classless society—which is much more difficult to envisage than people think—brings us into the area of conjecture. There are, however, some guesses which seem to me worth venturing.

The primary channel of transmission of culture is the family: no man wholly escapes from the kind, or wholly surpasses the degree, of culture which he acquired from his early environment. It would not do to suggest that this can be the *only* channel of transmission: in a society of any complexity it is supplemented and continued by other conduits of tradition. Even in relatively primitive societies this is so. In more civilised communities of specialised activities, in which not

[1] To avoid misunderstanding at this point, it should be observed that I do not assume that "good manners" should be peculiar to any one stratum of society. In a healthy society, good manners should be found throughout. But as we distinguish between the meanings of "culture" at the several levels, so we distinguish also between the meanings of more and less conscious "good manners."

all the sons would follow the occupation of their father, the apprentice (ideally, at least) did not merely serve his master, and did not merely learn from him as one would learn at a technical school—he became assimilated into a way of life which went with that particular trade or craft; and perhaps the lost secret of the craft is this, that not merely a skill but an entire way of life was transmitted. Culture—distinguishable from knowledge about culture—was transmitted by the older universities: young men have profited there who have been profitless students, and who have acquired no taste for learning, or for Gothic architecture, or for college ritual and form. I suppose that something of the same sort is transmitted also by societies of the masonic type: for initiation is an introduction into a way of life, of however restricted viability, received from the past and to be perpetuated in the future. But by far the most important channel of transmission of culture remains the family: and when family life fails to play its part, we must expect our culture to deteriorate. Now the family is an institution of which nearly everybody speaks well: but it is advisable to remember that this is a term that may vary in extension. In the present age it means little more than the living members. Even of living members, it is a rare exception when an advertisement depicts a large family or three generations: the usual family on the hoardings consists of two parents and one or two young children. What is held up for admiration is not devotion to a family, but personal affection between the members of it: and the smaller the family, the more easily can this personal affection be sentimentalised. But when I speak of the family, I have in mind a bond which embraces a longer period of time than this: a piety towards the dead, however obscure, and a solicitude for the unborn, however remote. Unless this reverence for past and future is cultivated in the home, it can never be more than a verbal convention in the community. Such an interest in the past is different from the vanities and pretensions of genealogy;

such a responsibility for the future is different from that of the builder of social programmes.

I should say then that in a vigorous society there will be both class and élite, with some overlapping and constant interaction between them. An élite, if it is a governing élite, and so far as the natural impulse to pass on to one's offspring both power and prestige is not artificially checked, will tend to establish itself as a class—it is this metamorphosis, I think, which leads to what appears to me an oversight on the part of Dr. Mannheim. But an élite which thus transforms itself tends to lose its function as élite, for the qualities by which the original members won their position will not all be transmitted equally to their descendants. On the other hand, we have to consider what would be the consequence when the converse took place, and we had a society in which the functions of class were assumed by élites. Dr. Mannheim seems to have believed that this will happen; he showed himself, as a passage which I have quoted indicates, aware of the dangers; and he does not appear to have been ready to propose definite safeguards against them.

The situation of a society without classes, and dominated exclusively by élites is, I submit, one about which we have no reliable evidence. By such a society, I suppose we must mean one in which every individual starts without advantage or handicap; and in which, by some mechanism set up by the best designers of such machinery, everybody will find his way, or be directed, to that station of life which he is best fitted to fill, and every position will be occupied by the man or woman best fitted for it. Of course, not even the most sanguine would expect the system to work as well as that: if, by and large, it seemed to come nearer to putting the right people in the right places than any previous system, we should all be satisfied. When I say "dominated," rather than "governed" by élites, I mean that such a society must not be content to be *governed* by the right people: it must see that the ablest artists and architects rise to the top, influence taste, and execute the important public commissions; it must do the same by the other arts and by science; and above all, perhaps, it must be such that the ablest minds will find expression in speculative thought. The system must not only do all this for society in a particular situation—it must *go on* doing it, generation after generation. It would be folly to deny that in a particular phase of a country's development, and *for a limited purpose,* an élite can do a very good job. It may, by expelling a previous governing group, which in contrast to itself may be a *class,* save or reform or revitalise the national life. Such things have happened. But we have very little evidence about the perpetuation of government by élite, and such as we have is unsatisfactory. A considerable time must elapse before we can draw any illustration from Russia. Russia is a rude and vigorous country; it is also a very big country; and it will need a long period of peace and internal development. Three things may happen. Russia may show us how a stable government and a flourishing culture can be transmitted only through élites; it may lapse into oriental lethargy; or the governing élite may follow the course of other governing élites and become a governing class. Nor can we rely upon any evidence from the United States of America. The real revolution in that country was not what is called the Revolution in the history books, but is a consequence of the Civil War; after which arose a plutocratic élite; after which the expansion and material development of the country was accelerated; after which was swollen that stream of mixed immigration, bringing (or rather multiplying) the danger of development into a *caste* system [1] which has not yet been quite dispelled. For the sociologist, the evidence from America is not yet ripe. Our other evidence for government by élite

---

[1] I believe that the essential difference between a caste and a class system is that the basis of the former is a difference such that the dominant class comes to consider itself a superior *race.*

comes chiefly from France. A governing class, which, during a long period in which the Throne was all-powerful, had ceased to govern, was reduced to the ordinary level of citizenship. Modern France has had no governing class: her political life in the Third Republic, whatever else we may say of it, was *unsettled*. And here we may remark that when a dominant class, however badly it has performed its function, is forcibly removed, its function is not wholly taken over by any other. The "flight of the wild geese" is perhaps a symbol of the harm that England has done to Ireland—more serious, from this point of view, than the massacres of Cromwell, or any of the grievances which the Irish most gladly recall. It may be, too, that England has done more harm to Wales and Scotland by gently attracting their upper classes to certain public schools, than by the wrongs (some real, some imaginary, some misunderstood) voiced by their respective nationalists. But here again, I wish to reserve judgment about Russia. That country, at the time of its revolution, may still have been at so early a stage of its development, that the removal of its upper class may prove not only not to have arrested that development but to have stimulated it. There are, however, some grounds for believing that the elimination of an upper class at a more developed stage can be a disaster for a country: and most certainly when that removal is due to the intervention of another nation.

I have, in the preceding paragraphs, been speaking mainly of the "governing class" and the "governing élite." But I must remind the reader again that in concerning ourselves with class *versus* élite, we are concerned with the total culture of a country, and that involves a good deal more than government. We can yield ourselves with some confidence to a governing élite, as the republican Romans surrendered power to dictators, so long as we have in view a *defined purpose* in a crisis—and a crisis may last a long time. This limited purpose also makes it possible to choose the élite, for we know what we are choosing it for. But, if we are looking for a way to select the right people to constitute every élite, for an indefinite future, by what mechanism are we to do this? If our "purpose" is only to get the best people, in every walk of life, to the top, we lack a criterion of who are the best people; or, if we impose a criterion, it will have an oppressive effect upon novelty. The new work of genius, whether in art, science or philosophy, frequently meets with opposition.

All that concerns me at the moment is the question whether, by education alone, we can ensure the transmission of culture in a society in which some educationists appear indifferent to class distinctions, and from which some other educationists appear to want to remove class distinctions altogether. There is, in any case, a danger of interpreting "education" to cover both too much and too little: too little, when it implies that education is limited to what can be taught; too much, when it implies that everything worth preserving can be transmitted by teaching. In the society desired by some reformers, what the family can transmit will be limited to the minimum, especially if the child is to be, as Mr. H. C. Dent hopes, manipulated by a unified educational system "from the cradle to the grave." And unless the child is classified, by the officials who will have the task of sorting him out, as being just like his father, he will be brought up in a different—not necessarily a better, because all will be equally good, but a different—school environment, and trained on what the official opinion of the moment considers to be "the genuinely democratic lines." The élites, in consequence, will consist solely of individuals whose only common bond will be their professional interest: with no social cohesion, with no social continuity. They will be united only by a part, and that the most conscious part, of their personalities; they will meet like committees. The greater part of their "culture" will be only what they share with all the other individuals composing their nation.

The case for a society with a class structure, the affirmation that it is, in some sense, the "natural" society, is prejudiced if we allow ourselves to be hypnotised by the two contrasted terms *aristocracy* and *democracy*. The whole problem is falsified if we use these terms antithetically. What I have advanced is not a "defence of aristocracy"—an emphasis upon the importance of one organ of society. Rather it is a plea on behalf of a form of society in which an aristocracy should have a peculiar and essential function, as peculiar and essential as the function of any other part of society. What is important is a structure of society in which there will be, from "top" to "bottom," a continuous gradation of cultural levels: it is important to remember that we should not consider the upper levels as possessing *more* culture than the lower, but as representing a more conscious culture and a greater specialisation of culture. I incline to believe that no true democracy can maintain itself unless it contains these different levels of culture. The levels of culture may also be seen as levels of power, to the extent that a smaller group at a higher level will have equal power with a larger group at a lower level; for it may be argued that complete equality means universal irresponsibility; and in such a society as I envisage, each individual would inherit greater or less responsibility towards the commonwealth, according to the position in society which he inherited—each class would have somewhat different responsibilities. A democracy in which everybody had an equal responsibility in everything would be oppressive for the conscientious and licentious for the rest.

There are other grounds upon which a graded society can be defended; and I hope, in general, that this essay will suggest lines of thought that I shall not myself explore; but I must constantly remind the reader of the limits of my subject. If we agree that the primary vehicle for the transmission of culture is the family, and if we agree that in a more highly civilised society there must be different levels of culture, then it follows that to ensure the transmission of the culture of these different levels there must be groups of families persisting, from generation to generation, each in the same way of life.

And once again I must repeat, that the "conditions of culture" which I set forth do not necessarily produce the higher civilisation: I assert only that when they are absent, the higher civilisation is unlikely to be found.

CHAPTER III

Unity and Diversity: The Region

> *A diversification among human communities is essential for the provision of the incentive and material for the Odyssey of the human spirit. Other nations of different habits are not enemies: they are godsends. Men require of their neighbours something sufficiently akin to be understood, something sufficiently different to provoke attention, and something great enough to command admiration.*
> A. N. WHITEHEAD: Science and the Modern World

IT is a recurrent theme of this essay, that a people should be neither too united nor too divided, if its culture is to flourish. Excess of unity may be due to barbarism and may lead to tyranny; excess of division may be due to decadence and may also lead to tyranny: either excess will prevent further development in culture. The proper degree of unity and of diversity cannot be determined for all peoples at all times. We can only state and illustrate some departments in which excess or defect is dangerous: what is necessary, beneficial or deleterious for a particular people at a particular time, must be left to the wisdom of the sage and the insight of the statesman. Neither a classless society, nor a society of strict and impenetrable social barriers is good; each class should have constant additions and defections; the classes, while remaining distinct, should be able to mix freely; and they should all have a community of culture with each other which will give them something in common, more fundamental than the community which each class has with its counterpart in another society. In the previous chapter we considered the special developments of culture by class: we have now to consider the special developments of culture by region.

Of the advantages of administrative and sentimental unity we hardly need to be reminded, after the experience of war; but it is often assumed that the unity of wartime should be preserved in time of peace. Amongst any people engaged in warfare, especially when the war appears, or can be made to appear, purely defensive, we may expect a spontaneous unity of sentiment which is genuine, an affectation of it on the part of those who merely wish to escape odium, and, from all, submission to the commands of the constituted authorities. We should hope to find the same harmony and docility among the survivors of a shipwreck adrift in a lifeboat. People often express regret that the same unity, self-sacrifice and fraternity which prevail in an emergency, cannot survive the emergency itself. Most audiences at Barrie's play, *The Admirable Crichton,* have drawn the inference that the social organisation on the island was right, and that the social organisation at the country seat was wrong: I am not sure that Barrie's play is not susceptible of a different interpretation. We must distinguish at all events between the kind of unity which is necessary in an emergency, and that which is appropriate for the development of culture in a nation at peace. It is conceivable, of course, that a period of "peace" may be a period of preparation for war, or of continuation of warfare in another form: in which situation we may expect a deliberate stimulation of patriotic sentiment and a rigorous central government control. It might be expected, too, in such a period, that "economic warfare" would be conducted by strict government discipline, not left to the guerillas and privateers of enterprise. But I am concerned here with the kind and degree of unity desirable in a country which is at peace with other countries: for if we cannot have periods of real peace, it is futile to hope for culture at all. The kind of unity with which I am concerned is not expressible as a common enthusiasm or a common purpose: enthusiasms and purposes are always transient.

The unity with which I am concerned must be largely unconscious, and therefore can perhaps be best approached through a consideration of the useful diversities. Here I have to do with diversity of region. It is important that a man should feel himself to be, not merely a citizen of a particular nation, but a citizen of a particular part of his country, with local loyalties. These, like loyalty to class, arise out of loyalty to the family. Certainly, an individual may develop the warmest devotion to a place in which he was not born, and to a community with which he has no ancestral ties. But I think we should agree that there would be something artificial, something a little too conscious, about a community of people with strong local feeling, all of whom had come from somewhere else. I think we should say that we must wait for a generation or two for a loyalty which the inhabitants had inherited, and which was not the result of a conscious choice. On the whole, it would appear to be for the best that the great majority of human beings should go on living in the place in which they were born. Family, class and local loyalty all support each other; and if one of these decays, the others will suffer also.

The problem of "regionalism" is seldom contemplated in its proper perspective. I introduce the term "regionalism" deliberately, because of the associations which it is apt to conjure up. It means, I think, to most people, the conception of some small group of local malcontents conducting a political agitation which, because it is not formidable, is regarded as ludicrous—for any movement for what is assumed to be a lost cause always excites ridicule. We expect to find "regionalists" attempting to revive some language which is disappearing and ought to disappear; or to revive customs of a bygone age which have lost all significance; or to obstruct the inevitable and accepted progress of mechanisation and large-scale industry. The champions of local tradition, indeed, often fail to make the best of their case; and when, as sometimes happens, they are most vigorously opposed and derided by others among their own people, the outsider feels that he has no reason to take them seriously. They sometimes misconceive their own case. They are inclined to formulate the remedy wholly in political terms; and as they may be politically inexperienced, and at the same time are agitated by deeper than political motives, their programmes may be patently impracticable. And when they put forward an economic programme, there, too, they are handicapped by having motives which go deeper than economics, in contrast with men who have the reputation of being practical. Furthermore, the usual regionalist is concerned solely with the interests of his own region, and thereby suggests to his neighbour across the border, that what is to the interest of one must be to the disadvantage of the other. The Englishman, for instance, does not ordinarily think of England as a "region" in the way that a Scottish or Welsh national can think of Scotland or Wales; and as it is not made clear to him that his interests also are involved, his sympathies are not enlisted. Thus the Englishman may identify his own interests with a tendency to obliterate local and racial distinctions, which is as harmful to his own culture as to those of his neighbours. Until the case is generalised, therefore, it is not likely to meet with a fair hearing.

At this point the professed regionalist, if he reads these pages, may suspect that I am playing a trick which he sees through. What I am up to, he may think, is trying to deny him the political and economic autonomy of his region, and appease him by offering him a substitute, "cultural autonomy," which, because it is divorced from political and economic power, will only be a shadow of the real thing. I am quite aware that the political, the economic and the cultural problems cannot be isolated from each other. I am quite aware that any local "cultural revival" which left the political and economic framework unaffected, would hardly be more than an artificially sustained antiquarianism: what is wanted is not to restore a vanished, or to revive a vanishing culture under modern conditions which make it impossible, but to grow a contemporary culture from the old roots. But the political and economic conditions of healthy regionalism are not the concern of the present essay; nor are they matters on which I am qualified to pronounce. Nor, I think, should the political or the economic problem be the *primary* concern of the true regionalist. The *absolute* value is that each area should have its characteristic culture, which should also harmonise with, and enrich, the cultures of the neighbouring areas. In order to realise this value it is necessary to investigate political and economic alternatives to centralisation in London or elsewhere: and here, it is a question of the possible—of what can be done which will support this absolute value of culture, without injury to the island as a whole and by consequence to that part of it also in which the regionalist is interested. But this is beyond my scope.

We are, you will have noticed, primarily concerned with the particular constellation of cultures which is found in the British Isles. The clearest among the differences to be considered is that of the areas which still possess languages of their own. Even this division is not so simple as it looks: for a people (like the English-speaking Irish) which has lost its language may preserve enough of the structure, idiom, intonation and rhythm of its original tongue (vocabulary is of minor importance) for its speech and writing to have qualities not elsewhere found in the language of its adoption. And on the other hand a "dialect" may preserve the vestiges, on the lowest level of culture, of a variety of the language which once had equal status with any. But the unmistakable *satellite* culture is one which preserves its language, but which is so closely associated with, and dependent upon, another, that not only certain classes of the population, but all of them, have to be bi-lingual. It differs from the culture of the independent small nation in this respect, that in the latter it is usually only necessary for some classes to know another language; and in the independent small nation, those who need to know one foreign language are likely to need two or three: so that the pull towards one foreign culture will be balanced by the attraction of at least one other. A nation of weaker culture may be under the influence of one or another stronger culture at different periods: a true satellite culture is one which, for geographical and other reasons, has a permanent relation to a stronger one.

When we consider what I call the satellite culture, we find two reasons against consenting to its complete absorption into the stronger culture. The first objection is one so profound that it must simply be accepted: it is the instinct of every living thing to persist in its own being. The resentment against absorption is sometimes most strongly felt, and most loudly voiced, by those individuals in whom it is united with an unacknowledged awareness of inferiority or failure; and on the other hand it is often repudiated by those individuals for whom adoption into the stronger culture has meant success—greater power, prestige or wealth than could have been theirs had their fortunes been circumscribed by their area of origin.[1] But when the testimony of both these types of individual has been discounted, we may say that any vigorous small people wants to preserve its individuality.

The other reason for the preservation of local culture is one which is also a reason for the satellite culture continuing

---

[1] It is not unknown, however, that the successful self-exile sometimes manifests an exaggerated sentiment towards his native region, to which he may return for his holidays, or to enjoy the affluent retirement of his declining years.

to be satellite, and not going so far as to try to cut itself off completely. It is that the satellite exercises a considerable influence upon the stronger culture; and so plays a larger part in the world at large than it could in isolation. For Ireland, Scotland and Wales to cut themselves off completely from England would be to cut themselves off from Europe and the world, and no talk of auld alliances would help matters. But it is the other side of the question that interests me more, for it is the side that has received less acknowledgment. It is that the survival of the satellite culture is of very great value to the stronger culture. It would be no gain whatever for English culture, for the Welsh, Scots and Irish to become indistinguishable from Englishmen—what *would* happen, of course, is that we should all become indistinguishable featureless "Britons," at a lower lever of culture than that of any of the separate regions. On the contrary, it is of great advantage for English culture to be constantly influenced from Scotland, Ireland and Wales.

A people is judged by history according to its contribution to the culture of other peoples flourishing at the same time and according to its contribution to the cultures which arise afterwards. It is from this point of view that I look at the question of the preservation of languages—I am not interested in languages in an advanced state of decay (that is to say, when they are no longer adequate to the needs of expression of the more educated members of the community). It is sometimes considered an advantage, and a source of glory, that one's own language should be a necessary medium for as many foreigners as possible: I am not sure that this popularity is without grave dangers for any language. A less dubious advantage of certain languages which are native to large numbers of people, is that they have become, because of the work done by scientists and philosophers who have thought in those languages, and because of the traditions thus created, better vehicles than others for scientific and abstract thought. The case for the more restricted languages must be put on grounds which have less immediate appeal.

The question we may ask about such a language as Welsh, is whether it is of any value to the world at large, that it should be used in Wales. But this is really as much as to ask whether the Welsh, *qua* Welsh, are of any use? not, of course, as human beings, but as the preservers and continuers of a culture which is not English. The direct contribution to poetry by Welshmen and men of Welsh extraction, writing in English, is very considerable; and considerable also is the influence of their poetry upon poets of different racial origins. The fact that an extensive amount of poetry has been written in the Welsh language, in the ages when the English language was unknown in Wales, is of less direct importance: for there appears no reason why this should not be studied by those who will take the trouble to learn the language, on the same terms as poetry written in Latin or Greek. On the surface, there would seem to be every reason why Welsh poets should compose in the English language exclusively: for I know of no instance of a poet having reached the first rank in both languages; and the Welsh influence upon English poetry has been the work chiefly of Welsh poets who wrote only in English. But it must be remembered, that for the transmission of a culture—a peculiar way of thinking, feeling and behaving—and for its maintenance, there is no safeguard more reliable than a language. And to survive for this purpose it must continue to be a literary language—not necessarily a scientific language but certainly a poetic one: otherwise the spread of education will extinguish it. The literature written in that language will not, of course, make any direct impact upon the world at large; but if it is no longer cultivated, the people to whom it belongs (we are considering particularly the Welsh) will tend to lose their racial character. The Welsh will be less Welsh; and their poets will cease to have any contribution to make to English literature, beyond their individual genius.

And I am of opinion, that the benefits which Scottish, Welsh and Irish writers have conferred upon English literature are far in excess of what the contribution of all these individual men of genius would have been had they, let us say, all been adopted in early infancy by English foster-parents.

I am not concerned, in an essay which aims at least at the merit of brevity, to defend the thesis, that it is desirable that the English should continue to be English. I am obliged to take that for granted: and if this assumption is called into question, I must defend it on another occasion. But if I can defend with any success the thesis, that it is to the advantage of England that the Welsh should continue to be Welsh, the Scots Scots and the Irish Irish, then the reader should be disposed to agree that there may be some advantage to other peoples in the English continuing to be English. It is an essential part of my case, that if the other cultures of the British Isles were wholly superseded by English culture, English culture would disappear too. Many people seem to take for granted that English culture is something self-sufficient and secure; that it will persist whatever happens. While some refuse to admit that any foreign influence can be bad, others assume complacently that English culture could flourish in complete isolation from the Continent. To many it has never occurred to reflect that the disappearance of the peripheral cultures of England (to say nothing of the more humble local peculiarities within England itself) might be a calamity. We have not given enough attention to the ecology of cultures. It is probable, I think, that complete uniformity of culture throughout these islands would bring about a lower grade of culture altogether.

It should be clear that I attempt no solution of the regional problem; and the "solution" would have in any case to vary indefinitely according to local needs and possibilities. I am trying only to take apart, and leave to others to reassemble, the elements in the problem. I neither support nor dispute any specific proposals for particular regional reforms. Most attempts to solve the problem seem to me to suffer from a failure to examine closely either the unity, or the differences, between the cultural, political and economic aspects. To deal with one of these aspects, to the exclusion of the others, is to produce a programme which will, because of its inadequacy, appear a little absurd. If the nationalistic motive in regionalism were pushed very far, it certainly would lead to absurdity. The close association of the Bretons with the French, and of the Welsh with the English, is to the advantage of everybody: an association of Brittany and Wales which ruptured their connexions with France and England respectively, would be an unqualified misfortune. For a national culture, if it is to flourish, should be a constellation of cultures, the constituents of which, benefiting each other, benefit the whole.

At this point I introduce a new notion: that of the vital importance for a society of *friction* between its parts. Accustomed as we are to think in figures of speech taken from machinery, we assume that a society, like a machine, should be as well oiled as possible, provided with ball bearings of the best steel. We think of friction as waste of energy. I shall not attempt to substitute any other imagery: perhaps at this point the less we think in analogies the better. In the last chapter I suggested that in any society which became permanently established in either a caste or a classless system, the culture would decay: one might even put it that a classless society should always be emerging into class, and a class society should be tending towards obliteration of its class distinctions. I now suggest that both class and region, by dividing the inhabitants of a country into two different kinds of groups, lead to a conflict favourable to creativeness and progress. And (to remind the reader of what I said in my introduction) these are only two of an indefinite number of conflicts and jealousies which should be profitable to society. Indeed, the more the better: so that everyone should be an ally of everyone else in some respects, and an opponent in several others, and no one conflict, envy or fear will dominate.

As individuals, we find that our development depends upon the people whom we meet in the course of our lives. (These people include the authors whose books we read, and characters in works of fiction and history.) The benefit of these meetings is due as much to the differences as to the resemblances; to the conflict, as well as the sympathy, between persons. Fortunate the man who, at the right moment, meets the right friend; fortunate also the man who at the right moment meets the right enemy. I do not approve the extermination of the enemy: the policy of exterminating or, as is barbarously said, liquidating enemies, is one of the most alarming developments of modern war and peace, from the point of view of those who desire the survival of culture. One needs the enemy. So, within limits, the friction, not only between individuals but between groups, seems to me quite necessary for civilisation. The universality of irritation is the best assurance of peace. A country within which the divisions have gone too far is a danger to itself: a country which is too well united—whether by nature or by device, by honest purpose or by fraud and oppression—is a menace to others. In Italy and in Germany, we have seen that a unity with politico-economic aims, imposed violently and too rapidly, had unfortunate effects upon both nations. Their cultures had developed in the course of a history of extreme, and extremely sub-divided regionalism: the attempt to teach Germans to think of themselves as Germans first, and the attempt to teach Italians to think of themselves as Italians first, rather than as natives of a particular small principality or city, was to disturb the traditional culture from which alone any future culture could grow.

I may put the idea of the importance of conflict within a nation more positively by insisting on the importance of various and sometimes conflicting loyalties. If we consider these two divisions alone, of class and region, these ought to some extent to operate against each other: a man should have certain interests and sympathies in common with other men of the same local culture as against those of his own class elsewhere; and interests and sympathies in common with others of his class, irrespective of place. Numerous cross-divisions favour peace within a nation, by dispersing and confusing animosities; they favour peace between nations, by giving every man enough antagonism at home to exercise all his aggressiveness. The majority of men commonly dislike foreigners, and are easily inflamed against them; and it is not possible for the majority to know much about foreign peoples. A nation which has gradations of class seems to me, other things being equal, likely to be more tolerant and pacific than one which is not so organised.

So far, we have proceeded from the greater to the less, finding a national culture to be the resultant of an indefinite number of local cultures which, when themselves analysed, are composed of still smaller local cultures. Ideally, each village, and of course more visibly the larger towns, should have each its peculiar character. But I have already suggested that a national culture is the better for being in contact with outside cultures, both giving and receiving: and we shall now proceed in the opposite direction, from the smaller to the larger. As we go in this direction, we find that the content of the term *culture* undergoes some change: the word *means* something rather different, if we are speaking of the culture of a village, of a small region, of an island like Britain which comprehends several distinct racial cultures; and the meaning is altered much more when we come to speak of "European culture." We have to abandon most of the political associations, for whereas in such smaller units of culture as I have just mentioned there is normally a certain unity of government, the unity of government of the Holy Roman Empire was, throughout most of the period covered by the term, both precarious and largely nominal. Of the nature of the unity of culture in Western Europe, I have written in the three broadcast talks—composed for another audience and therefore in a somewhat different style from the body of this essay—which I have added as an appendix under the title of "The Unity of European Culture." I shall not attempt to cover the same ground in this chapter, but shall proceed to enquire what meaning, if any, can be attached to the term "world culture." The investigation of a possible "world culture" should be of particular interest to those who champion any of the various schemes for world-federation, or for a world government: for, obviously, so long as there exist cultures which are beyond some point antagonistic to each other, antagonistic to the point of irreconcilability, all attempts at politico-economic unification will be in vain. I say "beyond some point," because in the relations of any two cultures there will be two opposite forces balancing each other: attraction and repulsion—without the attraction they could not affect each other, and without the repulsion they could not survive as distinct cultures; one would absorb the other, or both would be fused into one culture. Now the zealots of world-government seem to me sometimes to assume, unconsciously, that their unity of organisation has an absolute value, and that if differences between cultures stand in the way, these must be abolished. If these zealots are of the humanitarian type, they will assume that this process will take place naturally and painlessly: they may, without knowing it, take for granted that the final world-culture will be simply an extension of that to which they belong themselves. Our Russian friends, who are more realistic, if not in the long run any more practical, are much more conscious of irreconcilability between cultures; and appear to hold the view that any culture incompatible with their own should be forcibly uprooted.

The world-planners who are both serious and humane, however, might—if we believed that their methods would

succeed—be as grave a menace to culture as those who practise
more violent methods. For it must follow from what I have
already pleaded about the value of local cultures, that a world
culture which was simply a *uniform* culture would be no culture at all. We should have a humanity de-humanised. It
would be a nightmare. But on the other hand, we cannot re-
sign the idea of world-culture altogether. For if we content
ourselves with the ideal of "European culture" we shall still
be unable to fix any definite frontiers. European culture has
an area, but no definite frontiers: and you cannot build
Chinese walls. The notion of a purely self-contained European
culture would be as fatal as the notion of a self-contained
national culture: in the end as absurd as the notion of preserving a local uncontaminated culture in a single county or
village of England. We are therefore pressed to maintain the
ideal of a world culture, while admitting that it is something
we cannot *imagine*. We can only conceive it, as the logical term
of relations between cultures. Just as we recognise that the
parts of Britain must have in one sense, a common culture,
though this common culture is only actual in diverse local
manifestations, so we must aspire to a common world culture,
which will yet not diminish the particularity of the constituent parts. And here, of course, we are finally up against religion, which so far, in the consideration of local differences
within the same area, we have not had to face. Ultimately,
antagonistic religions must mean antagonistic cultures; and
ultimately, religions cannot be reconciled. From the official
Russian point of view there are two objections to religion:
first, of course, that religion is apt to provide another loyalty
than that claimed by the State; and second, that there are several religions in the world still firmly maintained by many
believers. The second objection is perhaps even more serious
than the first: for where there is only one religion, it is always
possible that that religion may be subtly altered, so that it

will enjoin conformity rather than stimulate resistance to the State.

We are the more likely to be able to stay loyal to the ideal of the unimaginable world culture, if we recognise all the difficulties, the practical impossibility, of its realisation. And there are further difficulties which cannot be ignored. We have so far considered cultures as if they had all come into being by the same process of growth: the same people in the same place. But there is the *colonial* problem, and the *colonisation* problem: it is a pity that the world "colony" has had to do duty for two quite different meanings. The colonial problem is that of the relation between an indigenous native culture and a foreign culture, when a higher foreign culture has been imposed, often by force, upon a lower. This problem is insoluble, and takes several forms. There is one problem when we come into contact with a lower culture for the first time: there are very few places in the world where this is still possible. There is another problem where a native culture has already begun to disintegrate under foreign influence, and where a native population has already taken in more of the foreign culture than it can ever expel. There is a third problem where, as in some of the West Indies, several uprooted peoples have been haphazardly mixed. And these problems are insoluble, in the sense that, whatever we do towards their solution or mitigation, we do not altogether know what we are doing. We must be aware of them; we must do what we can, so far as our understanding will take us; but many more forces enter into the changes of the culture of a people than we can grasp and control; and any positive and excellent development of culture is always a miracle when it happens.

The colonisation problem arises from migration. When peoples migrated across Asia and Europe in pre-historic and early times, it was a whole tribe, or at least a wholly representative part of it, that moved together. Therefore, it was a total culture that moved. In the migrations of modern times, the emigrants have come from countries already highly civilised. They came from countries where the development of social organisation was already complex. The people who migrated have never represented the whole of the culture of the country from which they came, or they have represented it in quite different proportions. They have transplanted themselves according to some social, religious, economic or political determination, or some peculiar mixture of these. There has therefore been something in the removements analogous in nature to religious schism. The people have taken with them only a part of the total culture in which, so long as they remained at home, they participated. The culture which develops on the new soil must therefore be bafflingly alike and different from the parent culture: it will be complicated sometimes by whatever relations are established with some native race, and further by immigration from other than the original source. In this way, peculiar types of culture-sympathy and culture-clash appear, between the areas populated by colonisation and the countries of Europe from which the migrants came.

There is finally the peculiar case of India, where almost every complication is found to defeat the culture-planner. There is stratification of society which is not purely social but to some extent racial, in a Hindu world which comprehends peoples with an ancient tradition of high civilisation, and tribesmen of very primitive culture indeed. There is Brahminism and there is Islam. There are two or more important cultures on completely different religious foundations. Into this confused world came the British, with their assurance that their own culture was the best in the world, their ignorance of the relation between culture and religion, and (at least since the nineteenth century) their bland assumption that religion was a secondary matter. It is human, when we do not understand another human being, and cannot ignore him, to exert an unconscious pressure on that person to turn him into something that we *can* understand: many husbands and wives exert this pressure on each other. The effect on the person so influenced is liable to be the repression and distortion, rather than the improvement, of the personality; and no man is good enough to have the right to make another over in his own image. The benefits of British rule will soon be lost, but the ill effects of the disturbance of a native culture by an alien one will remain. To offer another people your culture first, and your religion second, is a reversal of values: and while every European represents, for good or ill, the culture to which he belongs, only a small minority are worthy representatives of its religious faith.[1] The only prospect of stability in India seems the alternative of a development, let us hope under peaceful conditions, into a loose federation of kingdoms, or to a mass uniformity attainable only at the price of the abolition of class distinctions and the abandonment of all religion—which would mean the disappearance of Indian culture.

I have thought it necessary to make this brief excursion into the several types of culture relation between one nation and the different kinds of foreign area, because the regional problem within the nation has to be seen in this larger context. There can be, of course, no one simple solution. As I have said, the improvement and transmission of culture can never be the direct object of any of our practical activities: all we can do is to try to keep in mind that whatever we do will affect our own culture or that of some other people. We can also learn to respect every other culture as a whole, however inferior to our own it may appear, or however justly we may disapprove of some features of it: the deliberate

---

[1] It is interesting to speculate, even though we cannot prove our conclusions, what would have happened to Western Europe had the Roman conquest imposed a culture pattern which left the religious beliefs and practices unaffected.

destruction of another culture as a whole is an irreparable wrong, almost as evil as to treat human beings like animals. But it is when we give our attention to the question of unity and diversity within the limited area that we know best, and within which we have the most frequent opportunities for right action, that we can combat the hopelessness that invades us, when we linger too long upon perplexities so far beyond our measure.

It was necessary to remind ourselves of those considerable areas of the globe, in which the problem takes a different form from ours: of those areas particularly, in which two or more distinct cultures are so inextricably involved with each other, in propinquity and in the ordinary business of living, that "regionalism," as we conceive it in Britain, would be a mockery. For such areas it is probable that a very different type of political philosophy should inspire political action, from that in terms of which we are accustomed to think and act in this part of the world. It is as well to have these differences at the back of our mind, that we may appreciate better the conditions with which we have to deal at home. These conditions are those of a homogeneous general culture, associated with the traditions of one religion: given these conditions, we can maintain the conception of a national culture which will draw its vitality from the cultures of its several areas, within each of which again there will be smaller units of culture having their own local peculiarities.

CHAPTER IV

Unity and Diversity: Sect and Cult

I N the first chapter I tried to place myself at a point of view from which the same phenomena appear both religious and cultural. In this chapter I shall be concerned with the cultural significance of religious divisions. While the considerations put forward should, if worthy of being taken seriously, have a particular interest for those Christians who are perplexed over the problem of Christian reunion, they are primarily intended to show that Christian divisions, and therefore schemes for Christian reunion, should be of concern not only to Christians, but to everybody except those who advocate a kind of society which would break completely with the Christian tradition.

I asserted, in the first chapter, that in the most primitive societies no clear distinction is visible between religious and non-religious activities; and that as we proceed to examine the more developed societies, we perceive a greater distinction, and finally contrast and opposition, between these activities. The sort of identity of religion and culture which we observe amongst peoples of very low development cannot recur except in the New Jerusalem. A higher religion is one which is much more difficult to believe. For the more conscious becomes the belief, so the more conscious becomes unbelief: indifference, doubt and scepticism appear, and the endeavour to adapt the tenets of religion to what people in each age find easiest to believe. In the higher religion, it is more difficult also to make behaviour conform to the moral laws of the religion. A higher religion imposes a conflict, a division, torment and struggle within the individual; a conflict sometimes between the laity and the priesthood; a conflict eventually between Church and State.

The reader may have difficulty in reconciling these asser-tions with the point of view set forth in my first chapter, according to which there is always, even in the most con-scious and highly developed societies that we know, an aspect of identity between the religion and the culture. I wish to maintain *both* these points of view. We do not leave the earlier stage of development behind us: it is that upon which we build. The identity of religion and culture remains on the unconscious level, upon which we have superimposed a conscious structure wherein religion and culture are con-trasted and can be opposed. The *meaning* of the terms "reli-gion" and "culture" is of course altered between these two levels. To the unconscious level we constantly tend to re-vert, as we find consciousness an excessive burden; and the tendency towards reversion may explain the powerful attrac-tion which totalitarian philosophy and practice can exert upon humanity. Totalitarianism appeals to the desire to re-turn to the womb. The contrast between religion and culture imposes a strain: we escape from this strain by attempting to revert to an identity of religion and culture which prevailed at a more primitive stage; as when we indulge in alcohol as an anodyne, we consciously seek unconsciousness. It is only by unremitting effort that we can persist in being individuals in a society, instead of merely members of a disciplined crowd. Yet we remain members of the crowd, even when we succeed in being individuals. Hence, for the purposes of this essay, I am obliged to maintain two contradictory propositions: that religion and culture are aspects of one unity, and that they are two different and contrasted things.

I attempt, as far as possible, to contemplate my problems from the point of view of the sociologist, and not from that of the Christian apologist. Most of my generalisations are intended to have some applicability to all religion, and not only to Christianity; and when, as in what follows in this chapter, I discuss Christian matters, that is because I am particularly concerned with Christian culture, with the Western World, with Europe, and with England. In saying that I aim at taking, as consistently as I can, the sociological point of view, I must make clear that I do not think that the difference between the religious and the sociological point of view is so easily maintained as the difference between a couple of adjectives might lead us to suppose. We may here define the religious point of view, as that from which we ask the question, whether the tenets of a religion are true or false. It follows that we shall be taking the religious point of view, if we are atheists whose thinking is based on the assumption that all religions are untrue. From the sociological point of view, the truth or falsity is irrelevant: we are concerned only with the comparative effects of different religious structures upon culture. Now, if students of the subject could be neatly divided into theologians, including atheists, and sociologists, the problem would be very different from what it is. But, for one thing, no religion can be wholly "understood" from the outside—even the sociologist's purposes. For another, no one can wholly escape the religious point of view, because in the end one either believes or disbelieves. Therefore, no one can be as wholly detached and disinterested as the ideal sociologist should be. The reader accordingly must try, not only to make allowance for the religious views of the author, but, what is more difficult, to make allowance for his own—and he may never have examined thoroughly his own mind. So both writer and reader must be on guard against assuming that they are wholly detached.[1]

We have now to consider unity and diversity in religious belief and practice, and enquire what is the situation most favourable to the preservation and improvement of culture. I have suggested in my first chapter that those among the "higher religions" which are most likely to continue to stimulate culture, are those which are capable of being accepted by peoples of different cultures: those which have the greatest universality—though potential universality by itself may be no criterion of a "higher religion." Such religions can provide a ground pattern of common belief and behaviour, upon which a variety of local patterns can be embroidered; and they will encourage a reciprocal influence of peoples upon each other, such that any cultural progress in one area may quicken development in another. In certain historical conditions, a fierce exclusiveness may be a necessary condition for the preservation of a culture: the Old Testament bears witness to this.[2] In spite of this particular historical situation, we should be able to agree that the practice of a common religion, by peoples each having its own cultural character, should usually promote the exchange of influence to their reciprocal advantage. It is of course conceivable that a religion may be too easily accommodated to a variety of cultures, and become assimilated without assimilating; and that this weakness may tend to bring about the opposite result, if the religion breaks

[1] See a valuable article by Professor Evans-Pritchard on "Social Anthropology" in *Blackfriars* for November 1946. He remarks: "The answer would seem to be that the sociologist should also be a moral philosopher and that, as such, he should have a set of definite beliefs and values in terms of which he evaluates the facts he studies as a sociologist."

[2] Since the diaspora, and the scattering of Jews amongst peoples holding the Christian Faith, it may have been unfortunate both for these peoples and for the Jews themselves, that the culture-contact between them has had to be within those neutral zones of culture in which religion could be ignored: and the effect may have been to strengthen the illusion that there can be culture without religion.

up into branches or sects so opposed that they cease to influence each other. Christianity and Buddhism have been exposed to this danger.

From this point it is with Christianity alone that I am to be concerned; in particular with the relation of Catholicism and Protestantism in Europe and the diversity of sects within Protestantism. We must try to start without any bias for, or against, unity or reunion or the maintenance of the separate corporate identity of religious denominations. We must take note of whatever injury appears to have been done to European culture, and to the culture of any part of Europe, by division into sects. On the other hand, we must acknowledge that many of the most remarkable achievements of culture have been made since the sixteenth century, in conditions of disunity: and that some, indeed, as in nineteenth-century France, appear after the religious foundations for culture seem to have crumbled away. We cannot affirm that if the religious unity of Europe had continued, these or equally brilliant achievements would have been realised. Either religious unity or religious division may coincide with cultural efflorescence or cultural decay.

From this point of view, we may take a moderate satisfaction, which should not be allowed to settle into complacency, when we review the history of England. In a nation in which no *tendency* to Protestantism appeared, or in which it was negligible, there must always be a danger of religious petrifaction, and of aggressive unbelief. In a nation in which the relations of Church and State run too smoothly, it does not matter much, from our present point of view, whether the cause is ecclesiasticism, the dominance of State by Church, or erastianism, the dominance of Church by State. Indeed, it is not always easy to distinguish between the two conditions. The effect equally may be, that every disaffected person, and every sufferer from injustice, will attribute his misfortunes to the inherent evil of the Church, or to an inherent evil in Christianity itself. Formal obedience to the Roman See is itself no assurance that, in a wholly Catholic nation, religion and culture will not become too closely identified. Elements of local culture—even of local barbarism—may become invested with the sanctity of religious observances, and superstition may flourish under the guise of piety: a people may tend to slip back towards the unity of religion and culture that pertains to primitive communities. The result of the unquestioned dominance of one cult, when a people is passive, may be torpor: when a people is quick and self-assertive, the result may be chaos. For, as discontent turns to disaffection, the anti-clerical bias may become an anti-religious tradition; a distinct and hostile culture grows and flourishes, and a nation is divided against itself. The factions have to continue to live with each other; and the common language and ways of life which they retain, far from mollifying animosity, may only exasperate it. The religious division becomes a symbol for a group of associated differences, often rationally unrelated; around these differences swarm a host of private grievances, fears and interests; and the contest for an indivisible heritage may terminate only in exhaustion.

It would here be irrelevant to review those sanguinary passages of civil strife, such as the Thirty Years War, in which Catholics and Protestants fought over such an heritage. Explicit theological contentions between Christians no longer attract to themselves those other irreconcilable interests which seek a decision by arms. The deepest causes of division may still be religious, but they become conscious, not in theological but in political, social and economic doctrines. Certainly, in those countries in which the prevailing faith has been Protestant, anti-clericalism seldom takes a violent form. In such countries, both faith and infidelity tend to be mild and inoffensive; as the culture has become secularised, the cultural differences between faithful and infidel are minimal; the boundary between belief and unbelief is vague; the Christianity is more pliant, the atheism more negative; and all parties live in amity, so long as they continue to accept some common moral conventions.

The situation in England, however, differs from that in other countries, whether Catholic or Protestant. In England, as in other Protestant countries, atheism has been mostly of a passive kind. No statistician could produce an estimate of the numbers of Christians and non-Christians. Many people live on an unmarked frontier enveloped in dense fog; and those who dwell beyond it are more numerous in the dark waste of ignorance and indifference, than in the well-lighted desert of atheism. The English unbeliever, of some social status however humble, is likely to conform to the practices of Christianity on the occasions of birth, death and the first venture in matrimony. Atheists in this country are not yet culturally united: their types of atheism will vary according to the culture of the religious communion in which they, or their parents, or their grandparents were reared. The chief cultural differences in England have, in the past, been those between Anglicanism and the more important Protestant sects; and even these differences are far from clearly defined: first, because the Church of England itself has comprehended wider variations of belief and cult than a foreign observer would believe it possible for one institution to contain without bursting; and second, because of the number and variety of the sects separated from it.

If my contentions in the first chapter are accepted, it will be agreed that the formation of a religion is also the formation of a culture. From this it should follow that, as a religion divides into sects, and as these sects develop from generation to generation, a variety of cultures will be propagated. And, as the intimacy of religion and culture is such that we may expect what happens one way to happen the other, we are prepared to find that the division between Christian cultures will stimulate further differentiations of belief and cult. It

does not fall within my purpose to consider the Great Schism
between East and West which corresponds to the shifting
geographical boundary between two cultures. When we consider the Western World, we must recognise that the main cultural tradition has been that corresponding to the Church of
Rome. Only within the last four hundred years has any other
manifested itself; and anyone with a sense of centre and pe-
riphery must admit that the western tradition has been Latin,
and Latin means Rome. There are countless testimonies of
art and thought and manners; and among these we must include the work of all men born and educated in a Catholic
society, whatever their individual beliefs. From this point of
view, the separation of Northern Europe, and of England in
particular, from communion with Rome represents a diver-
sion from the main stream of culture. To pronounce, upon
this separation, any judgment of value, to assume that it was
a good or a bad thing, is what in this investigation we must try
to avoid; for that would be to pass from the sociological to the
theological point of view. And as I must at this point introduce the term *sub-culture* to signify the culture which pertains to the area of a divided part of Christendom, we must be
careful not to assume that a sub-culture is necessarily an inferior culture; remembering also that while a sub-culture may
suffer loss in being separated from the main body, the main
body may also be mutilated by the loss of a member of itself.

We must recognise next, that where a sub-culture has in
time become established as the main culture *of a particular
territory*, it tends to change places, for that territory, with
the main European culture. In this respect it differs from
those sub-cultures representing sects the members of which
share a region with the main culture. In England, the main
cultural tradition has for several centuries been Anglican.
Roman Catholics in England are, of course, in a more central
European tradition than are Anglicans; yet, because the main
tradition of England has been Anglican, they are in another

aspect more outside of the tradition than are Protestant dis·
senters. It is Protestant dissent which is, in relation to Anglicanism, a congeries of sub-cultures: or, when we regard Anglicanism itself as a sub-culture, we might refer to it as a congeries of "sub-sub-cultures"—as this term is too clownish to
be admitted into good company, we can only say "secondary
sub-cultures." By Protestant dissent I mean those bodies which
recognise each other as "the Free Churches," together with
the Society of Friends, which has an isolated but distinguished
history: all minor religious entities are culturally negligible.
The variations of character among the chief religious bodies,
have to some extent to do with the peculiar circumstances of
their origins, and the length of the separation. It is of some
interest that Congregationalism, which has a long history,
numbers several distinguished theologians; whereas Methodism, with a briefer history, and less theological justification
for its separate existence, appears to rely chiefly on its
hymnology, and to need no independent theological structure of its own. But whether we consider a territorial sub-culture, or a secondary sub-culture within a territory or scattered
over several territories, we may find ourselves led to the conclusion, that every sub-culture is dependent upon that from
which it is an offshoot. The life of Protestantism depends upon
the survival of that against which it protests; and just as the
culture of Protestant dissent would perish of inanition
without the persistence of Anglican culture, so the maintenance of English culture is contingent upon the health of
the culture of Latin Europe, and upon continuing to draw
sustenance from that Latin culture.

There is, however, a difference between the division of
Canterbury from Rome, and the division of Free Protestantism from Canterbury, which is important for my purposes.
It corresponds to a difference presented in the previous chapter, between colonisation by mass migration (as in the early
movements westwards across Europe) and colonisation by cer·

tain elements separating themselves from a culture which remains at home (as in the colonisation of the Dominions and
the Americas). The separation precipitated by Henry VIII
had the immediate cause of personal motives in high quarters;
it was reinforced by tendencies strong in England and in
Northern Europe, of more respectable origin. Once released,
the forces of Protestantism went further than Henry himself
intended or would have approved. But, although the Reformation in England was, like any other revolution, the work of a
minority, and although it met with several local movements
of stubborn resistance, it eventually carried with it the greater
part of the nation irrespective of class or region. The Protestant sects, on the other hand, represent certain elements in
English culture to the exclusion of others: class and occupation played a large part in their formation. It would probably be impossible for the closest student to pronounce how
far it is adherence to dissenting tenets that forms a sub-culture,
and how far it is the formation of a sub-culture that inspires
the finding of reasons for dissent. The solution of that enigma
is fortunately not necessary for my purpose. The result, in any
case, was a stratification of England by sects, in some measure
proceeding from, in some measure aggravating, the cultural
distinctions between classes.

It might be possible for a profound student of ethnology
and of the history of early settlement in this island, to argue
the existence of causes of a more stubborn and more primitive nature, for the tendencies to religious fission. He might
trace them to ineradicable differences between the culture
of the several tribes, races and languages which from time
to time held sway or contested for supremacy. He might,
furthermore, take the view that cultural mixture does not
necessarily follow the same course as biological mixture; and
that, even if we assumed every person of purely English
descent to have the blood of all the successive invaders
mingled in his veins in exactly the same proportions, it need

not follow that cultural fusion ensued. He might therefore discover, in the tendency of various elements in the population to express their faith in different ways, to prefer different types of communal organisation and different styles of worship, a reflection of early divisions between dominant and subject races. Such speculations, which I am too unlearned to support or oppose, lie outside of my scope; but it is as well for both writer and readers to remind themselves that there may be deeper levels than that upon which the enquiry is being conducted. If differences persisting to the present day could be established in descent from primitive differences of culture, this would only reinforce the case for the unity of religion and culture propounded in my first chapter.

However this may be, there are curiosities enough to occupy our attention in the mixture of motives and interests in the dissensions of religious parties within the period of modern history. One need not be a cynic to be amused, or a devotee to be saddened, by the spectacle of the self-deception, as well as the frequent hypocrisy, of the attackers and defenders of one or another form of the Christian Faith. But from the point of view of my essay, both mirth and sorrow are irrelevant, because this confusion is just what one must expect, being inherent in the human condition. There are, certainly, situations in history in which a religious contest can be attributed to a purely religious motive. The life-long battle of St. Athanasius against the Arians and Eutychians need not be regarded in any other light than the light of theology: the scholar who endeavoured to demonstrate that it represented a culture-clash between Alexandria and Antioch, or some similar ingenuity, would appear to us at best to be talking about something else. Even the purest theological issue, however, will in the long run have cultural consequences: a superficial acquaintance with the career of Athanasius should be enough to assure us that he was one of the great builders of western civilisation. And, for the most part, it is *inevitable* that we should, when we defend our religion, be defending at the same time our culture, and vice versa: we are obeying the fundamental instinct to preserve our existence. And in so doing, in the course of time we make many errors and commit many crimes—most of which may be simplified into the one error, of identifying our religion and our culture on a level on which we ought to distinguish them from each other.

Such considerations are relevant not only to the history of religious strife and separation: they are equally pertinent when we come to entertain schemes for reunion. The importance of stopping to examine cultural peculiarities, to disentangle religious from cultural hindrances, has hitherto been overlooked—and I should say more than overlooked: deliberately though unconsciously ignored—in the schemes of reunion between Christian bodies adopted or put forward. Hence the appearance of disingenuousness, of agreement upon formulae to which the contracting parties can give different interpretations, which provokes a comparison with treaties between governments.

The reader unacquainted with the details of "oecumenicity," should be reminded of the difference between *inter-communion* and *reunion*. An arrangement of inter-communion between two national churches—such as the Church of England and the Church of Sweden—or between the Church of England and one of the Eastern Churches, or between the Church of England and a body such as the "Old Catholics" found in Holland and elsewhere on the Continent, does not necessarily look any further than what the term implies: a reciprocal recognition of the "validity of orders" and of the orthodoxy of tenets; with the consequence that the members of each church can communicate, the priests celebrate and preach, in the churches of the other country. An agreement of inter-communion could only lead toward reunion in one of two events: the unlikely event of a political union of the two nations, or the ultimate event of a world-wide reunion of Christians. Reunion, on the other hand, means in effect either reunion of one or another body having episcopal government, with the Church of Rome, or reunion between bodies separated from each other in the same areas. The movements towards reunion which are at the present time most active, are of the second kind: reunion between the Anglican Church and one or more of the "Free Church" bodies. It is with the cultural implications of this latter kind of reunion that we are here specially concerned. There can be no question of reunion between the Church of England and, let us say, the Presbyterians or Methodists in America: any reunion would be of American Presbyterians with the Episcopal Church in America, and of English Presbyterians with the Church of England.

It should be obvious, from the considerations advanced in my first chapter, that complete reunion involves community of culture—some common culture already existing, and the potentiality of its further development consequent upon official reunion. The ideal reunion of all Christians does not, of course, imply an eventual *uniform* culture the world over: it implies simply a "Christian culture" of which all local cultures should be variants—and they would and should vary very widely indeed. We can already distinguish between a "local culture" and a "European culture"; when we use the latter term we recognise the local differences; similarly a universal "Christian culture" should not be taken to ignore or override the differences between the cultures of the several continents. But the existence of a strong community of culture between various Christian bodies in the same area (we must remember that we here mean "culture" as distinguished from "religion") not only facilitates reunion of Christians in that area, but exposes such reunion to peculiar dangers.

I have put forward the view that every division of a Christian people into sects brings about or aggravates the develop-

ment of "sub-cultures" amongst that people; and I have asked
the reader to examine Anglicanism and the Free Churches
for confirmation of this view. But it should now be added,
that the cultural divisions between Anglicans and Free
Churchmen have, under changing social and economic conditions, become attenuated. The organisation of rural society
from which the Church of England drew much of its cultural
strength is in decay; the landed gentry have less security, less
power and less influence; the families which have risen in
trade and in many places succeeded to territorial proprietor-
ship are themselves progressively reduced and impoverished.
A diminishing number of Anglican clergy come from public
schools or the old universities, or are educated at their
families' expense; bishops are not wealthy men, and are embarrassed in keeping up palaces. Anglican and Free Church
laymen have been educated at the same universities and often
at the same schools. And finally, they are all exposed to the
same environment of a culture severed from religion. When
men of different religious persuasions are drawn together by
common interests and common anxieties, by their awareness
of an increasingly oppressive non-Christian world, and by
their unawareness of the extent to which they are themselves
penetrated by non-Christian influences and by a neutral culture, it is only to be expected that the vestiges of the distinctions between their several Christian cultures should seem to
them of minor significance.

With the dangers of reunion on erroneous or evasive terms
I am not here concerned; but I am much concerned with the
danger that reunion facilitated by the disappearance of the
cultural characteristics of the several bodies reunited might
accelerate and confirm the general lowering of culture. The
refinement or crudity of theological and philosophical thinking is itself, of course, one of the measures of the state of our
culture; and the tendency in some quarters to reduce theology
to such principles as a child can understand or a Socinian
accept, is itself indicative of cultural debility. But there is a

further danger, from our point of view, in schemes of reunion which attempt to remove the difficulties, and protect the self-assertiveness, of everybody. In an age like our own, when it has become a point of politeness to dissimulate social distinctions, and to pretend that the highest degree of "culture" ought to be made accessible to everybody—in an age of cultural levelling, it will be denied that the several Christian fragments to be re-united represent any cultural differences. There is certain to be a strong pressure towards a reunion on terms of complete cultural equality. Too much account may even be taken of the relative numbers of the membership of the uniting bodies: for a main culture will remain a main culture, and a sub-culture will remain a sub-culture, even if the latter attracts more adherents than the former. It is always the main religious body which is the guardian of more of the remains of the higher developments of culture preserved from a past time before the division took place. Not only is it the main religious body which has the more elaborated theology; it is the main religious body which is the least alienated from the best intellectual and artistic activity of its time. Hence it is that the convert—and I think not only of conversion from one form of Christianity to another, but indeed primarily of conversion from indifference to Christian belief and practice—the convert of the intellectual or sensitive type is drawn towards the more Catholic type of worship and doctrine. This attraction, which may occur before the prospective convert has begun to inform himself about Christianity at all, may be cited by the outsider as evidence that the convert has become a Christian for the wrong reasons, or that he is guilty of insincerity and affectation. Every sin that can be imagined has been practised, and the pretence of religious faith may often enough have cloaked intellectual or esthetic vanity and self-indulgence; but, on the view of the intimacy of religion and culture which is the starting point of my examination, such phenomena as the progress to religious faith through cultural attraction are both natural and acceptable.

After the considerations now reviewed, I must attempt to link the chapter to the two preceding chapters, by enquiring what is the ideal pattern of unity and diversity between Christian nations and between the several strata in each nation. It should be obvious that the sociological point of view cannot lead us to those conclusions which can properly be reached only by theological premisses; and the reader of the previous chapters will be prepared to find no solution in any rigid and unchangeable scheme. No security against cultural deterioration is offered by any of the three chief types of religious organisation: the international church with a central government, the national church, or the separated sect. The danger of freedom is deliquescence; the danger of strict order is petrifaction. Nor can we judge from the history of any particular society, whether a different religious history would have resulted in a more healthy culture today. The disastrous effects of armed religious strife within a people, as in England in the seventeenth century or in the German States in the sixteenth, need no emphasis; the disintegrating effect of sectarian division has already been touched upon. Yet we may ask whether Methodism did not, in the period of its greatest fervour, revive the spiritual life of the English, and prepare the way for the Evangelical Movement and even for the Oxford Movement. Furthermore, Dissent made it possible for "working class" Christians (though perhaps it might have done more than it has for "labouring class" Christians) to play that part, which all zealous and socially active Christians should wish to play, in the conduct of their local church and the social and charitable organisations connected with it.[1] The actual choice, at times, has been between sectarianism and indifference; and those who chose the former were, in so doing, keeping alive the culture of certain social strata. And,

[1] See two valuable Supplements to *The Christian News-Letter:* "Ecumenical Christianity and the Working Classes" by W. G. Symons, July 30, 1941; and "The Free Churches and Working Class Culture" by John Marsh, May 20, 1942.

as I have said at the beginning, the appropriate culture of each stratum is of equal importance.

As in the relation between the social classes, and as in the relation of the several regions of a country to each other and to the central power, it would seem that a constant struggle between the centripetal and the centrifugal forces is desirable. For without the struggle no balance can be maintained; and if either force won the result would be deplorable. The conclusions to which we are justified in coming, from our premisses and from the sociologist's point of view, appear to me to be as follows. Christendom should be one: the form of organisation and the locus of powers in that unity are questions upon which we cannot pronounce. But within that unity there should be an endless conflict between ideas—for it is only by the struggle against constantly appearing false ideas that the truth is enlarged and clarified, and in the conflict with heresy that orthodoxy is developed to meet the needs of the times; an endless effort also on the part of each region to shape its Christianity to suit itself, an effort which should neither be wholly suppressed nor left wholly unchecked. The local temperament must express its particularity in its form of Christianity, and so must the social stratum, so that the culture proper to each area and each class may flourish; but there must also be a force holding these areas and these classes together. If this corrective force in the direction of uniformity of belief and practice is lacking, then the culture of each part will suffer. We have already found that the culture of a nation prospers with the prosperity of the culture of its several constituents, both geographical and social; but that it also needs to be itself a part of a larger culture, which requires the ultimate ideal, however unrealisable, of a "world culture" in a sense different from that implicit in the schemes of world-federationists. And without a common faith, all efforts towards drawing nations closer together in culture can produce only an illusion of unity.

CHAPTER V

A Note on Culture and Politics

Politics did not, however, so much engage him as to withhold his thoughts from things of more importance.

SAMUEL JOHNSON on GEORGE LYTTELTON

WE observe nowadays that "culture" attracts the attention of men of politics: not that politicians are always "men of culture," but that "culture" is recognised both as an instrument of policy and as something socially desirable which it is the business of the State to promote. We not only hear, from high political quarters, that "cultural relations" between nations are of great importance, but find that bureaux are founded, and officials appointed, for the express purpose of attending to these relations, which are presumed to foster international amity. The fact that culture has become, in some sense, a department of politics, should not obscure in our memory the fact that at other periods politics has been an activity pursued within a culture, and between representatives of different cultures. It is therefore not impertinent to attempt to indicate the place of politics within a culture united and divided according to the kind of unity and division which we have been considering.

We may assume, I think, that in a society so articulated the practice of politics and an active interest in public affairs would not be the business of everybody, or of everybody to the same degree; and that not everybody should concern himself, except at moments of crisis, with the conduct of the nation as a whole. In a healthily *regional* society, public affairs would be the business of everybody, or of the great majority, only within very small social units; and would be the business of a progressively smaller number of men in the larger units within which the smaller were comprehended. In a healthily *stratified* society, public affairs would be a responsibility not equally borne: a greater responsibility would be inherited by those who inherited special advantages, and in whom self-interest, and interest for the sake of their families ("a stake in the country") should cohere with public spirit. The governing élite, of the nation as a whole, would consist of those whose responsibility was inherited with their affluence and position, and whose forces were constantly increased, and often led, by rising individuals of exceptional talents. But when we speak of a governing élite, we must safeguard ourselves against thinking of an élite sharply divided from the other élites of society.

The relation of the political élite—by which we mean the leading members of *all* the effective and recognised political groups: for the survival of a parliamentary system requires a constant *dining with the Opposition* [1]—to the other élites would be put too crudely if described as communication between men of action and men of thought. It is rather a relation between men of different types of mind and different areas of thought and action. A sharp distinction between thought and action is no more tenable for the political than for the religious life, in which the contemplative must have his own activity, and the secular priest must not be wholly unpractised in meditation. There is no plane of active life on which thought is negligible, except that of the merest

[1] I seem to remember that some such phrase was either attributed to Sir William Vernon Harcourt, or used about him.

automatic execution of orders; and there is no species of
thinking which can be quite without effect upon action.

I have suggested elsewhere [1] that a society is in danger of
disintegration when there is a lack of contact between people
of different areas of activity—between the political, the scientific, the artistic, the philosophical and the religious minds.
This separation cannot be repaired merely by public organisation. It is not a question of assembling into committees
representatives of different types of knowledge and experience, of calling in everybody to advise everybody else. The
élite should be something different, something much more
organically composed, than a panel of bonzes, caciques and
tycoons. Men who meet only for definite serious purposes, and
on official occasions, do not wholly meet. They may have some
common concern very much at heart; they may, in the course
of repeated contacts, come to share a vocabulary and an idiom
which appear to communicate every shade of meaning necessary for their common purpose; but they will continue to
retire from these encounters each to his private social world
as well as to his solitary world. Everyone has observed that
the possibilities of contented silence, of a mutual happy awareness when engaged upon a common task, or an underlying
seriousness and significance in the enjoyment of a silly joke,
are characteristics of any close personal intimacy; and the congeniality of any circle of friends depends upon a common
social convention, a common ritual, and common pleasures of
relaxation. These aids to intimacy are no less important for
the communication of meaning in words, than the possession
of a common subject upon which the several parties are informed. It is unfortunate for a man when his friends and his
business associates are two unrelated groups; it is also narrow-
ing when they are one and the same group.

Such observations upon personal intimacy cannot pretend

[1] *The Idea of a Christian Society*, p. 32.

to any novelty: the only possible novelty is in calling attention to them in this context. They point to the desirability of
a society in which persons of every superior activity can meet
without merely talking shop or being at pains to talk each
other's shop. In order correctly to appraise a man of action
we must meet him: or we must at least have known enough
men of similar pursuits to be able to draw a shrewd guess
about one whom we have not met. And to meet a man of
thought, and to form an impression of his personality, may be
of great assistance in judging his ideas. This is not wholly
improper even in the field of art, though with important
reservations, and though the impressions of an artist's personality often affect opinion of his work quite irrelevantly—for
every artist must have remarked, that while a small number
of people dislike his work more strongly after meeting him,
there are also many who are more friendly disposed towards
his work if they find him a pleasant fellow. These advantages
persist however they may offend the reason, and in spite of the
fact that in modern societies of large numbers, it is impossible
for everyone to know everyone else.

In our time, we read too many new books, or are oppressed
by the thought of the new books which we are neglecting to
read; we read many books, because we cannot know enough
people; we cannot know everybody whom it would be to our
benefit to know, because there are too many of them. Consequently, if we have the skill to put words together and the
fortune to get them printed, we communicate by writing more
books. It is often those writers whom we are lucky enough to
know, whose books we can ignore; and the better we know
them personally, the less need we may feel to read what they
write. We are encumbered not only with too many new books:
we are further embarrassed by too many periodicals, reports
and privately circulated memoranda. In the endeavour to
keep up with the most intelligent of these publications we
may sacrifice the three permanent reasons for reading: the

acquisition of wisdom, the enjoyment of art, and the pleasure of entertainment. Meanwhile, the professional politician has too much to do to have leisure for serious reading, even on politics. He has far too little time for exchange of ideas and information with men of distinction in other walks of life. In a society of smaller size (a society, therefore, which was less feverishly *busy*) there might be more conversation and fewer books; and we should not find the tendency—of which this essay provides one example—for those who have acquired some reputation, to write books outside the subject on which they have made that reputation.

It is unlikely, in all the mass of letterpress, that the profoundest and most original works will reach the eye or command the attention of a large public, or even of a good number of the readers who are qualified to appreciate them. The ideas which flatter a current tendency or emotional attitude will go farthest; and some others will be distorted to fit in with what is already accepted. The residuum in the public mind is hardly likely to be a distillation of the best and wisest: it is more likely to represent the common prejudices of the majority of editors and reviewers. In this way are formed the *idées reçues*—more precisely the *mots reçus* —which, because of their emotional influence upon that part of the public which is influenced by printed matter, have to be taken into account by the professional politician, and treated with respect in his public utterances. It is unnecessary, for the simultaneous reception of these "ideas," that they should be consistent among themselves; and, however they contradict each other, the practical politician must handle them with as much deference as if they were the constructions of informed sagacity, the intuitions of genius, or the accumulated wisdom of ages. He has not, as a rule, inhaled any fragrance they may have had when they were fresh; he only noses them when they have already begun to stink.

In a society so graded as to have several levels of culture, and several levels of power and authority, the politician might at least be restrained, in his use of language, by his respect for the judgment, and fear of the ridicule, of a smaller and more critical public, among which was maintained some standard of prose style. If it were also a decentralised society, a society in which local cultures continued to flourish, and in which the majority of problems were local problems on which local populations could form an opinion from their own experience and from conversation with their neighbours, political utterances might also tend to manifest greater clarity and be susceptible of fewer variations of interpretation. A local speech on a local issue is likely to be more intelligible than one addressed to a whole nation, and we observe that the greatest muster of ambiguities and obscure generalities is usually to be found in speeches which are addressed to the whole world.

It is always desirable that a part of the education of those persons who are either born into, or qualified by their abilities to enter, the superior political grades of society, should be instruction in history, and that a part of the study of history should be the history of political theory. The advantage of the study of Greek history and Greek political theory, as a preliminary to the study of other history and other theory, is its *manageability*: it has to do with a small area, with men rather than masses, and with the human passions of individuals rather than with those vast impersonal forces which in our modern society are a necessary convenience of thought, and the study of which tends to obscure the study of human beings. The reader of Greek philosophy, moreover, is unlikely to be over-sanguine about the effects of political theory; for he will observe that the study of political forms appears to have arisen out of the failure of political systems; and that neither Plato nor Aristotle was much concerned with prediction, or very optimistic about the future.

The kind of political theory which has arisen in quite modern times is less concerned with human nature, which it is inclined to treat as something which can always be re-fashioned to fit whatever political form is regarded as most desirable. Its real data are impersonal forces which may have originated in the conflict and combination of human wills but have come to supersede them. As a part of academic discipline for the young, it suffers from several drawbacks. It tends, of course, to form minds which will be set to think only in terms of impersonal and inhuman forces, and thereby to de-humanise its students. Being occupied with humanity only in the mass, it tends to separate itself from ethics; being occupied only with that recent period of history during which humanity can most easily be shown to have been ruled by impersonal forces, it reduces the proper study of mankind to the last two or three hundred years of man. It too often inculcates a belief in a future inflexibly determined and at the same time in a future which we are wholly free to shape as we like. Modern political thought, inextricably involved with economics and with sociology, preempts to itself the position of queen of the sciences. For the exact and experimental sciences are judged according to their utility, and are valued in so far as they produce results—either for making life more comfortable and less laborious, or for making it more precarious and ending it more quickly. Culture itself is regarded either as a negligible by-product which can be left to itself, or as a department of life to be organised in accordance with the particular scheme we favour. I am thinking not only of the more dogmatic and totalitarian philosophies of the present day, but of assumptions which colour thinking in every country and tend to be shared by the most opposed parties.

An important document in the history of the political direction of culture will be Leon Trotsky's essay, *Literature and Revolution,* of which an English translation appeared in

1925.[1] The conviction, which seems to be deeply implanted in the Muscovite mind, that it is the role of Mother Russia to contribute not merely ideas and political forms, but a total way of life for the rest of the world, has gone far to make us all more politically culture-conscious. But there have been other causes than the Russian Revolution for this consciousness. The researches and the theories of anthropologists have played their part, and have led us to study the relations of imperial powers and subject peoples with a new attention. Governments are more aware of the necessity of taking account of cultural differences; and to the degree to which colonial administration is controlled from the imperial centre, these differences become of increasing importance. One people in isolation is not aware of having a "culture" at all. And the differences between the several European nations in the past were not wide enough to make their peoples see their cultures as different to the point of conflict and incompatibility: culture-consciousness as a means of uniting a nation against other nations was first exploited by the late rulers of Germany. Today, we have become culture-conscious in a way which nourishes nazism, communism and nationalism all at once; in a way which emphasises separation without helping us to overcome it. At this point a few remarks on the cultural effects of empire (in the most comprehensive sense) may not be amiss.

The early British rulers of India were content to rule; some of them, through long residence and continuous absence from Britain, assimilated themselves to the mentality of the

---

[1] Published by International Publishers, New York. A book which merits republication. It does not give the impression that Trotsky was very sensitive to literature; but he was, from his own point of view, very intelligent about it. Like all his writings, the book is encumbered with discussion of minor Russian personalities of which the foreigner is ignorant and in which he is not interested; but this indulgence in detail, while it contributes a flavour of provinciality, gives the work all the more appearance of genuineness, as having been written rather to speak his mind than with an eye to a foreign audience.

people they governed. A later type of rulers, explicitly and increasingly the servants of Whitehall, and serving only for a limited period (after which they returned to their native country, either to retirement or to some other activity) aimed rather to bring to India the benefits of western civilisation. They did not intend to uproot, or to impose, a total "culture": but the superiority of western political and social organisation, of English education, of English justice, of western "enlightenment" and science seemed to them so self-evident that the desire to do good would alone have been a sufficient motive for introducing these things. The Briton, unconscious of the importance of religion in the formation of his own culture, could hardly be expected to recognise its importance in the preservation of another. In the piece-meal imposition of a foreign culture—an imposition in which force plays only a small part: the appeal to ambition, and the temptation to which the native is exposed, to admire the wrong things in western civilisation, and for the wrong reasons, are much more decisive—the motives of arrogance and generosity are always inextricably mixed; there is at the same time an assertion of superiority and a desire to communicate the way of life upon which that assumed superiority is based; so that the native acquires a taste for western ways, a jealous admiration of material power, and a resentment against his tutors. The partial success of westernisation, of which some members of an Eastern society are quick to seize the apparent advantages, has tended to make the Oriental more discontented with his own civilisation and more resentful of that which has caused this discontent; has made him more conscious of differences, at the same time that it has obliterated some of these differences; and has broken up the native culture on its highest level, without penetrating the mass. And we are left with the melancholy reflection that the cause of this disintegration is not corruption, brutality or maladministration: such ills have played but a small part, and no ruling nation has had less to be ashamed of than Britain in these particulars; corruption, brutality and maladministration were too prevalent in India before the British arrived, for commission of them to disturb the fabric of Indian life. The cause lies in the fact that there can be no permanent compromise between the extremes of an external rule which is content to keep order and leave the social structure unaltered, and a complete cultural assimilation. The failure to arrive at the latter is a religious failure.[1]

To point to the damage that has been done to native cultures in the process of imperial expansion is by no means an indictment of empire itself, as the advocates of imperial dissolution are only too apt to infer. Indeed, it is often these same anti-imperialists who, being liberals, are the most complacent believers in the superiority of western civilisation, and at one and the same time blind to the benefits conferred by imperial government and to the injury done by the destruction of native culture. According to such enthusiasts, we do well to intrude ourselves upon another civilisation, equip the members of it with our mechanical contrivances, our systems of government, education, law, medicine and finance, inspire them with a contempt for their own customs and with an enlightened attitude towards religious superstition—and then leave them to stew in the broth which we have brewed for them.

[1] An interesting survey of the effects of culture-contact in the East is to be found in *The British in Asia* by Guy Wint. Mr. Wint's occasional suggestions of the effect of India upon the British are no less suggestive than his account of the effect of the British upon India. For example:

"How the English colour prejudice began—whether it was inherited from the Portuguese in India, or was an infection from the Hindu caste system or, as has been suggested, began with the arrival of insular and suburban wives of civil servants, or came from some other cause—is not certain. The British in India were the British middle class living in the artificial condition of having above them no upper class of their own people, and below them no lower class of their own people. It was a state of existence which led to a combined arrogance and defensiveness." P. 209.

It is noticeable that the most vehement criticism, or abuse, of British imperialism often comes from representatives of societies which practise a different form of imperialism—that is to say, of expansion which brings material benefits and extends the influence of culture. America has tended to impose its way of life chiefly in the course of doing business, and creating a taste for its commodities. Even the humblest material artefact, which is the product and the symbol of a particular civilisation, is an emissary of the culture out of which it comes: I mention that influential and inflammable article the celluloid film. American economic expansion can be also, in its way, the cause of disintegration of cultures which it touches.

The newest type of imperialism, that of Russia, is probably the most ingenious, and the best calculated to flourish according to the temper of the present age. The Russian Empire appears to be sedulous to avoid the weaknesses of the empires which have preceded it: it is at the same time more ruthless and more careful of the vanity of subject peoples. The official doctrine is one of complete racial equality—an appearance easier for Russia to preserve in Asia, because of the oriental cast of the Russian mind and because of the backwardness of Russian development according to western standards. Attempts appear to be made to preserve the similitude of local self-government and autonomy: the aim, I suspect, is to give the several local republics and satellite states the illusion of a kind of independence, while the real power is exercised from Moscow. The illusion must sometimes fade, when a local republic is suddenly and ignominiously reduced to the status of a kind of province or crown colony; but it is maintained—and this is what is most interesting from our point of view—by a careful fostering of local "culture," culture in the reduced sense of the word, as everything that is picturesque, harmless and separable from politics, such as language and literature, local arts and customs. But as Soviet Russia must maintain the subordination of culture to political theory, the success of her imperialism seems likely to lead to a sense of superiority on the part of that one of her peoples in which her political theory has been formed; so that we might expect, so long as the Russian Empire holds together, to find the increasing assertion of one dominant Muscovite culture, with subordinate races surviving, not as peoples each with its own cultural pattern, but as inferior castes. However that may be, the Russians have been the first modern people to practise the political direction of culture consciously, and to attack at every point the culture of any people whom they wish to dominate. The more highly developed is any alien culture, the more thorough the attempts to extirpate it by elimination of those elements in the subject population in which that culture is most conscious.

The dangers arising from "culture-consciousness" in the West are at present of a different kind. Our motives, in attempting to do something about our culture, are not yet consciously political. They arise from the consciousness that our culture is not in very good health and from the feeling that we must take steps to improve its condition. This consciousness has transformed the problem of education, by either identifying culture with education, or turning to education as the one instrument for improving our culture. As for the intervention of the State, or of some quasi-official body subventioned by the State, in assistance of the arts and sciences, we can see only too well the need, under present conditions, for such support. A body like the British Council, by constantly sending representatives of the arts and sciences abroad, and inviting foreign representatives to this country, is in our time invaluable—but we must not come to accept as permanent or normal and healthy the conditions which make such direction necessary. We are prepared to believe that there will, under any conditions, be useful work for the British Council to perform; but we should not like to be assured that never again will it be possible for the intellectual élite of all countries to travel as private citizens and make each other's acquaintance without the approval and support of some official organisation. Some important activities, it is likely enough, will never again be possible without official backing of some kind. The progress of the experimental sciences now requires vast and expensive equipment; and the practice of the arts has no longer, on any large scale, the benefit of private patronage. Some safeguard may be provided, against increasing centralisation of control and politicisation of the arts and sciences, by encouraging local initiative and responsibility; and, as far as possible, separating the central source of funds from control over their use. We should do well also to refer to the subsidised and artificially stimulated activities each by its name: let us do what is necessary for painting and sculpture, or architecture, or the theatre, or music, or one or another science or department of intellectual exercise, speaking of each by its name, and restraining ourselves from using the word "culture" as a comprehensive term. For thus we slip into the assumption that culture can be planned. Culture can never be wholly conscious—there is always more to it than we are conscious of; and it cannot be planned because it is also the unconscious background of all our planning.

CHAPTER VI

Notes on Education and Culture: and Conc'usion

D URING the recent war an exceptional number of books were published on the subject of education; there were also voluminous reports of commissions, and an incalculable number of contributions on this subject in periodicals. It is not my business, nor is it within my competence, to review the whole of current educational theory; but a few comments on it are in place, because of the close association, in many minds, between education and culture. What is of interest to my thesis is the kind of assumption which is made by those who write about education. The notes which follow comment on a few such prevalent assumptions.

1. *That, before entering upon any discussion of Education, the purpose of Education must be stated.*

This is a very different thing from defining the word "education." The Oxford Dictionary tells us that education is "the process of bringing up (young persons)"; that it is "the systematic instruction, schooling or training given to the young (and, by extension, to adults) in preparation for the work of life"; that it is also "culture or development of powers, formation of character." We learn that the first of these defini

tions is according to the use of the sixteenth century; and that
the third use appears to have arisen in the nineteenth. In
short, the dictionary tells you what you know already, and I
do not see how a dictionary could do more. But when writers
attempt to state the *purpose* of education, they are doing one
of two things: they are eliciting what they believe to have
been the unconscious purpose always, and thereby giving their
own meaning to the history of the subject; or they are formu-
lating what may not have been, or may have been only fit-
fully, the real purpose in the past, but should in their opinion
be the purpose directing development in the future. Let us
look at a few of these statements of the purpose of education.
In *The Churches Survey Their Task,* a volume published in
connexion with the Oxford Conference on Church, Community and State in 1937, we find the following:

> Education is the process by which the community seeks to open its
> life to all the individuals within it and enable them to take their
> part in it. It attempts to pass on to them its culture, including the
> standards by which it would have them live. Where that culture is
> regarded as final the attempt is made to impose it on younger minds.
> Where it is viewed as a stage in development, younger minds are
> trained both to receive it and to criticise and improve upon it.
>   This culture is composed of various elements. It runs from rudi-
> mentary skill and knowledge up to the interpretation of the universe
> and of man by which the community lives . . .

The purpose of education, it seems, is to transmit culture: so
culture (which has not been defined) is likely to be limited
to what can be transmitted by education. While "education"
is perhaps allowed to be more comprehensive than "the
educational system," we must observe that the assumption
that culture can be summed up as skills and interpretations
controverts the more comprehensive view of culture which
I have endeavoured to take. Incidentally, we should keep a
sharp eye on this personified "community" which is the repository of authority.

Another account of the purpose of education is that which sees it in terms of political and social change. This, if I have understood him, is the purpose which fires Mr. H. C. Dent. "Our ideal," he says in *A New Order in English Education,* "is a full democracy." Full democracy is not defined; and, if full democracy is attained, we should like to know what is to be our next ideal for education after this ideal has been realised.

Mr. Herbert Read gives his account of the purpose of education in *Education Through Art.* I do not think that Mr. Read could see quite eye to eye with Mr. Dent, for whereas Mr. Dent wants a "full democracy," Mr. Read says that he "elects for a libertarian conception of democracy," which I suspect is a very different democracy from Mr. Dent's. Mr. Read (in spite of *elects for*) is a good deal more precise in his use of words than Mr. Dent; so, while he is less likely to confuse the hasty reader, he is more likely to confound the diligent one. It is in electing for a libertarian conception of democracy, he says, that we answer the question, "What is the purpose of education?" This purpose is further defined as "the reconciliation of individual uniqueness with social unity."

Another kind of account of the purpose of education is the uncompleted account, of which Dr. F. C. Happold (in *Towards a New Aristocracy*) gives us a specimen. The fundamental task of education, he tells us, is "training the sort of men and women the age needs." If we believe that there are some sorts of men and women which are needed by every age, we may remark that there should be permanence as well as change in education. But the account is incomplete, in that we are left wondering who is to determine what are the needs of the age.

One of the most frequent answers to the question "what is the purpose of education?" is "happiness." Mr. Herbert Read gives us this answer too, in a pamphlet called *The Education*

of Free Men, by saying that he knows of no better definition
of the aims of education than that of William Godwin: "the
true object of education . . . is the generation of happiness."
"The Government's purpose," said the White Paper which
heralded the latest Education Act, "is to secure for children
a happier childhood and a better start in life." Happiness is
often associated with "the full development of personality."

Dr. C. E. M. Joad, showing more prudence than most of
those who attempt to answer this question, holds the view,
which seems to me a very sensible one, that education has a
number of ends. Of these he lists three (in *About Education,*
one of the most readable books on the subject that I have
consulted):

1. To enable a boy or girl to earn his or her living. . . .
2. To equip him to play his part as the citizen of a democracy.
3. To enable him to develop all the latent powers and faculties
   of his nature and so enjoy a good life.

It is a relief, at this point, to have presented to us the simple
and intelligible notion that equipment to earn one's living
is one of the purposes of education. We again note the close
association between education and democracy; here also Dr.
Joad is perhaps more prudent than Mr. Dent or Mr. Read
in not qualifying his "democracy" by an adjective. "To develop all the latent powers and faculties" appears to be a
variant of "the full development of personality": but Dr.
Joad is sagacious in avoiding the use of that puzzling word
"personality."

Some, no doubt, will disagree with Dr. Joad's selection of
purposes. And we may, with more reason, complain that none
of them takes us very far without getting us into trouble. They
all contain some truth: but as each of them needs to be corrected by the others, it is possible that they all need to be
adjusted to other purposes as well. Each of them needs some
qualification. A particular course of education may, in the

world in which a young person finds himself, be exactly what is needed to develop his peculiar gifts and yet impair his ability to earn a living. Education of the young to play their part in a democracy is a necessary adaptation of individual to environment, if a democracy is what they are going to play their part in: if not, it is making the pupil instrumental to the accomplishment of a social change which the educator has at heart—and this is not education but something else. I am not denying that a democracy is the best form of society, but by introducing this standard for education, Dr. Joad, with other writers, is leaving it open to those who believe in some other form of society which Dr. Joad might not like, to substitute (and so far as he is talking about education only, Dr. Joad could not confute them) some account like the following: "One of the purposes of education is to equip a boy or girl to play his or her part as the subject of a despotic government." Finally, as for developing all the latent powers and faculties of one's nature, I am not sure that anyone should hope for that: it may be that we can only develop some powers and faculties at the expense of others, and that there must be some choice, as well as inevitably some accident, in the direction which anyone's development takes. And as for the good life, there is some ambiguity in the sense in which we shall "enjoy" it; and what the good life is, has been a subject of discussion from early times to the present day.

What we remark especially about the educational thought of the last few years, is the enthusiasm with which education has been taken up as an instrument for the realisation of social ideals. It would be a pity if we overlooked the possibilities of education as a means of acquiring *wisdom;* if we belittled the acquisition of *knowledge* for the satisfaction of curiosity, without any further motive than the desire to know; and if we lost our respect for *learning.* So much for the purpose of education. I proceed to the next assumption.

2. *That Education makes people happier.*

We have already found that the purpose of education has been defined as the making people happier. The assumption that it *does* make people happier needs to be considered separately. That the educated person is happier than the uneducated is by no means self-evident. Those who are conscious of their lack of education are discontented, if they cherish ambitions to excel in occupations for which they are not qualified; they are sometimes discontented, simply because they have been given to understand that more education would have made them happier. Many of us feel some grievance against our elders, our schools or our universities for not having done better by us: this can be a way of extenuating our own shortcomings and excusing our failures. On the other hand, to be educated above the level of those whose social habits and tastes one has inherited, may cause a division within a man which interferes with happiness; even though, when the individual is of superior intellect, it may bring him a fuller and more useful life. And to be trained, taught or instructed above the level of one's abilities and strength may be disastrous; for education is a strain, and can impose greater burdens upon a mind than that mind can bear. Too much education, like too little education, can produce unhappiness.

3. *That Education is something that everyone wants.*

People can be persuaded to desire almost anything, for a time, if they are constantly told that it is something to which they are entitled and which is unjustly withheld from them. The spontaneous desire for education is greater in some communities than in others; it is generally agreed to be stronger in the North than in the South of England, and stronger still in Scotland. It is possible that the desire for education is greater where there are difficulties in the way of obtaining it—difficulties not insuperable but only to be surmounted at the cost of some sacrifice and privation. If this is so, we may conjecture that facility of education will lead to indifference to it; and that the universal imposition of education up to the years of maturity will lead to hostility towards it. A high average of general education is perhaps less necessary for a civil society than is a respect for learning.

4. *That Education should be organised so as to give "equality of opportunity."* [1]

It follows from what has been said in an earlier chapter about classes and élites, that education should help to preserve the class and to select the élite. It is right that the exceptional individual should have the opportunity to elevate himself in the social scale and attain a position in which he can exercise his talents to the greatest benefit of himself and of society. But the ideal of an educational system which would automatically sort out everyone according to his native capacities is unattainable in practice; and if we made it our chief aim, would disorganise society and debase education. It would disorganise society, by substituting for classes, élites of brains, or perhaps only of sharp wits. Any educational system aiming at a complete adjustment between education and society will tend both to restrict education to what will lead to success in the world, and to restrict success in the world to those persons who have been good pupils of the system. The pros-

---

[1] This may be called Jacobinism in Education. Jacobinism, according to one who had given some attention to it, consisted "in taking the people as equal individuals, without any corporate name or description, without attention to property, without division of powers, and forming the government of delegates from a number of men, so constituted; in destroying or confiscating property, and bribing the public creditors, or the poor, with the spoils, now of one part of the community, now of another, without regard to prescription or profession."—Burke: *Remarks on the Policy of the Allies.*

pect of a society ruled and directed only by those who have
passed certain examinations or satisfied tests devised by psy-
chologists is not reassuring: while it might give scope to
talents hitherto obscured, it would probably obscure others,
and reduce to impotence some who should have rendered
high service. Furthermore, the ideal of a uniform system such
that no one capable of receiving higher education could fail
to get it, leads imperceptibly to the education of too many
people, and consequently to the lowering of standards to
whatever this swollen number of candidates is able to reach.

Nothing is more moving in Dr. Joad's treatise than the
passage in which he expatiates on the amenities of Winchester and Oxford. Dr. Joad paid a visit to Winchester; and
while there, he wandered into a delightful garden. One sus-
pects that he may have got into the garden of the Deanery,
but he does not know what garden it was. This garden set
him to ruminating about the College, and its "blend of the
works of nature and man." "What I see," he said to himself,
"is the end-product of a long-continuing tradition, running
back through our history, in this particular case, to the
Tudors." (I cannot see why he stopped at the Tudors, but
that was far enough to sustain the emotion with which his
mind was suffused.) It was not only nature and architecture that impressed him; he was aware also of "a long tradition of secure men leading dignified and leisured lives."
From Winchester his mind passed to Oxford, to the Oxford
which he had known as an undergraduate; and again, it was
not merely architecture and gardens upon which his mind
dwelt, but also men:

But even in my own time . . . when democracy was already
knocking at the gates of the citadel it was so soon to capture, some
faint aftermath of the Greek sunset could be observed. At Balliol,
in 1911 there was a group of young men centring upon the Grenfells
and John Manners, many of whom were killed in the last war, who
took it for granted that they should row in the College boat, play

hockey or rugger for the College or even for the University, act for the O.U.D.S., get tight at College Gaudies, spend part of the night talking in the company of their friends, while at the same time getting their scholarships and prizes and Firsts in Greats. The First in Greats was taken, as it were, in their stride. I have not seen such men before or since. It may be that they were the last representatives of a tradition which died with them. . . .

It seems strange, after these wistful reflections, that Dr. Joad should end his chapter by supporting a proposal of Mr. R. H. Tawney: that the public schools should be taken over by the State and used as boarding schools to accommodate for two or three years the intellectually abler secondary school boys from the ages of sixteen to eighteen. For the conditions over which he pronounces such a tearful valedictory were not brought about by equality of opportunity. They were not brought about, either, by mere privilege; but by a happy combination of privilege and opportunity, in the *blend* he so savours, of which no Education Act will ever find the secret.

5. *The Mute Inglorious Milton dogma.*

The Equality of Opportunity dogma, which is associated with the belief that superiority is always superiority of intellect, that some infallible method can be designed for the detection of intellect, and that a system can be devised which will infallibly nourish it, derives emotional reinforcement from the belief in the mute inglorious Milton. This myth assumes that a great deal of first-rate ability—not merely ability, but genius—is being wasted for lack of education; or, alternatively, that if even one potential Milton has been suppressed in the course of centuries, from deprivation of formal teaching, it is still worth while to turn education topsy-turvy so that it may not happen again. (It might be embarrassing to have a great many Miltons and Shakespeares, but that danger is remote.) In justice to Thomas Gray, we should remind ourselves of the last and finest line of the quatrain, and remember that we may also have escaped some Cromwell *guilty* of his country's blood. The proposition that we have lost a number of Miltons and Cromwells through our tardiness in providing a comprehensive state system of education, cannot be either proved or disproved: it has a strong attraction for many ardent reforming spirits.

This completes my brief list—which is not intended to be exhaustive—of current beliefs. The dogma of equal opportunity is the most influential of all, and is maintained stoutly by some who would shrink from what seem to me its probable consequences. It is an ideal which can only be fully realised when the institution of the family is no longer respected, and when parental control and responsibility passes to the State. Any system which puts it into effect must see that no advantages of family fortune, no advantages due to the foresight, the self-sacrifice or the ambition of parents are allowed to obtain for any child or young person an education superior to that to which the system finds him to be entitled. The popularity of the belief is perhaps an indication that the depression of the family is accepted, and that the disintegration of classes is far advanced. This disintegration of classes had already led to an exaggerated estimate of the social importance of the right school and the right college at the right university, as giving a status which formerly pertained to mere birth. In a more articulated society—which is *not* a society in which social classes are isolated from each other: that is itself a kind of decay—the social distinction of the right school or college would not be so coveted, for social position would be marked in other ways. The envy of those who are "better born" than oneself is a feeble velleity, with only a shadow of the passion with which material advantages are envied. No sane person can be consumed with bitterness at not having had more exalted ancestors, for that would be to wish to be another person than the person one is: but the advantage of the status conferred by education at a more fashionable school is one which we can readily imagine ourselves as having enjoyed also. The disintegration of class has induced the expansion of envy, which provides ample fuel for the flame of "equal opportunity."

Besides the motive of giving everyone as much education as possible, because education is in itself desirable, there are other motives affecting educational legislation: motives which may be praiseworthy, or which simply recognise the inevitable, and which we need mention here only as a reminder of the complexity of the legislative problem. One motive, for instance, for raising the age-limit of compulsory schooling is the laudable desire to protect the adolescent, and fortify him against the more degrading influences to which he is exposed on entering the ranks of industry. We should be candid about such a motive; and instead of affirming what is to be doubted, that everyone will profit by as many years of tuition as we can give him, admit that the conditions of life in modern industrial society are so deplorable, and the moral restraints so weak, that we must prolong the schooling of young people simply because we are at our wits' end to know what to do to save them. Instead of congratulating ourselves on our progress, whenever the school assumes another responsibility hitherto left to parents, we might do better to admit that we have arrived at a stage of civilisation at which the family is irresponsible, or incompetent, or helpless; at which parents cannot be expected to train their children properly; at which many parents cannot afford to feed them properly, and would not know how, even if they had the means; and that Education must step in and make the best of a bad job.[1]

[1] I hope, however, that the reader of these lines has read, or will immediately read, *The Peckham Experiment*, as an illustration of what can be done, under modern conditions, to help the family to help itself.

Mr. D. R. Hardman [1] observed that:

The age of industrialism and democracy had brought to an end most of the great cultural traditions of Europe, and not least that of architecture. In the contemporary world, in which the majority were half-educated and many not even a quarter-educated, and in which large fortunes and enormous power could be obtained by exploiting ignorance and appetite, there was a vast cultural breakdown which stretched from America to Europe and from Europe to the East.

This is true, though there are a few inferences which might be improperly drawn. The exploitation of ignorance and appetite is not an activity only of commercial adventurers making large fortunes: it can be pursued more thoroughly and on a larger scale by governments. The cultural breakdown is not a kind of infection which began in America, spread to Europe, and from Europe has contaminated the East (Mr. Hardman may not have meant that, but his words might be so interpreted). But what is important is to remember that "half-education" is a modern phenomenon. In earlier ages the majority could not be said to have been "half-educated" or less: people had the education necessary for the functions they were called upon to perform. It would be incorrect to refer to a member of a primitive society, or to a skilled agricultural labourer in any age, as half-educated or quarter-educated or educated to any smaller fraction. *Education* in the modern sense implies a disintegrated society, in which it has come to be assumed that there must be one measure of education according to which everyone is educated simply more or less. Hence *Education* has become an abstraction.

Once we have arrived at this abstraction, remote from life, it is easy to proceed to the conclusion—for we all agree about the "cultural breakdown"—that education for every-

[1] As Parliamentary Secretary to the Ministry of Education, speaking on January 12, 1946, at the general meeting of the Middlesex Head Teachers' Association.

body is the means we must employ for putting civilisation together again. Now so long as we mean by "education" everything that goes to form the good individual in a good society, we are in accord, though the conclusion does not appear to get us anywhere; but when we come to mean by "education" that limited system of instruction which the Ministry of Education controls, or aims to control, the remedy is manifestly and ludicrously inadequate. The same may be said of the definition of the purpose of education which we have already found in *The Churches Survey Their Task*. According to this definition, education is the process by which the community attempts to pass on to all its members its culture, including the standards by which it would have them live. The community, in this definition, is an unconscious collective mind, very different from the mind of the Ministry of Education, or the Head Masters' Association, or the mind of any of the numerous bodies concerned with education. If we include as education all the influences of family and environment, we are going far beyond what professional educators can control—though their sway can extend very far indeed; but if we mean that culture is what is passed on by our elementary and secondary schools, or by our preparatory and public schools, then we are asserting that an organ is a whole organism. For the schools can transmit only a part, and they can only transmit this part effectively, if the outside influences, not only of family and environment, but of work and play, of newsprint and spectacles and entertainment and sport, are in harmony with them.

Error creeps in again and again through our tendency to think of culture as group culture exclusively, the culture of the "cultured" classes and élites. We then proceed to think of the humbler part of society as having culture only in so far as it participates in this superior and more conscious culture. To treat the "uneducated" mass of the population as we might treat some innocent tribe of savages to whom we are impelled to deliver the true faith, is to encourage them to neglect or despise that culture which they should possess and from which the more conscious part of culture draws vitality; and to aim to make everyone share in the appreciation of the fruits of the more conscious part of culture is to adulterate and cheapen what you give. For it is an essential condition of the preservation of the quality of the culture of the minority, that it should continue to be a minority culture. No number of Young Peoples' Colleges will compensate for the deterioration of Oxford and Cambridge, and for the disappearance of that "blend" which Dr. Joad relishes. A "mass-culture" will always be a substitute-culture; and sooner or later the deception will become apparent to the more intelligent of those upon whom this culture has been palmed off.

I am not questioning the usefulness, or deriding the dignity of Young Peoples' Colleges, or of any other particular new construction. In so far as these institutions can be good, they are more likely to be good, and not to deliver disappointment, if we are frankly aware of the limits of what we can do with them, and if we combat the delusion that the maladies of the modern world can be put right by a system of instruction. A measure which is desirable as a palliative, may be injurious if presented as a cure. My main point is the same as that which I tried to make in the previous chapter, when I spoke of the tendency of politics to dominate culture, instead of keeping to its place within a culture. There is also the danger that education—which indeed comes under the influence of politics —will take upon itself the reformation and direction of culture, instead of keeping to its place as one of the activities through which a culture realises itself. Culture cannot altogether be brought to consciousness; and the culture of which we are wholly conscious is never the whole of culture: the effective culture is that which is directing the activities of those who are manipulating that which they *call* culture.

So the instructive point is this, that the more education

arrogates to itself the responsibility, the more systematically will it betray culture. The definition of the purpose of education in *The Churches Survey Their Task* returns to plague us like the laughter of hyaenas at a funeral. *Where that culture is regarded as final, the attempt is made to impose it on younger minds. Where it is viewed as a stage in development, younger minds are trained to receive it and to improve upon it.* These are cosseting phrases which reprove our cultural ancestors—including those of Greece, Rome, Italy and France —who had no notion of the extent to which their culture was going to be improved upon after the Oxford Conference on Church, Community and State in 1937. We know now that the highest achievements of the past, in art, in wisdom, in holiness, were but "stages in development" which we can teach our springalds to improve upon. We must not train them merely to receive the culture of the past, for that would be to regard the culture of the past as final. We must not impose culture upon the young, though we may impose upon them whatever political and social philosophy is in vogue. And yet the culture of Europe has deteriorated visibly within the memory of many who are by no means the oldest among us. And we know, that whether education can foster and improve culture or not, it can surely adulterate and degrade it. For there is no doubt that in our headlong rush to educate everybody, we are lowering our standards, and more and more abandoning the study of those subjects by which the essentials of our culture—of that part of it which is transmissible by education—are transmitted; destroying our ancient edifices to make ready the ground upon which the barbarian nomads of the future will encamp in their mechanised caravans.

The previous paragraph is to be considered only as an incidental flourish to relieve the feelings of the writer and perhaps of a few of his more sympathetic readers. It is no longer possible, as it might have been a hundred years ago, to find consolation in prophetic gloom; and such a means of escape would betray the intentions of this essay as stated in my introduction. If the reader goes so far as to agree that the kind of organisation of society which I have indicated is likely to be that most favourable to the growth and survival of a superior culture, he should then consider whether the *means* are themselves desirable as *ends:* for I have maintained that we cannot directly set about to create or improve culture—we can only will the means which are favourable to culture, and to do this we must be convinced that these means are themselves socially desirable. And beyond that point, we must proceed to consider how far these conditions of culture are possible, or even, in a particular situation at a particular time, compatible with all the immediate and pressing needs of an emergency. For one thing to avoid is a *universalised* planning; one thing to ascertain is the limits of the plannable. My enquiry, therefore, has been directed on the meaning of the word *culture:* so that everyone should at least pause to examine what this word means to him, and what it means to him in each particular context before using it. Even this modest aspiration might, if realised, have consequences in the policy and conduct of our "cultural" enterprises.

The Unity of European Culture

I

THIS is the first time that I have ever addressed a German-speaking audience, and before speaking on such a large subject, I think that I should present my credentials. For the unity of European culture is a very large subject indeed, and no one should try to speak about it, unless he has some particular knowledge or experience. Then he should start from that knowledge and experience and show what bearing it has on the general subject. I am a poet and a critic of poetry; I was also, from 1922 to 1939, the editor of a quarterly review. In this first talk I shall try to show what the first of these two professions has to do with my subject, and what conclusions my experience has led me to draw. So this is a series of talks about the unity of European culture from the point of view of a man of letters.

It has often been claimed that English, of all the languages of modern Europe, is the richest for the purposes of writing poetry. I think that this claim is justified. But please notice that when I say "richest for the purposes of writing poetry" I have been careful in my words: I do not mean that England has produced the greatest poets, or the greatest amount of great poetry. That is another question altogether. There are as great poets in other languages: Dante is certainly greater than Milton, and at least as great as Shakespeare. And even for the quantity of great poetry, I am not concerned to maintain that England has produced more. I simply say that the English language is the most remarkable medium for the poet to play with. It has the largest vocabulary: so large, that the command of it by any one poet seems meagre in comparison with its total wealth. But this is not the reason why it is the richest language for poetry: it is only a consequence of the real reason. This reason, in my opinion, is the variety of the elements of which English is made up. First, of course, there is the Germanic foundation, the element that you and we have in common. After this we find a considerable Scandinavian element, due in the first place to the Danish conquest. Then there is the Norman French element, after the Norman conquest. After this there followed a succession of French influences, traceable through words adopted at different periods. The sixteenth century saw a great increase of new words coined from the Latin; and the development of the language from the early sixteenth century to the middle of the seventeenth, was largely a process of testing new Latin words, assimilating some and rejecting others. And there is another element in English, not so easy to trace, but I think of considerable importance, the Celtic. But I am not thinking, in all this history, only of the Words, I am thinking, for poetry, primarily of the Rhythms. Each of these languages brought its own music: and the richness of the English language for poetry is first of all in its variety of metrical elements. There is the rhythm of early Saxon verse, the rhythm of the Norman French, the rhythm of the Welsh, and also the influence of generations of study of Latin and Greek poetry. And even today, the English language enjoys constant possibilities of refreshment from its several centres: apart from the vocabulary, poems by Englishmen, Welshmen, Scots and Irishmen, all written in English, continue to show differences in their Music.

I have not taken the trouble to talk to you in order to praise my own language; my reason for discussing it is that I think the reason why English is such a good language for poetry is that it is a composite from so many different European sources. As I have said, this does not imply that England must have produced the greatest poets. Art, as Goethe said, is in limitation: and a great poet is one who makes the most of the language that is given him. The truly great poet makes his language a great language. It is true, however, that we tend to think of each of the greater peoples as excelling in one art rather than another: Italy and then France in painting, Germany in music, and England in poetry. But, in the first place, no art has ever been the exclusive possession of any one country of Europe. And in the second place, there have been periods in which some other country than England has taken the lead in poetry. For instance, in the final years of the eighteenth century and the first quarter of the nineteenth, the Romantic movement in English poetry certainly dominated. But in the second half of the nineteenth century the greatest contribution to European poetry was certainly made in France. I refer to the tradition which starts with Baudelaire, and culminates in Paul Valéry. I venture to say that without this French tradition the work of three poets in other languages—and three very different from each other—I refer to W. B. Yeats, to Rainer Maria Rilke, and, if I may, to myself—would hardly be conceivable. And, so complicated are these literary influences, we must remember that this French movement itself owed a good deal to an American of Irish extraction: Edgar Allan Poe. And, even when one country and language leads all others, we must not assume that the poets to whom this is due are necessarily the greatest poets. I have spoken of the Romantic movement in England. But at that time Goethe was writing. I do not know of any standard by which one could gauge the relative greatness of Goethe and Wordsworth as poets, but the total work of Goethe has a scope which makes him a greater man. And no English poet contemporary with Wordsworth can enter into comparison with Goethe at all.

I have been leading up to another important truth about poetry in Europe. This is, that no one nation, no one language, would have achieved what it has, if the same art had not been cultivated in neighbouring countries and in different languages. We cannot understand any one European literature without knowing a good deal about the others. When we examine the history of poetry in Europe, we find a tissue of influences woven to and fro. There have been good poets who knew no language but their own, but even they have been subject to influences taken in and disseminated by other writers among their own people. Now, the possibility of each literature renewing itself, proceeding to new creative activity, making new discoveries in the use of words, depends on two things. First, its ability to receive and assimilate influences from abroad. Second, its ability to go back and learn from its own sources. As for the first, when the several countries of Europe are cut off from each other, when poets no longer read any literature but that in their own language, poetry in every country must deteriorate. As for the second, I wish to make this point especially: that every literature must have some sources which are peculiarly its own, deep in its own history; but, also, and at least equally important, are the sources which we share in common: that is, the literature of Rome, of Greece and of Israel.

There is a question which ought to be asked at this point, and which ought to be answered. What of the influences from outside Europe, of the great literature of Asia?

In the literature of Asia is great poetry. There is also profound wisdom and some very difficult metaphysics; but at the moment I am only concerned with poetry. I have no knowledge whatever of the Arabic, Persian, or Chinese languages. Long ago I studied the ancient Indian languages, and while I was chiefly interested at that time in Philosophy, I read a little poetry too; and I know that my own poetry shows the influence of Indian thought and sensibility. But generally, poets are not oriental scholars—I was never a scholar myself; and the influence of oriental literature upon poets is usually through translations. That there has been some influence of poetry of the East in the last century and a half is undeniable: to instance only English poetry, and in our own time, the poetical translations from the Chinese made by Ezra Pound, and those made by Arthur Waley, have probably been read by every poet writing in English. It is obvious that through individual interpreters, specially gifted for appreciating a remote culture, every literature may influence every other; and I emphasise this. For when I speak of the unity of European culture, I do not want to give the impression that I regard European culture as something cut off from every other. The frontiers of culture are not, and should not be, closed. But history makes a difference. Those countries which share the most history, are the most important to each other, with respect to their future literature. We have our common classics, of Greece and Rome; we have a common classic even in our several translations of the Bible.

What I have said of poetry is I think true of the other arts as well. The painter or the composer perhaps enjoys greater freedom, in that he is not limited by a particular language spoken only in one part of Europe: but in the practice of every art I think you find the same three elements: the local tradition, the common European tradition, and the influence of the art of one European country upon another. I only put this as a suggestion. I must limit myself to the art which I know most about. In poetry at least, no one country can be consistently highly creative for an indefinite period. Each country must have its secondary epochs, when no remarkable new development takes place: and so the centre of activity will shift to and fro between one country and another. And in poetry there is no such thing as complete originality, owing nothing to the past. Whenever a Virgil, a Dante, a Shake-speare, a Goethe is born, the whole future of European poetry is altered. When a great poet has lived, certain things have been done once for all, and cannot be achieved again; but, on the other hand, every great poet adds something to the complex material out of which future poetry will be written.

I have been speaking of the unity of European culture as illustrated by the arts and among the arts by the only one on which I am qualified to speak. I want to talk next time about the unity of European culture as illustrated by ideas. I mentioned at the beginning that during the period between the wars I had edited a quarterly review. My experience in this capacity, and my reflections upon it, will provide the starting point for my next talk.

II

I mentioned in my last talk that I had started and edited, between the wars, a literary review. I mentioned it first as one of my qualifications for speaking on this general subject. But also the history of this review illustrates some of the points that I want to make. So I hope that, after I have told you a little about it, you will begin to see its relevance to the subject of these talks.

We produced the first number of this review in the autumn of 1922, and decided to bring it to an end with the first number of the year 1939. So you see that its life covered nearly the same period that we call the years of peace. Except for a period of six months during which I tried the experiment of producing it monthly, its appearance was four times a year. In starting this review, I had the aim of bringing together the best in new thinking and new writing in its time, from all the countries of Europe that had anything to contribute to the common good. Of course it was designed primarily for English readers, and therefore all foreign contributions had to appear in an English translation. There may be a function for reviews published in two or more languages, and in two or more countries simultaneously. But even such reviews, searching all Europe for contributions, must contain some pieces of translation, if they are to be read by everybody. And they cannot take the place of those periodicals which appear in each country and which are intended primarily for the readers in that country. So my review was an ordinary English periodical, only of international scope. I sought, therefore, first to find out who were the best writers, unknown or little known outside of their own country, whose work deserved to be known more widely. Second, I tried to establish relations with those literary periodicals abroad, the aims of which corresponded most nearly to my own. I mention, as instances, the *Nouvelle Revue Française* (then edited by Jacques Rivière, and subsequently by Jean Paulhan), the *Neue Rundschau,* the *Neue Schweizer Rundschau,* the *Revista de Occidente* in Spain, *Il Convegno* and others in Italy. These connexions developed very satisfactorily, and it was no fault of any of the editors concerned, if they subsequently languished. I am still of the opinion, twenty-three years after I began, and seven years after I ended, that the existence of such a network of independent reviews, at least one in every capital of Europe, is necessary for the transmission of ideas— and to make possible the circulation of ideas while they are still fresh. The editors of such reviews, and if possible the more regular contributors, should be able to get to know each other personally, to visit each other, to entertain each other, and to exchange ideas in conversation. In any one such periodical, of course, there must be much that will be of interest only to readers of its own nation and language. But their co-operation should continually stimulate that circulation of influence of thought and sensibility, between nation and nation in Europe, which fertilises and renovates from abroad the literature of each one of them. And through such co-operation, and the friendships between men of letters which ensue from it, should emerge into public view those works of literature which are not only of local, but of European significance.

The particular point, however, of my talking about my aims, in relation to a review which has been dead for seven years, is that in the end they failed. And I attribute this failure chiefly to the gradual closing of the mental frontiers of Europe. A kind of cultural autarchy followed inevitably upon political and economic autarchy. This did not merely interrupt communications: I believe that it had a numbing effect upon creative activity within every country. The blight fell first upon our friends in Italy. And after 1933 contributions from Germany became more and more difficult to find. Some of our friends died; some disappeared; some merely became silent. Some went abroad, cut off from their own cultural roots. One of the latest found and the last lost, was that great critic and good European, who died a few months ago: Theodor Haecker. And, from much of the German writing that I saw in the 30's, by authors previously unknown to me, I formed the opinion that the newer German writers had less and less to say to Europe; that they were more and more saying what could be understood, if understood at all, only in Germany. What happened in Spain is more confused; the tumult of the civil war was hardly favourable to thought and creative writing; and that war divided and scattered, even when it did not destroy, many of her ablest writers. In France there was still free intellectual activity, but more and more harassed and limited by political anxieties and forebodings, and by the internal divisions which political prepossessions set up. England, though manifesting some symptoms of the same malady, remained apparently intact. But I think that our literature of that period suffered by being more and more restricted to its own resources, as well as by the obsession with politics.

Now the first comment I have to make on this story of a literary review which had clearly failed of its purpose several years before events brought it to an end, is this. A universal concern with politics 'loes not unite, it divides. It unites those politically minded folk who agree, across the frontiers of nations, against some other international group who hold opposed views. But it tends to destroy the cultural unity of Europe. *The Criterion,* for that is the name of the review which I edited, had, I believe, a definite character and cohesion, although its contributors were men holding the most diverse political, social and religious views. I think also that it had a definite congeniality with the foreign periodicals with which it associated itself. The question of a writer's political, social or religious views simply did not enter into our calculations, or into those of our foreign colleagues. What the common basis was, both at home and abroad, is not easy to define. In those days it was unnecessary to formulate it; at the present time it becomes impossible to formulate. I should say that it was a common concern for the highest standards both of thought and of expression, that it was a common curiosity and openness of mind to new ideas. The ideas with which you did not agree, the opinions which you could not accept, were as important to you as those which you found immediately acceptable. You examined them without hostility, and with the assurance that you could learn from them. In other words, we could take for granted an interest, a delight, in ideas for their own sake, in the free play of intellect. And I think that also, among our chief contributors and colleagues, there was something which was not so much a consciously held belief, but an unconscious assumption. Something which had never been doubted, and therefore had no need to rise to the conscious level of affirmation. It was the assumption that there existed an international fraternity of men of letters, within Europe: a bond which did not replace. but was perfectly compatible with,

national loyalties, religious loyalties, and differences of political philosophy. And that it was our business not so much to
make any particular ideas prevail, as to maintain intellectual
activity on the highest level.

I do not think that *The Criterion,* in its final years, wholly
succeeded in living up to this ideal. I think that in the later
years it tended to reflect a particular point of view, rather
than to illustrate a variety of views on that plane. But I do
not think that this was altogether the fault of the editor: I
think that it came about partly from the pressure of circumstances of which I have spoken.

I am not pretending that politics and culture have nothing
to do with each other. If they could be kept completely apart,
the problem might be simpler than it is. A nation's political
structure affects its culture, and in turn is affected by that
culture. But nowadays we take too much interest in each
other's domestic politics, and at the same time have very
little contact with each other's culture. The confusion of
culture and politics may lead in two different directions. It
may make a nation intolerant of every culture but its own,
so that it feels impelled to stamp out, or to remould, every
culture surrounding it. An error of the Germany of Hitler
was to assume that every other culture than that of Germany was either decadent or barbaric. Let us have an end of
such assumptions. The other direction in which the confusion of culture and politics may lead, is towards the ideal of a
world state in which there will, in the end, be only one uniform world culture. I am not here criticising any schemes
for world organisation. Such schemes belong to the plane of
engineering, of devising machinery. Machinery is necessary,
and the more perfect the machine the better. But culture is
something that must grow; you cannot build a tree, you can
only plant it, and care for it, and wait for it to mature in its
due time; and when it is grown you must not complain if
you find that from an acorn has come an oak, and not an

elm-tree. And a political structure is partly construction, and partly growth; partly machinery, and the same machinery, if good, is equally good for all peoples; and partly growing with and from the nation's culture, and in that respect different from tnat of other nations. For the health of the culture of Europe two conditions are required: that the culture of each country should be unique, and that the different cultures should recognise their relationship to each other, so that each should be susceptible of influence from the others. And this is possible because there is a common element in European culture, an interrelated history of thought and feeling and behaviour, an interchange of arts and of ideas.

In my last talk I shall try to define this common element more closely: and I think that will require my saying a little more about the meaning that I give to this word "Culture," which I have been using so constantly.

III

I said at the end of my second talk that I should want to make a little clearer what I mean when I use the term culture. Like "democracy," this is a term which needs to be, not only defined, but illustrated, almost every time we use it. And it is necessary to be clear about what we mean by "culture," so that we may be clear about the distinction between the material organisation of Europe, and the spiritual organism of Europe. If the latter dies, then what you organise will not be Europe, but merely a mass of human beings speaking several different languages. And there will be no longer any justification for their continuing to speak different languages, for they will no longer have anything to say which cannot be said equally well in any language: they will, in short, have no longer anything to say in poetry. I have already affirmed that there can be no "European" culture if the several countries are isolated from each other: I add now that there can be no European culture if these countries are reduced to identity. We need variety in unity: not the unity of organisation, but the unity of nature.

By "culture," then, I mean first of all what the anthropologists mean: the way of life of a particular people living together in one place. That culture is made visible in their arts, in their social system, in their habits and customs, in their religion. But these things added together do not consti-tute the culture, though we often speak for convenience as if they did. These things are simply the parts into which a culture can be anatomised, as a human body can. But just as a man is something more than an assemblage of the various constituent parts of his body, so a culture is more than the assemblage of its arts, customs, and religious beliefs. These things all act upon each other, and fully to understand one you have to understand all. Now there are of course higher cultures and lower cultures, and the higher cultures in general are distinguished by differentiation of function, so that you can speak of the less cultured and the more cultured strata of society, and finally, you can speak of individuals as being exceptionally cultured. The culture of an artist or a philosopher is distinct from that of a mine worker or field labourer; the culture of a poet will be somewhat different from that of a politician; but in a healthy society these are all parts of the same culture; and the artist, the poet, the philosopher, the politician and the labourer will have a cul-ture in common, which they do not share with other people of the same occupations in other countries.

Now it is obvious that one unity of culture is that of the people who live together and speak the same language: be-cause speaking the same language means thinking, and feel-ing, and having emotions, rather differently from people who use a different language. But the cultures of different peoples do affect each other: in the world of the future it looks as if every part of the world would affect every other part. I have suggested earlier, that the cultures of the different countries of Europe have in the past derived very great benefit from their influence upon each other. I have suggested that the national culture which isolates itself voluntarily, or the national culture which is cut off from others by circumstances which it cannot control, suffers from this isolation. Also, that the country which receives culture from abroad, without having anything to give in return, and the country which aims to impose its culture on another, without accepting anything in return, will both suffer from this lack of reciprocity.

There is something more than a general exchange of culture influences, however. You cannot even attempt to trade equally with every other nation: there will be some who need the kind of goods that you produce, more than others do, and there will be some who produce the goods you need yourselves, and others who do not. So cultures of people speaking different languages can be more or less closely related: and sometimes so closely related that we can speak of their having a common culture. Now when we speak of "European culture," we mean the identities which we can discover in the various national cultures; and of course even within Europe, some cultures are more closely related than others. Also, one culture within a group of cultures can be closely related, on different sides, to two cultures which are not closely related to each other. Your cousins are not all cousins of each other, for some are on the father's side and some on the mother's. Now, just as I have refused to consider the culture of Europe simply as the sum of a number of unrelated cultures in the same area, so I refused to separate the world into quite unrelated cultural groups; I refused to draw any absolute line between East and West, between Europe and Asia. There are, however, certain common features in Europe, which make it possible to speak of a European culture. What are they?

The dominant force in creating a common culture between peoples each of which has its distinct culture, is religion. Please do not, at this point, make a mistake in anticipating my meaning. This is not a religious talk, and I am not setting out to convert anybody. I am simply stating a fact. I am not so much concerned with the communion of Christian believers today; I am talking about the common tradition of Christianity which has made Europe what it is, and about the common cultural elements which this common Christianity has brought with it. If Asia were converted to Christianity tomorrow, it would not thereby become a part of Europe. It is in Christianity that our arts have developed; it is in Christianity that the laws of Europe have —until recently—been rooted. It is against a background of Christianity that all our thought has significance. An individual European may not believe that the Christian Faith is true, and yet what he says, and makes, and does, will all spring out of his heritage of Christian culture and depend upon that culture for its meaning. Only a Christian culture could have produced a Voltaire or a Nietzsche. I do not believe that the culture of Europe could survive the complete disappearance of the Christian Faith. And I am convinced of that, not merely because I am a Christian myself, but as a student of social biology. If Christianity goes, the whole of our culture goes. Then you must start painfully again, and you cannot put on a new culture ready made. You must wait for the grass to grow to feed the sheep to give the wool out of which your new coat will be made. You must pass through many centuries of barbarism. We should not live to see the new culture, nor would our great-great-great-grandchildren: and if we did, not one of us would be happy in it.

To our Christian heritage we owe many things besides religious faith. Through it we trace the evolution of our arts, through it we have our conception of Roman Law which has done so much to shape the Western World, through it we have our conceptions of private and public morality. And through it we have our common standards of literature, in the literatures of Greece and Rome. The Western World has its unity in this heritage, in Christianity and in the ancient civilisations of Greece, Rome and Israel, from which, owing to two thousand years of Christianity, we trace our descent. I shall not elaborate this point. What I wish to say is, that this unity in the common elements of culture, throughout many centuries, is the true bond between us. No political and economic organisation, however much goodwill it commands, can supply what this culture unity gives. If we dissipate or throw away our common patrimony of culture, then all the organisation and planning of the most ingenious minds will not help us, or bring us closer together.

The unity of culture, in contrast to the unity of political organisation, does not require us all to have only one loyalty: it means that there will be a variety of loyalties. It is wrong that the only duty of the individual should be held to be towards the State; it is fantastic to hold that the supreme duty of every individual should be towards a Super-State. I will give one instance of what I mean by a variety of loyalties. No university ought to be merely a national institution, even if it is supported by the nation. The universities of Europe should have their common ideals, they should have their obligations towards each other. They should be independent of the governments of the countries in which they are situated. They should not be institutions for the training of an efficient bureaucracy, or for equipping scientists to get the better of foreign scientists; they should stand for the preservation of learning, for the pursuit of truth, and in so far as men are capable of it, the attainment of wisdom.

There is much more that I should have liked to say in this last talk, but I must now be very brief. My last appeal is to the men of letters of Europe, who have a special responsibility for the preservation and transmission of our common culture. We may hold very different political views: our common responsibility is to preserve our common culture uncontaminated by political influences. It is not a question of sentiment: it does not matter so much whether we like each other, or praise each other's writings. What matters is that we should recognise our relationship and mutual dependence upon each other. What matters is our inability, without each other, to produce those excellent works which mark a superior civilisation. We cannot, at present, hold much communication with each other. We cannot visit each other as private individuals; if we travel at all, it can only be through government agencies and with official duties. But we can at least try to save something of those goods of which we are the common trustees: the legacy of Greece, Rome and Israel, and the legacy of Europe throughout the last 2,000 years. In a world which has seen such material devastation as ours, these spiritual possessions are also in imminent peril.

in a year, but no one could prove it, so Bosco and his trainer Benny Kean won the cup and made a killing from the bookie. Donal ended up winning a thousand euro, which he split with Jimmy. Everyone was heading to the local pub for celebration drinks, but as they were driving out Donal turned left instead of right like everyone else.

"Where are we going?" asked Lucy.

"As a reward for being a good sport in the rain all day, I'm taking you to the Sanderson Hotel in Tipperary for a hot bath, dinner, drinks and, hopefully, if I get you drunk enough, a night of passion."

And that was exactly what happened. . . .

TWENTY-FIVE

I began to take the clomiphene and, having eagerly swallowed the first tablet, I decided to read the accompanying leaflet. It described the possible side effects of the drug, which included ovarian hyperstimulation and enlargement, possible rupture, visual disturbances, hot flashes, abdominal discomfort, nausea and vomiting, depression, insomnia, weight gain, rashes, dizziness and hair loss. I stared at it in shock. Jesus Christ! I was going to be bald, sweaty, fat and depressive. I rang Dr. Reynolds in a panic. He assured me that these were extreme side effects that rarely—if ever—affected his patients and especially not on the low dose of fifty milligrams that he had started me on.

Feeling calmer, I decided to throw out the information leaflet in case James found it. I knew he'd make me come off the drugs immediately if he read those symptoms. I'd wait until he found a clump of my hair on the pillow before I went into any explanations. For the next four days I took my drugs, and later, on day nine, I went into the clinic for my first follicle-tracking examination.

Once again I found myself naked from the waist down, flat on my back with my legs akimbo. The male radiologist, Tom, was young, fit and extremely good-looking, which made it all even more uncomfortable. When I'm embarrassed I tend to overcompensate by talking incessantly in an overcheery manner. So when Tom began explaining the procedure to me, I kept interrupting him with crummy lines. It was pathetic.

"As you are no doubt aware, follicle-tracking scans will show us if the ovaries are functioning correctly. With these scans we can—"

"Oh, I see, yes. Come on, the eggs, come on, the Easter bunny, ha-ha . . ."

He looked at me, smiled without smiling and continued. "—track the size of the follicles in the ovary over several days to predict timing of ovulation and advise you of the optimal time for conception."

"Will I have to bring my husband with me next time so we can get to it immediately in the broom cupboard, ha-ha-ha?"

It was awful. I knew I was making a fool of myself, but I couldn't control it. I was just so nervous.

Tom was a real pro and once again continued his flow as though I had never interrupted him. "We'll also be measuring the thickness of the womb lining. This gives an indication of egg quality and likelihood of a successful pregnancy."

He then took a big tube of lubricant jelly and squidged a lump of it over the top of one of those large vibrator-type things and inserted it into my vagina. The bad Tommy Cooper impressions ended there and then. I was shocked into silence. A computer screen was turned toward me and as Tom twisted the camera thing around, he began clicking furiously with the mouse, dragging measuring lines across the screen and printing out little black photos. All I could see was a big black mass with the occasional black blob. He was intent on measuring any black blobs that appeared on the screen. After about five minutes of frenzied measuring, clicking and printing, the camera was taken out and I was handed a tissue by the nurse to wipe away the lubricant while Tom politely turned his back . . . gross.

Once I was dressed, Tom sat me down and began showing me the printouts. They were small, dark and blurry. I had no idea what I was looking at. "You can see here," he said, pointing to a cluster of blobs, "that the follicles appear to be similar in size. When one grows significantly bigger than the others, we can be confident that you're ovulating and an egg will be released. It's too soon to tell with your follicles yet. I'll make an appointment for you to come back in two days' time."

"What if in two days' time I still have no big one?"

"It could mean that you're ovulating later in your cycle or that you're not ovulating at all. We won't know until we've tracked you a few more times this cycle."

"What if I don't ovulate?"

"Well, then, Dr. Reynolds will probably increase the dosage of clomiphene."

Great—more drugs. I'd be a fat, sweaty baldy in no time. So much for the sex: James wouldn't want to go near me.

Two days later I was back in the clinic and a different radiologist was doing the same test. I had to answer the same questions about how long I'd been trying to get pregnant and how long I'd been taking clomiphene.

"Where's Tom?" I asked, annoyed.

"We rotate," said Judy, the new radiologist. "There are three of us so we do different days each week. Now, tell me, what dosage of clomiphene are you taking?"

When she had all my details she inserted the ultrasound camera and we stared at the screen. No big blobs. She made an appointment for me to come back in two days' time on day thirteen of my cycle. Two days later I went through the same process with Liz, the third radiologist. We went over the same questions and again stared at a screen with no obvious big blobs appearing. I was told to come back in two days' time—on day fifteen—to see if I was ovulating later in my cycle. On day fifteen it was Judy again and there were still no big blobs.

"I'm afraid, Emma, it doesn't look like you're going to ovulate this month. I'll send a report to Dr. Reynolds and he'll discuss your options with you."

I left the clinic feeling despondent. What the hell was wrong with me? Why couldn't my stupid ovaries produce eggs? How come everyone in the world was able to get pregnant except me? Was I barren and they just couldn't figure out why? Was it ever going to happen? Should I just hang up my boots and pack it all in?

When I got home a package was waiting for me. It was a box with Dutch stamps on it. I didn't remember ordering anything. Maybe it was a present from James. I opened the box and un-wrapped the gift. It was a large pink bunny rabbit with beads. . . . Oh my God, it was a vibrator! I looked at the message inside the box: "To brighten up your sex life. Sorry for calling you barren at Christmas. Babs."

I had never been one of those modern women who had vibrators in their bedside tables. I suppose I had always had some kind of boyfriend/leper/loser on the scene, and thus a fairly regular sex life so I had never felt the urge. My pre-trying-for-a-baby sex life with James had been extremely active, frisky and fun—we couldn't keep our hands off each other. We didn't need battery-operated devices: we were doing just fine using the equipment God had given us.

Mind you, I'd been tempted to try a vibrator after Lucy told me that hers gave her better results than any man she had slept with. This one was called the Rampant Rabbit Pearl vibrator. I switched it on and giggled as the little beads spun 'round and the rabbit ears vibrated. The promotional leaflet claimed:

> *There is a good reason that this is the most popular sex toy in the world, just ask any woman who has one. A long, thick jelly-finish shaft, vibrating, rotating pearls, multispeed vibration and the soft bunny ears to tease the clitoris—it's fantastic.*

I hid it in my wardrobe. After all my internal tests, I couldn't face inserting anything else inside me for the time being, but maybe at a later date . . .

Having analyzed the tests, Dr. Reynolds decided to increase my dose of clomiphene to one hundred milligrams. I went for four more internal ultrasounds and still no big blobs appeared. A month later my dosage was increased to one-hundred-fifty milligrams—still nothing, so it went up to two-hundred milligrams. I could now feel the side effects. The sweating was the worst. One minute I'd be completely normal and the next I'd be drenched in sweat and my face would be bright red. Truth be told, my mood swings were getting worse too.

I was doing my regular makeup job with Amanda Nolan on *Afternoon with Amanda* the morning I was due to go in for my first ultrasound on day nine of the new two-hundred-milligrams dose. I arrived late, having had to buy a shirt on the way in because a particularly violent hot flash had left me dripping. As I was putting on Amanda's mascara, I began to think about the test and how desperately I wanted one of the blobs to be bigger than the other when I heard Amanda squeal.

"Ouch."

Shit! I had stabbed her in the eye with the mascara wand. "I'm sorry, Amanda. Are you okay?" I asked, handing her a tissue. "God, I'm really sorry—let me see your eye."

"I'm fine, Emma, but what's wrong with you? You're like a cat on a hot tin roof. You can't seem to concentrate for more than ten seconds these days. Sit down and tell me what's going on."

I told her about my treatment and how invasive it was and how I hated the tests and how after four months on the drugs my blobs were not getting bigger and how I was all sweaty and hot and bothered all the time and how I felt weepy at the slightest thing. "In fact, I pretty much feel either blind rage with the world or just really tearful, like now," I said, beginning to cry. "There's no happy medium. I ate the face off James last night because he'd bought round teabags instead of pyramid-shaped ones. I'm turning into a monster and now I'll probably lose my job because I've just blinded the star of the show."

"No you won't," said Amanda, passing me a tissue and patting my arm. "Come on now, Emma, give yourself a break. This is extremely hard on you. It's harder for the woman than the man because she's the one who has to have all the dreadful tests and take the nasty drugs. You're not to beat yourself up. It's perfectly normal to be feeling emotional—you're taking hormone-inducing drugs, for goodness' sake. But you'll have to do something to help yourself along. Are you having acupuncture?"

"No."

"Well, you need to start immediately. Acupuncture is known to help fertility. Now, I go to a great girl called Sheila who treats me for my hay fever. Here's her number. Call her and tell her you're a friend of mine. She's a miracle worker and it'll help you unwind from all those other tests."

"Thanks, Amanda," I said weepily. "Thanks for being so nice."

"Come on now, blow your nose and make me look beautiful. Only this time try not to injure me in the process."

I booked an appointment with Sheila on day eleven. I arrived feeling very sorry for myself. I had just been for another ultrasound, and as usual no big blobs had appeared on the screen. Sheila answered the door in a floor-length turquoise kaftan. She had long red hair tied back in a big plait and she smelled of incense. "Hello, Emma, come on in," she said, beaming at me.

I followed her into a room at the front of her house. It was painted a pale shade of lilac and smelled of lavender. Sheila sat me down and gently talked me through the last year and a half of my life. It was like therapy. I felt I could tell her anything. I talked and talked, and she nodded sympathetically and took notes, lots of notes, pages and pages of notes—I had a lot to say. We discussed my digestion, lifestyle, stress levels, eating habits, drinking habits, sleep patterns . . . my whole medical history as well as my family's.

I wanted to move in with Sheila and spend the rest of my life in this calm, lavender-scented room. She was totally sympathetic and said all the symptoms I was feeling were normal and a lot of her patients were having the same treatment I was and finding it equally stressful. She explained that acupuncture had been practiced in China for many thousands of years, but had only become known in the West fairly recently. She said that the success rate of acupuncture in aiding fertility was extremely high, especially when done in conjunction with hormone treatment. She added that every individual was treated uniquely as the exact combination of causes of imbalance within the body is different for everyone.

"A number of factors have to be taken into consideration, and that's why I had to ask you about any treatment you've had, your family's medical history and your current emotional state. Now, I'm going to ask you to lie back while I do a pulse reading to determine the flow of energy in your body and I'll also check your tongue."

"My tongue?" Shit, I hadn't washed my teeth before coming—what if my breath smelled?

"Yes, we can learn a lot from the tongue. Its texture and coating will indicate your general state of health."

"Okay, but what about the needles? I'm not very good with needles. Does it hurt?"

"You will feel only the tiniest pinprick, I promise."

Normally—particularly in light of the recent lies I'd been spun about tests not being painful—I wouldn't have believed her. But something about Sheila made me trust her. Besides, she was a woman and women don't lie to one another about pain.

I lay back on the bed in the middle of the room and tried to breathe deeply as instructed. Sheila looked at my tongue and didn't recoil, so my breath mustn't have been too bad, and then she felt my pulse. She told me that my qi—which was my vital energy and is made up of yin and yang—did not feel balanced. My energy was not flowing freely and evenly. My flow of qi was blocked due to the emotional and physical stress I was under.

She didn't need to look at my tongue to figure that one out. One look at my blotchy face was a dead giveaway. I tried to slow down my breathing and relax.

Then Sheila took out her needles and began inserting them into my arms, hands, feet, ankles, tummy and head. The only time I winced was when she came at me with a needle that she wanted to insert into my face—between my eyebrows. I thought she was going to stab me in the eye. My arm jerked up to stop her. The needle ended up impaled in the palm of my hand which—judging by the look of horror on Sheila's face—was not one of the energy points she was targeting. She extracted it and reminded me of the importance of remaining calm. Then, wedging the offending hand down with her leg, she inserted the needle in my forehead.

She turned down the lights and told me to relax. Within five minutes, despite the fact that I was half-naked, with needles sticking out of all corners of my body, I fell asleep. Twenty minutes later Sheila had to wake me up. I felt wonderful, as if I was floating. I felt relaxed and at peace. It was fantastic. I loved Sheila. I loved acupuncture. I felt positive for the first time in ages. It was going to work. Now that my qi was unblocked, my blobs would get bigger.

TWENTY-SIX

*I*t was a miracle. Two days after the acupuncture, when I went for my next internal ultrasound, I saw a big black blob on the screen. Tom measured it and smiled. "It looks good, Emma. It's significantly bigger than the others. Come back in two days and we should know for sure."

I was elated. I was going to live in China forever. Acupuncture was the way forward. Sheila had performed a miracle.

Two days later and the blob was huge. I was ovulating. Alleluia. I raced home and rang James. "I'm ovulating. Come on, quick, come home, we need to have sex now."

"I'm in the middle of a meeting. I'll call you back when I'm finished."

"*No.* I need you to come home now, James."

What was he doing? It was vital that we had sex now. Right now, while I was ovulating.

"I'll call you later."

"No, James, come—"

He'd hung up. I flung the phone across the room. It had taken four and a half months to get to this stage and now he was going to ruin it by coming home late and the egg would be gone, or shrunk or whatever. We needed to have sex now. I was hyperventilating as I paced the room. The hot flashes were coming fast and furious. I was damned if I was going to wait another minute. I grabbed my car keys and drove like a lunatic to the rugby club. Grannies dived into bushes for cover as I rammed the car up on the pavement to overtake slow drivers. I was bright red and sweaty by the time I got there. I stomped up the stairs to James's office.

I could hear voices, but nothing was going to stand in my way. I was a woman with a mission. I flung open the door. James and two older men in suits turned to stare at me.

"Hi, sorry to disturb you, but I need to speak to James urgently," I said, glaring at James, who was glaring back.

"Sorry, gentlemen, will you excuse me, please?" said James, coming over to me and frog-marching me out of the room. "What the hell are you doing, Emma? I'm in a very important meeting. I told you I'd call you back later."

"I don't give a toss about your stupid meeting. I've spent the last four-and-a-half months taking hormones and undergoing the humiliation of having my legs constantly in stirrups. I've just been told that I'm ovulating, so we need to have sex now. Not later on, not in an hour—*now.*"

"Keep your voice down," said James, dragging me farther away from his office. "I'm in the middle of a meeting with my boss. We're discussing the revamp of the clubhouse. I can't leave the meeting, so will you please just go home. I'll talk to you later."

"I don't care about your stupid boss. We have to have sex now. Come on, stop talking and come into the loo with me. It'll only take a minute," I said, dragging him toward the ladies'.

"*Emma,*" said James, now as red in the face as I was. "Go home and calm down. An hour or two will make no difference."

"That's the whole bloody point. It does make a difference. Come on, just come in here for a quickie."

I grabbed his shirt and began to tug. James pulled away and we began a tug of war, until I heard a rip and fell backward onto the ground with half of James's shirt in my hand. Buttons flew everywhere. James looked down at his now exposed chest.

"Well, that's just fantastic. Thanks, Emma. You've managed to make a complete fool of me. I have to go back into that meeting with a ripped shirt," said James, trying to tuck the shreds of his shirt back into his trousers.

"I'm sorry, but—"

"I don't want to hear it. Just go home," snapped my fed-up husband, as he stomped off holding his shirt closed with both hands.

I went and sat in the car and cried. I knew I was turning into a nutter, but we did need to have sex as soon as possible. What was the point of going through the treatment if we weren't going to follow it up with the sex? Part of me was annoyed with James for not understanding how important it was to get our timing exactly right. But I knew I'd have to make it up with him if there was any hope of having sex that day so I bought him a new shirt and when he came home I was wearing just the shirt and a pair of high heels. He walked straight by me—ripped shirt flapping—and went upstairs to have a shower. He was obviously still raging. I waited for him to come out and contemplated whether to bring out the Rampant Rabbit to surprise him, but decided against it. James wasn't a sex toy–type of guy—at least, I didn't think he was. As I tried to picture him in leather chaps brandishing a whip, the real James came into the room wrapped in a towel.

"Sorry about earlier. I got you a new shirt. D'you like it?"

James had his "serious chat" face on.

"Emma, this has got to stop. I understand that the drugs are making you moody, but storming into my office and ripping my shirt off in front of my boss is just not on. You have got to calm down."

"I know I went too far today, but I can't help it, James. I'm pumped full of hormones. Do you have any idea what that's like for me? I think half the time I'm going insane. I'm either sweating like a racehorse or crying or wanting to murder someone for looking at me sideways. I don't know if I'm coming or going. It's like I have no control over my emotions. I'm sorry about today, but what's the point of putting myself through this hell if we don't have the sex?"

"We will, just not in the middle of a meeting. A couple of hours isn't going to make any difference. You've got to get that into your head. And getting yourself into a state about it isn't going to help either. Larry said his wife went through IVF and the most important thing of all is to be relaxed and positive."

"Larry?"

"The architect who was in my office today with my boss."

"You discussed our private business with a complete stranger?" I said—turning into my mother.

"It was hardly private after you stormed into my meeting and ripped my shirt off. I had to explain why I was half-naked when I went back in. Thankfully, Larry had been through something similar so he understood because Eddie just looked shocked."

"Fuck Eddie and Larry and his stupid relaxed wife," I snapped, hormones taking over again.

"Eddie's my boss, Emma."

"I don't care, I—" I stopped. I realized that if we had another argument, we wouldn't have sex, and sex was more important than me trying to ram the point home that the hormones were making me crazy. Let's face it, he could see that.

"So do you like the shirt?" I purred, as I began to unbutton it.

"What?" said James, taken aback by the sudden U-turn in the conversation.

The phone rang.

"Leave it," I said, as James picked up the receiver.

"Hi . . . no. No plans . . . yeah, sounds good . . . see you there."

By the time he hung up I was having a savage hot flash and the shirt was stuck to my back. I was furious at the interruption. "Who was it?" I snapped.

"Donal. We're going to meet him and Lucy for drinks now, so you'd better hop into the shower."

"But we can't, James, we—"

"Emma," said James firmly, "we're going to go and have a few drinks, relax and enjoy ourselves, and when we come back we'll have sex. Now, go and get dressed."

I looked at my watch. It was now five hours since the test and by the time we got home it would be eight or nine hours. Still, it was better to have relaxed sex than fighting sex. I didn't want an angry baby. It would be nice to see Lucy. I hadn't seen much of her lately as she'd been traveling a lot with work and spending her spare time with Donal. They seemed to be getting on well. It would be the first time the four of us had been out together, so it would be fun, I thought, trying to jolt myself into a good mood.

Half an hour later we were sitting in the pub beside a cozy fire and I was feeling better. Lucy looked happy and comfortable with Donal. It was weird at first, seeing them together as a couple. They were in the honeymoon phase where nothing the other person did annoyed you. All the little idiosyncrasies that would later drive them 'round the twist were still "cute." It was like when I first met James and I thought the way he chewed each bite of food thirty times before swallowing it was sweet and now it drove me insane. I always finished my meal at least half an hour before James. He labored over every bite as if it was his last. Lately—no doubt due to the hormones—I had been tempted to put my hand into his mouth and shove the food down unchewed. At least I had managed to control that particular urge.

Donal was telling the story of Lucy meeting his niece Annie the week before, and how well they had got on and how Annie thought Lucy was beautiful and cool and glamorous. . . . I looked at Lucy as he was telling the story—she was positively glowing. It was nice to see her so happy. She looked at me and I beamed at her. She beamed back. I was thrilled for her: she so deserved to meet someone who thought the world of her. I nodded toward the loo and we both got up and went in for a chat.

"Oh my God, Lucy, he's besotted with you. It's great," I said, hugging her.

"Do you really think so?"

"Of course I do. The way he looks at you and talks about you— he's smitten."

"I really like him, Emma. I can't believe it because at first I thought he was such an oaf. But underneath it all he's lovely—all manly and protective. We still fight, but I'm definitely falling for him. Big-time."

"I'm so glad. You deserve to be happy. It's as if you've been going out for years. You're so yourself with him, it's great."

"It's the first time I can remember feeling totally relaxed with someone. I'm not constantly worried about holding my stomach in or wondering if my makeup is perfect or if I'm wearing the right clothes. I actually don't care because he doesn't care about that stuff. We've only been seeing each other properly since we went coursing and that's four months ago, but I feel as if I've known him for years . . . and the sex is fantastic."

"Four months? My God, Lucy, I can't believe we haven't seen each other in so long. It's crazy."

"I know, and chatting on the phone isn't the same as meeting up. It's just been really hectic with work and Donal."

"Look, you've been busy and so have I. I seem to spend all my spare time in hospital these days. We'll have to make a deal to meet up once a month for dinner. I want to know everything about you and Donal. He's obviously really serious about you—the fact that he introduced you to Annie is a huge sign."

"I was really pleased about that, and thank God she liked me."

"And why wouldn't she? You're fantastic. It's great, Lucy, it really is. You deserve every bit of it," I said, getting all tearful.

"Stop, you'll start me off," said Lucy, her eyes welling as she gave me a hug. "Now, enough about me, how are things with you? Are you okay?"

I didn't want to moan. It wasn't fair for her to have to console me when she was so happy. "Fine, thanks. The hormones seem to be working at last, so fingers crossed."

"Good. I know it'll all work out for you, Emma. It will, honestly. You'll be a mum in no time."

I nodded, not trusting myself to speak, and we went back in.

Two drinks later and I felt really drunk. I was totally light-headed and slurring my words like George Best on a bad day. After three glasses of red wine it was a bit odd that I was so smashed. The others thought it was funny and laughed about what a cheap date I was, but I knew it was the drugs because I never normally got drunk so quickly. James decided he'd better bring me home, so we were back in our house at ten o'clock. Him, very slightly merry. Me, very drunk.

I stumbled upstairs, got undressed, put on the new shirt I'd bought him and the high heels and fished the Rampant Rabbit out of the wardrobe. I went downstairs, jumped on top of James, who was lying on the couch, and stuck the vibrating Rabbit ears up his nose. The look of shock on his face set me off and I fell off the couch laughing, the Rabbit still shaking in my hand.

"What the hell is that?"

"It's the . . . ha-ha . . . it's the . . . ha-ha . . . best-selling sex toy in the world. Look, it has different speeds," I said, howling as I increased the vibration.

"Where did you get it?"

"Babs ordered it on the Internet to spice up our sex life."

"Why does she think it needs spicing up?" said James, looking a bit put out.

"Dunno. 'Cos I'm not pregnant, I guess," I said, giggling at the jellyfish thing vibrating.

"I see. All right, then, up you come," said James, lifting me over his shoulder like a fireman, legs buckling under the weight. "Bring the Rabbit—I've always quite fancied a threesome."

TWENTY-SEVEN

I spent the next two weeks constantly poking my boobs, to see if they were tender, and feeling nauseous—although I didn't know if that was because of the drugs, stress or the longed-for pregnancy. As those weeks went by I felt different. I felt a change in my body. I was tired, my breasts were tender and I was convinced I had that funny metal taste in my mouth that pregnant women talk about—although it might have been my fillings. I had never been more sure of anything in my life: I was pregnant. So when my period was late, I charged out to buy two pregnancy tests.

This time I waited until I was three days overdue and then I did the first test. I waited a few minutes and looked at it—negative. I wasn't put out. I knew I was pregnant. I did the second test—negative. It doesn't matter, I told myself, this often happens. It's probably too early for the tests. I called Dr. Reynolds, told him I was overdue and wanted to check if I was pregnant. He told me to come in for blood and pregnancy tests.

I did. I wasn't pregnant.

I locked myself in the toilet of the Harwood Clinic and cried myself sick. I had been so sure, so positive . . . and now nothing. Back to square one. I was devastated. I left the clinic, not caring about my blotchy face and red nose, and was about to get into the car when my mobile rang. Thinking it was James, I answered it. I wanted him to tell me it was going to be all right.

It was Tony.

"Hey, Emma, just calling to say Jess gave birth to a bouncing boy last night. Eight pounds three. We're over the moon. I was secretly hoping for a boy, but you know the way you don't want to say anything. Anyway, we're going to call him Roy—after Roy Keane."

I held the phone away from me, as I threw up beside the car.

"Emma? Are you there?"

"Sorry, Tony, I dropped the phone. Great news," I said, trying not to gag on the chunks of vomit still in my mouth.

"Yeah, we're thrilled. Jess said you can come and visit any time. She's dying to show him off."

"Okay, yeah, I'll be in later."

"Great. I'd better go, I've a list of people to call. See you soon."

I sat in the car and tried to suppress the wail I could feel just below my chest. I knew that if I let it out I wouldn't be able to control it. I breathed deeply—in and out, in and out. As I calmed down, my anguish was replaced with anger and resentment. Why the hell did Jess have it all so easy? How come she was able to pop out kids like a rabbit? Why did it all go so smoothly for her and Imogen and everyone else in the whole bloody world? Why? Why? Why? Why? I'd have to go to the stupid hospital now and smile and coo and pretend it was the best news I'd ever heard. I wanted to kill someone. I wanted to drive the car into a wall. Aaaargh. How much more of this did I have to endure?

Stop it! I shouted at myself. Think of people worse off. Think of women who have had five miscarriages or their baby has died when it was six months old or they were in a car crash and are paralyzed. Think of poor Christopher Reeve in his wheelchair. Stop feeling sorry for yourself. This is not the end of the world. Think of the starving people of Africa. . . . I didn't feel better, I felt worse. Now I was beating myself up for being self-pitying and dramatic—so on top of feeling miserable, I now felt guilty about it.

When I got home, Lucy rang. "Hi, Tony just called."

"Yeah, it's great news," I said, failing miserably to sound cheerful.

"Are you okay?"

"Yeah, I'm fine."

"Really?"

"Yeah. I had a moment of feeling sorry for myself, but I'm fine now," I lied. "I'm going to pop in later to see her."

"I was going to go after work, about seven. Do you want to meet me for a drink first? Bit of Dutch courage?"

"Thanks, but after the last reaction I had to drink, I think I'd better stay off it. I'll meet you in the reception area at seven."

By the time seven o'clock came I had got my tardy period and was feeling even worse. I was going to call off the visit, but I felt that it would look like sour grapes. Jess knew I was trying to get pregnant. We had never discussed it, but she knew me well and my erratic behavior wasn't exactly subtle. Besides, she had said it to Lucy, who had said it to me. So I knew she knew, and she knew I knew she knew, but nothing had been said. I preferred it that way. What was there to discuss? She was fertile, I wasn't, end of story. I didn't want her to feel bad about having a baby and she didn't want me to feel bad about not being pregnant.

Lucy arrived at the hospital with a big pot of Clarins body-shaping cream, while I had brought a bunch of flowers.

"Body-shaping cream?" I asked.

"It's practical. She'll want to get back into shape quickly after this baby, considering the last time it took them eight months to have sex. It's supposed to be fabulous for reducing fat and puffiness in the waist and hips."

"Good thinking. Tony will be pleased anyway," I said, smiling.

"Are you ready?" she asked, squeezing my hand.

"Yeah, let's go."

As we walked through the maternity ward I began to understand why desperate women snatched babies. All around me tiny pink newborns were swaddled in blankets. Some were being held by their mothers, some were being fed, others just lay quietly in their cots, ready and waiting to be swiped as their exhausted mothers slept beside them. It would be so easy to stroll over, pretend I was a friend or relation and walk out the door with a baby of my own. I could tell James that it had been left on our doorstep in a basket with a note saying, "Please love me." I would persuade him to move back to England—away from the Irish police—and we would live happily ever after in a pretty cottage by the sea in Cornwall.

"Emma," said Lucy, tapping my shoulder, "it's this way."

I followed her into a room with two beds. In the far corner Jess was looking tired but happy. She was breast-feeding her little bundle of joy, staring down at him with her face full of unconditional love. I felt my stomach twist. I took a deep breath and plastered on a smile. "Hey, there. Congratulations. Oh, look, isn't he gorgeous? How are you feeling?"

"Fine. Thanks for coming in. The flowers are beautiful."

"I think Lucy's cream will probably come in more handy," I said, as Lucy handed it to her.

"Thanks, Lucy, I'll need this badly."

"Well, it's for Tony too," said Lucy, winking at Jess as Tony walked in carrying fresh romper suits for his son.

"What's for me?"

"Nothing," we all said, laughing.

"Birds!" said Tony, shrugging. "James not with you?" he asked me.

"No, he's training tonight."

"Pity. I'd murder a pint."

"Who said 'pint'?" said Mr. Curran, Jess's father, as he arrived with her mother. "Jesus, Jessica, do you have to do that in front of me?" he said, putting his hand over his eyes when he saw his daughter breast-feeding.

"What's she supposed to do, Dessie?" asked Mrs. Curran. "Starve the child so you feel more comfortable? Honestly . . ."

"Right, Tony, about that pint," said Mr. Curran.

"Thanks a lot, Dad, you've only just arrived. Would you like to see your grandson before you bolt out the door?" said Jess.

"I can see him from here. Sure he's a grand little fellow. We'll be back in an hour when you've finished all that and I'll have a squeeze of him then."

With that, Mr. Curran legged it out of the ward before anyone could stop him, Tony hot on his heels.

"Men!" said Mrs. Curran, raising her eyes to heaven. "Well, Jessica, he's a little dote, so he is. How are you feeling, pet?"

"Not too bad, Mum," said Jess, smiling at her mother. "It was easier this time."

Mrs. Curran nodded knowingly.

I had always loved Mrs. Curran. When we were growing up she was the mother who was always at home in the kitchen baking bread or cakes. I used to like going back to Jess's house after school because we'd always have hot scones fresh from the Aga or home-made brown bread. It was heaven. Because Babs was so much younger than me, Mum was always busy looking after her and didn't have time to bake. But Jess was the youngest in her family and Mrs. Curran was married to that Aga. It was a big red one and you had to shovel the coal into the little door on the left-hand side. You could see the fire burning away when you opened it. Mrs. Curran said that the Aga was the only way to cook real food. She thought microwaves were the curse of our generation.

"Emma, it's been ages since I saw you. You look wonderful. How's life treating you?"

"Well, thanks, Mrs. Curran."

"I hear you married a lovely Englishman. Isn't that great?"

"Yeah. I don't know how James puts up with me sometimes."

"I'm sure he's delighted with you. Any kids of your own?"

"No, not yet . . . you know . . . just sort of . . ."

"Mum!" snapped Jess. "Don't annoy Emma with stupid questions."

It was a conversation stopper if ever there was one. We all looked at the floor.

"I think I'll go and get us some coffee," said Mrs. Curran, breaking the silence. "Emma, will you give me a hand?"

We left the room and, when we were out of earshot, Mrs. Curran said, "I'm sorry, Emma, I didn't mean to be insensitive. I can tell I hit a nerve. It's not easy, is it? It's not always as straightforward as we hope. It took me a long time to have Jessica's brother. I had three miscarriages before I had him and I remember how hard it was to be around babies."

I nodded. I was afraid to speak. I could feel a lump forming in my throat. It would have been better if she had been horrible and insensitive. Being nice to me was dangerous territory.

"I didn't mean to upset you, pet. I know how hard it can be. But don't worry, it will happen for you. It will."

I had begun to cry. I knew that I had to get out of there before I really broke down. I managed to blurt out, "Have to go," and ran down the corridor, bumping into ecstatic fathers and mothers as I went. I couldn't breathe. I felt as if I was drowning. I made it to the car and tore out of the car park down the road. I was crying so much I couldn't see a thing. I just needed to get home before I completely fell apart. I needed the safety of my house. I jammed my foot down on the accelerator. Faster, I had to go faster.

It was only when the police car drove up beside me, siren blaring, and almost ran me off the road that I realized it was me it was after. A very angry policeman stormed over to my car and thumped on the window. I rolled it down.

"In a hurry, are we, madam? Step out of the car, please. Have you been drinking?"

I climbed out of the car and shook my head. "No. I was visiting a friend in hospital." The shock of being arrested had dried up my tears.

"Breathe in here, please," he said, pointing to a little tube attached to a bag.

The result was negative, but the policeman was still furious.

"I've been chasing you down for the last two miles. Did you think you were going to get away from me by driving faster? Do you know you were going at eighty miles an hour in a forty-mile speed limit? Think you can make up your own rules, do you? I'm going to charge you with reckless driving."

"But I didn't mean to . . . I just—"

"There's no excuse for driving like a maniac and endangering people's lives."

I couldn't control it. It had been coming all day. A wail of anguish escaped from my throat. I sat down on the side of the road and sobbed uncontrollably. The policeman was taken aback. He clearly hadn't dealt with a hysterical woman before.

"You don't understand . . . this has been the worst day of my life . . . seventeen months and nothing . . . no baby . . . and I went to see my friend and her new baby . . . and it was just so hard . . . so many mothers and babies . . . all so happy . . . the love in their eyes . . . so I had to leave . . . and I was crying and driving . . . I couldn't see 'cos of the crying . . . I have nothing . . . no baby . . . just horrible tests and drugs that make me go mad . . . and my husband hates me . . . well, he doesn't hate me, but I'm driving him mad . . . I'm driving myself mad . . . it's just so hard . . . why is it so hard to have a baby?"

The policeman's face softened. He sat down beside me and patted my shoulder. "There, there now. My wife went through the same thing. Three years of tests only to be told at the end of it that she couldn't have kids. So we adopted a little girl from Romania four years ago. A gorgeous little thing, she is. My wife went through hell. I know how hard it can be."

"Really? You adopted?"

"We were told we'd never have children naturally, so it was the only option for us. I'm sure you'll have some of your own. You're a lot younger than my wife was."

"I don't feel young, I feel about a zillion years old," I said, sighing.

"You're only a slip of a thing with your whole life ahead of you. It'll work itself out, these things always do. Come on now, we can't sit here all night, I've criminals to catch," he said, standing up.

I stood up too. "Are you going to arrest me? Am I going to have to go to prison and become a lesbian so I don't get killed?"

He laughed. "No, you aren't going to prison. I'm letting you off with a warning. Come on, I'll escort you home."

"Will you put on your siren? I've always wanted to have a police escort."

When James heard the siren he came rushing out of the house

thinking I'd been in an accident. Policeman Kieran Mooney escorted me to the front door and told James he had a wonderful wife and he was to look after me because I had had a very stressful day. Then he warned me never to drive when I was upset. Cry first, drive later.

TWENTY-EIGHT

A few weeks later I was sitting in the kitchen reading a book that taught you ways to remain calm. James had bought it for me after the police-escort incident. I was reading a page a day and some days I have to say it annoyed me more than calmed me down. The day before, I had read a piece on slowing down. The book recommended speaking at a more relaxed pace and slowing down your breathing to become instantly calmer. I had tried it on James when he came home, but he said I sounded like a stroke victim and it was far more scary than calm.

On this particular day the book was telling me how to relax my facial tension. I was following the instructions: "Slightly raise the eyebrows—this relaxes the brow muscles. Place your tongue against the roof of your mouth—this relaxes the jaw muscles, and then smile to relax the cheek muscles."

As I sat there grinning like a Cheshire cat with my tongue stuck up in the air, the doorbell rang. It was Babs sitting on an enormous pink suitcase, looking decidedly grumpy.

"What's going on?"

"Mum and Dad have thrown me out of the house with only the shirt on my back."

"Big shirt," I said, nodding at the suitcase.

"A few personal effects, that's all. You can't begin a new life without clothes or a hair straightener. I didn't bother bringing makeup 'cos I figured you'd be able to give me loads."

"Are you planning on staying for a while?"

"Only until I can get enough money together to buy my own place. By the way, can you lend me a tenner to pay for the taxi?"

I sighed and gave her the money. She came back beaming. "So, what'll we have for dinner? I fancy Indian."

"What did you do?" I asked, intrigued to know how far she had gone. It must be pretty bad if they had kicked her out.

"Nothing."

"Bullshit."

"Okay, well, it's all your stupid fault, anyway."

"What?"

Babs told me that Mum had decided to try to help me with my fertility issues so she had been looking at the *Encyclopaedia Britannica* for information on fertility drugs. "But sure those books she has date back to the dinosaurs, so she couldn't find anything helpful. Then she starts asking me about the Internet and how it works and how you get information and all that. I tried to explain it to her, but it was impossible. . . ."

Every time Babs showed Mum how to do something she was shouted at for going too quickly and not respecting her elders. Mum kept reminding her that when she was teaching Babs to read, she had spent hours sitting patiently with her as she struggled with each letter, and now her ungrateful pup of a daughter didn't have the decency to give her mother a few computer lessons. She accused Babs of deliberately using technical terminology to throw her off-guard.

"So I gave up and told her to get professional lessons. I even found her a course to do and she signed up. Then she decided to turn your room into a study and started to clear out your stuff and put it into my wardrobes. . . ."

Whereupon Mum had come across a small box buried under a spare duvet that she just happened to open and, to her horror, inside she found a stash of dope. Needless to say she hit the roof. By the time Babs got home from college that day, Dad had been summoned and she was met with a rare, but formidable, united front. A huge row ensued, which ended up with Babs packing her large pink suitcase and "running away" to my house.

As she finished telling me the story, the phone rang. We both looked at it and said, "Mum."

I picked it up and quickly held it away from my ear, so that my eardrum didn't perforate with the high-pitched squeal.

"DO YOU KNOW WHAT THAT BRAT HAS DONE? BROUGHT DRUGS INTO OUR HOME! HARD DRUGS!"

"Mum, calm down, it's not that bad—"

"WHAT? Not that bad. Don't give me your new-wave nonsense. I know drugs when I see them. I've seen *Crimewatch*—I've even seen that *Trainspotters* film. Don't try to pull the wool over my eyes. They all start with the pot and the next thing you know they're on heroin, lying in the gutter with a needle hanging out of their arm. Your sister has gone too far this time. Even your father is shocked. Hard drugs . . . in my home. The shame of it. A drug addict for a daughter. If Nuala gets wind of this I'll never be able to show my face in public again. Drugs are a slippery slope. No wonder she's thin, jigging away on those ecstatic pills, morning, noon and night. There are young girls dropping dead all over the country from taking those. I know all about those pills, Emma, I wasn't born yesterday. I know about these things."

"Mum, I realize you're upset about the pot, but it's a very mild drug. It'll be legalized soon. It's not a hard drug, it's only for fun. She's not a drug addict."

"For fun! Fun, is it, to throw away your life on drugs? Fun, is it, to fry your brain and end up dead or like that Ozzy Osbourne? Drugs kill, Emma, it's a well-known fact. Here's your father now. The poor man has aged twenty years since he found out that his youngest child is a drug addict."

Dad came on the phone, sounding very cheesed off. "Can you keep her there for a few days till your mother calms down?"

"Sure, but only a few days, I've enough on my plate without Babs lounging around my house sponging off me, thanks very much."

"Of all the effing times—this has to blow up the weekend of the Ryder Cup and I've a big bet on Europe to win it. I'll wring your sister's neck. I won't have a moment's peace for the next three days. It'll be a miracle if I get to see one bloody hole played. Your mother wants me to go to some shagging parents-against-drugs meeting tomorrow."

I stifled a giggle. Dad was clearly in no mood for humor. I did feel sorry for him: he was obsessed with golf. It was his one true love. Every two years, when the Ryder Cup was on, he took over the television for three days. No one was allowed even to look at the remote control. All soap operas, reality-TV shows and sitcoms were out of bounds. It was golf, golf and more golf. The only time I had ever seen my father cry was thirteen years ago when Bernhard Langer missed a six-foot putt on the very last hole in Europe's bid to retain the trophy. He went from being hailed as the "genius golfer from Germany" to "that feckin' useless Kraut."

I told him I'd keep Babs for a few days until Mum calmed down, then send her home to face a few months of daily urine and blood tests. He didn't even laugh at that. He was a broken man. His Ryder Cup weekend was in tatters.

When James came home he tripped over the pink suitcase.

"What the hell? Emma, what is this doing here?" he snapped,

assuming I had placed it there to test his aptitude at the hurdles on the way into the kitchen. Then he saw Babs and it became clear. "Ah, I see we have a visitor. I sincerely hope this is a farewell visit by you, Babs, as you are on your way to the airport to emigrate for . . . a year, judging by the size of that suitcase."

"Wrong. I got kicked out of home because my mother found some blow in my bedroom, so I'm moving in here for a few days while I decide where to go to begin my new life."

"Why don't you just go straight to South America and stay with some of your fellow barons in Colombia?" said James, finding himself very amusing as he grabbed a beer from the fridge.

"Ha-ha," said Babs, rolling her eyes. "I think I'll hide out here for a while first, thanks."

"Well, it's an ingenious plan. Interpol would never look for you in your sister's house."

"Hilarious! Don't give up the day job, James, Billy Connolly isn't exactly quaking in his boots."

"Oh God, please shut up. I'm not listening to this sniping for the next few days," I said, jumping in before they got worse. "Now, what do you fancy for dinner?"

"I'd like some of that revolting green tea and some tasty steamed vegetables," said Babs, pushing her luck.

The raging hormones kicked in. "You ungrateful little wench," I said, grabbing her suitcase and hurling it out the front door, in an amazing display of superhuman strength. It must have been another side effect of the drugs I hadn't previously noticed. Maybe that was what Bruce Banner took before he turned into the Incredible Hulk—plain old hormone enhancers. "Go on, piss off, I'm sick of you. I've enough shit to deal with without you annoying me."

Babs looked genuinely shocked and for once was speechless. She looked at James.

"Come on, Emma, she's sorry. Aren't you, Babs?"

"Yeah, I am. Sorry, Emma, I was just joking. If you want me to eat the vegetables I will, but can I at least have a beer to wash them down? I really don't think I can stomach drinking the green muck. Maybe it's because my nose is so big, but the smell of it makes me want to puke."

"I'll cook if you like," said James.

Christ! If Babs was apologizing and James was offering to cook, I must be really scary. Still, it made a nice change. "Okay, I'd like Szechuan beef."

"Did I say 'cook'? I meant 'pay for,' " said James, as he grabbed his car keys.

"You sit down and put your feet up, Emma, we'll be back in ten minutes," said my newly humbled sister.

This was great—I should roar at her more often.

Five days later I drove Babs home to face the music. Dad was furious with her for causing him to miss the entire Ryder Cup. Mum, meanwhile, had been watching every film on drugs she could find in the video shop—including *Goodfellas* and *The Basketball Diaries*—and had spent hours calling the "My child's a drug addict, what can I do?" helpline. She had just stopped short of buying a sniffer dog. Babs was frisked at the front door, then hustled into the house for some serious questioning, *NYPD Blue* style. For the first time in my life, I actually felt sorry for her.

TWENTY-NINE

A month and a useless big black blob later, I was still not pregnant. Our wedding anniversary was coming up, and I was trying to decide where to go for a nice romantic mini-break. Suddenly it came to me—I had to stop waiting for miracles to happen and go and find one. There was only one place I knew where miracles happened. I went to the travel agent and booked three days away as a surprise for James. Needless to say, I had planned the three-day break around my supposedly fertile time of the month. When James came home I handed him an envelope wrapped in a red bow. "Happy anniversary."

"But it's not until next week—or did I . . ." he said, looking panic-stricken at the thought of having forgotten an anniversary with a wife who currently went off the deep end if he brought home the wrong teabags.

"No, you haven't forgotten—it *is* next week. I just wanted to surprise you early with this little holiday so you can plan your training 'round it."

"Oh, right," said a relieved-looking James. "Where are we off to, then?"

He opened the envelope and pulled out the itinerary. "Two return flights to Paris. Fantastic, I love Paris. . . . Oh, hang on, and then onward by train to Lourdes. Lourdes?" asked James, looking at me.

"Yes."

"Joke?"

"No."

"We're going to Lourdes for our wedding anniversary?"

"Yes."

"This is a windup."

"No."

"Emma."

"What?"

"What the hell is this?"

"We're going to Lourdes for a few days. It's no big deal. I thought you'd be pleased. It's something a bit different and the weather should be nice. I've booked a hotel with a swimming pool. I think it's time we had some divine intervention. I know you're not Catholic and I'm a lapsed one, but God is all-loving and forgiving and miracles happen in Lourdes. Apparently if you have really bad skin diseases and multiple sclerosis and stuff, they dunk you in holy water and you're cured. So I think it's worth a shot for us to go to the baths and pray at the grotto to Our Lady. She can relate to having children. Sure, wasn't Jesus a miracle—a virgin birth and all that? So, anyway, I just think it might help and miracles do happen in Lourdes, I read about them, and Auntie Doreen says that pilgrimages are really inspiring—"

"I'm not going on some wild-goose chase to Lourdes to spend three days with a bunch of religious fanatics. We'll stay in Paris and have a nice, relaxing time drinking wine and chilling out."

"I can't drink on these stupid drugs and, as you well know, relaxing is not my forte these days. I have spent the last six months with my legs in stirrups drugged out of my mind to no avail. So I'm going in search of a miracle. This is the trip I want and this is where I'm going," I said, snatching the itinerary out of his hand.

"I see, and if this doesn't work, what's next? Fatima for Christmas? Medjugorje with your auntie Doreen for New Year's Eve?"

"There's no need to make a mockery of it. Just because you Prods don't believe that Mary was a vital part of the equation doesn't mean that She wasn't. In case you haven't noticed, it's Mary who performs the miracles. It's Mary who appears to people and gives them hope. Protestants are just too chauvinistic to appreciate the power of a woman in religion. In my world, Mary rocks," I said, in a speech that Sister Patricia would have been proud of.

"Oh, I'm well aware that She rocks. Didn't Doreen see Her rocking in some field a few years ago just before she turned into a pilgrimage junkie? I have the utmost respect for Mary, but I'm not spending three days in Lourdes waiting for Her to start swaying or dancing or whatever She does when She appears. Nor am I diving into dirty bathwater in some far-fetched belief that it will help us conceive. We'd be much better off in a nice hotel in Paris having lots of sex."

"James," I said, in my scary voice, "I'm going to Lourdes with or without you. My mind is made up. As an anniversary present to me I'd like you to come, but I'm going regardless. Miracles do happen and, anyway, maybe if I go to Lourdes and see really sick people and stuff, I'll stop feeling so miserable and be distracted and not even think about getting pregnant and then get pregnant. You know, reverse psychology. I want you to come with me. It'll be fun."

"Fun? In Lourdes with sick and dying pilgrims?"

"Okay, not fun exactly, but fulfilling and spiritual, and maybe we can help out with the sick while we're there."

"Now you're really selling it to me. Go to Lourdes and wipe people's arses. Why don't we leave now? Why waste any more time? Let's go tomorrow."

"Fine. Don't come. I'll go on my own. Just like I go to all my appointments on my own. Just like I take the drugs on my own. Just like I get the bad results on my own—"

"Okay! I'll go," said James, sensibly shutting me up before I blamed him for the hole in the ozone layer and the destruction of the Amazon rainforest. "But this is a once-off, Emma. Never again. Next year I'm booking the trip and we're going to watch United playing in Old Trafford."

"Of course. Next year we'll do whatever you want. Old Trafford sounds nice. Is it in the Cotswolds?"

James sighed and picked up the newspaper.

A week later we were on the TGV shooting across the French countryside, surrounded by young people with guitars singing folksy songs and talking excitedly about the wonder that was Lourdes. I thought it was nice and joined in with the few songs I recognized—"Bridge Over Troubled Water," "Annie's Song," "He Is Lord" . . . I nudged James to sing along, but he refused and spent the entire journey glaring out the window. He was obviously determined not to enjoy himself. Mind you, he had never been a sing-song person. When we had family gatherings and Dad got a bit drunk, he'd launch into his Tom Jones impression and sing "Delilah," hips swinging, and winking at his imaginary Las Vegas audience. We'd all sing along, but James always looked a bit uncomfortable, and when he was forced to sing something himself, he always sang that really annoying rugby song, "Swing Low, Swing Chariots," or whatever it's called: he knew we all hated it and that we would interrupt him after the first line. I always sang "The Sun'll Come Out Tomorrow" from *Annie*. Mum would sing a very emotional rendition of "Somewhere Over the Rainbow" in a high, squeaky voice, which always made us howl with laughter, although I'd say the ghost of Judy Garland was writhing in torment at the crucifixion of her song. Sean sang "The Piano Man" and, unlike the rest of us, he could sing. Babs thought singing was for dorks and always went to bed when it began. It was one thing she and James had in common.

When the train pulled in, I waved good-bye to the international do-gooders as they went off to comfort the sick. They told me that there was always help needed in Lourdes and said I was welcome to join them any time to lend a hand. James stood grumpily to the side, fiddling with his case. I could see he was worried that I was going to volunteer him for duty.

Our hotel was surprisingly nice. Not plush, but nice and clean and airy with a decent-size pool. It was on the outskirts of the town, and while there were statues and pictures of Mary in abundance, you didn't feel as though you were in the grotto. We dumped our bags and headed for a swim. It was lovely and warm outside and the pool was heated. James began to cheer up.

Later that evening, on our way to the grotto, I filled James in on Bernadette and the apparition. *The Song of Bernadette* had been my headmistress Sister Patricia's favorite film and we had been subjected to it at least five times a year in religion class. Personally I thought that at twenty-four Jennifer Jones was a little old to be playing the young Bernadette, but Hollywood had thought otherwise. I explained to James that on February 11, 1858, fourteen-year-old Bernadette had been minding her own business, focusing on her breathing—because she suffered from chronic asthma—when Mary appeared to her. It was the first of eighteen apparitions and soon people from all over were coming to the grotto of Massabielle. Bernadette became a nun and devoted her life to God. Well, she had to, really—it wouldn't have looked too good if she'd gone off to Paris to shake her booty at the Moulin Rouge.

There was a long line of people waiting to go past the grotto and pray for their special intentions. Everywhere you turned there were sick people, but everyone looked peaceful and serene. It was nice. Even I began to feel calm. We shuffled along and when we got to the grotto I prayed for my miracle. It was very soothing. By the time we had finished, the torchlight procession had begun. We sat on a wall and watched it go by. Everyone carried candles and sang in different languages. It was really beautiful.

When we got into bed later that night, I suddenly felt odd about having sex. It didn't feel right—even though it was day thirteen of my cycle. I had just been to one of the holiest places in the world and somehow sex seemed wrong, or bold, or something. I felt as if I was committing a crime. James said it was just my old Catholic guilt surfacing, but it was important to remember that I was married, trying to procreate and had left the Rampant Rabbit at home. I wasn't even just in it for the fun—I was actually trying to get pregnant. "Even the pope couldn't fault you, Emma. It's clean sex with your husband without contraceptives or sex toys."

He was right. Besides, it was day thirteen and I needed to focus. I got up and took down the picture of Mary and Saint Bernadette, and turned the statues lining the room to face the wall. Now at least I didn't feel we were being watched.

The next morning I dragged James out of bed early to go to the baths. I knew the queues got very long and I wanted to catch some sun in the afternoon, so we went down early. The queue for the men's baths was separate from the women's so we arranged to meet up for coffee afterward.

When I got to the top of my queue I was ushered into a crowded room, told to undress and tie a damp, ice-cold sheet 'round myself. Then I went into a freezing room with a bath in the middle and women on either side. I was unceremoniously dunked in the bath-water. It was subzero and my body was in total shock. I was told to go and get dressed, but offered no towel. The really weird thing was, I was dry. Bone dry. It was as if the water had vanished—a miracle in a way. Everyone in the changing room was looking at one another in wonder. I got dressed and ran to meet James. If Mary could make special nonwet water, surely She could give me a few good eggs. He was waiting for me, drinking coffee and reading the paper.

"Hi," I said breathlessly, slumping down into the seat opposite him. "Wasn't that just the most spiritual experience ever?"

"Yeah, absolutely," he said, just a little too enthusiastically.

"I mean the water. Isn't it incredible?"

"Mmm, yes, I thought so too."

"Were there men there to dunk you?"

"Oh, yes, there was dunking. Coffee, darling?"

"Yes, cappuccino, please."

James ordered me a coffee, then began to tell me about something he had just read in the paper.

"Isn't it amazing the way the water is so warm?" I interrupted.

"Amazing. Almost hot, if you think about it."

"You liar! James Hamilton, you're a big fat liar. You didn't go to the baths."

James knew he was sussed. "No, I didn't, and I have no intention of going. I didn't want to have an argument with you this morning about it, so I played along. But, Emma, I will never be having a bath here so don't start. I came to Lourdes to keep you company, not to convert."

I knew I was wasting my time so I let it go.

That afternoon, as we lounged by the pool, we saw a little boy in the shallow end, paddling around with armbands on. He looked about six and he was bald. He watched in awe as James swam the length of the pool under water. He beamed at him when he came up for air.

The poor little boy, I thought, my eyes welling with tears. He must have cancer. All his hair has fallen out. He's obviously come to Lourdes for a miracle cure. I felt like a fraud. Coming to Lourdes with my silly problems when this little boy was about to die.

"Hello," he said shyly to James.

"Hello to you," said James, wiping water out of his eyes.

"My name's Peter, I'm learning to swim. Soon I'll be able to swim like you," said the little boy, in a strong Scottish accent.

"Good for you," said James. "Do you want me to help you?" Peter's face lit up. "Yes, please."

A young girl in her early twenties came over to the edge of the pool and told Peter not to bother the nice man. James assured her that it would be his pleasure to help Peter learn to swim. She smiled at him and introduced herself. "I'm Peter's mum, Linda."

James introduced himself and I strolled over to meet them too. Linda looked pretty good in her bikini and I wanted to get a closer view. She was young and attractive, but looked worn out.

"Hi, I'm Emma. Your little boy is lovely."

"Thanks, he can be a handful at times, but I wouldn't be without him."

"Look, we're going to be here for the afternoon, so why don't you lie back and enjoy the sun while we keep an eye on him for you? Take a break, I'm sure you could do with one," I offered.

"Are you sure?"

"Positive."

"I won't say no. Thanks," she said, her face full of gratitude at my meager offer of help. I felt truly humbled as I watched her walk away and sink into her sun lounger. What a brave lady she was.

We spent the rest of the afternoon by the pool as James patiently taught Peter to swim while Linda read and dozed in the sun. My heart melted as I watched them together. James was brilliant with him and Peter worshiped him. It was perfect. James was really getting into the spirit of Lourdes. He was helping a dying child. Mary would definitely help us out now. By early evening Peter could do a few strokes on his own and he was chuffed to bits.

They were leaving at five the next morning so we said good-bye to Peter when Linda took him off to bed. He clung to James and began to cry. James lifted him up. "Hey, little man, no tears now. I want you to go home and practice your swimming. And when you win a gold medal at the Olympics for Great Britain, I want you to remember that I gave you your first lesson. And the gold medal goes to . . ." said James, swinging Peter upside down.

"Peter!" squealed the little boy.

"You've been great," said Linda, smiling at me. "Thanks for looking after him."

"It was a pleasure," I said. "He's such a lovely kid. How long has he been ill?"

"Ill?"

"Sick."

"Peter?"

"His hair and—"

"Oh, that. There was a lice outbreak at his school so I decided to shave his head so the little bastards couldn't fester in his hair.

Did you think he had cancer?" said Linda, throwing back her head and whooping.

"Well, I just thought because you were in Lourdes that—"

"Och, no. We just came with my nan for a bit of a break. She comes every year and my mum couldn't take her this year so we came instead. Come on, Petey, let's get you to bed."

THIRTY

A week after we got back, I was ironing in the kitchen when I saw something moving at the window. I looked closer, thinking it was a bird or a cat. It was a statue of Our Lady, dancing from side to side.

"Emmaaa, can you hear me? I want you to spread the word about religion."

I looked down to see Babs kneeling under the windowsill, giggling hysterically. "Very funny. Come on in," I shouted.

"Well?" she said, plonking herself at the kitchen table.

"Well what?"

"Did you see Her? Did She speak to you or at least sway for you?"

"Neither."

"Are you pregnant?"

"I won't know until next week."

"Do you think you are?"

"Dunno. One day I do. The next I don't."

"I can't believe James went with you. He must think you're mad. Going to Lourdes for your wedding anniversary! Even Mum thinks you've lost the plot. Still, at least if James leaves you, you can move to Lourdes and become a nun."

"It's great to see you too, Babs."

"I'm just telling you what everyone thinks. I even got a call from Sean! The first time he's ever called me for anything. He thinks you're losing it too."

"So you all think I'm going insane?"

"Pretty much, yeah."

"Well, you can go back and tell them all that I'm perfectly sane, and that next time they send an emissary they should choose more carefully."

"Look, I don't know about the baby stuff and how hard it is, but you have been pretty moody lately and you're always going mental for no reason. It can't be good for you or your marriage."

"So you're a marriage counselor now?"

"Fine, I'll butt out. I'm just filling you in on what's being said about you. To be honest, I'm delighted, it takes the pressure off me. Mum's so distracted about you that she hasn't had a go at me for weeks. She didn't even give out when I came home with my belly button pierced."

"Really?" I found it hard to believe that Mum hadn't hit the roof when she saw that.

"Yep. I'm telling you, her main concern now is you. It's great, so keep it up, sis. By the way, any chance you could do my makeup this Saturday? I'm going to a ball and I want to look sensational. My next boyfriend is going to be there."

"Ex?"

"No, next. I spotted him last week. Very sexy and knows it, so I have to look really good and you have to do lots of shading to make my nose look smaller. Okay?"

"Okay. If I decide to stick my head in the oven before then, I'll let you know so you can make alternative arrangements."

"Well, at least you haven't totally lost your sense of humor. I'll tell Mum, she'll be pleased. See ya."

" 'Bye."

* * *

The next day when I went to open my post, there was a letter from Sean. I recognized his handwriting. He hadn't written to me since I went on a French exchange to Toulouse, aged fifteen, and hated it. Mum had made him write to me every day to cheer me up. The family I was sent to were friends of friends of my auntie Tara's. They were awful. The girl—Cécile—was a stick insect with no personality. The mother kept telling me I was fat and fed me nothing but steamed vegetables and lettuce. I've never been so hungry in my life. The undernourished Cécile spent half the day weighing herself and shoving her fingers down her throat after every meal, and the other half lying on her bed and discussing diets on the phone with her equally obsessed friends. I hung out with the housekeeper, Dominique: she used to sneak me in chocolate bars to keep me going, until Madame Leroux caught her and fired her. So I ended up starving and feeling guilty because I had lost the lovely Dominique her job. Eventually after I'd cried to my mother on the phone every night for two weeks—even she grew weary of telling me it was character-building—she changed my ticket and I flew home early.

Sean's letter said:

Dear Sis,

Hope you don't mind me sending you this. I'm not trying to stick my oar in, but Mum tells me—on a daily basis—that you are having a tough time with this pregnancy lark and I saw this in a magazine in the dentist's yesterday, so I ripped it out—much to the bemusement of the receptionist. If you are interested I'd be happy to pay for the consultation and treatment. Let's face it, I can't even hold down a relationship, so the chances of me being a father are slim to none. Your kids will be the closest thing I get to parenthood, so I'm doing this for selfish reasons too. Anyway, see what you think and let me know. The offer is there. This woman seems to be doing great things and all the stars go to her so you'd be in good company! Keep away from the aspirin.

Sean

Inside was an article about a woman called Zita West. She was a midwife who had been one of the first people to take acupuncture into NHS hospitals. Her clients included Kate Winslet, Cate Blanchett and Davina McCall—sounded good to me. I was still going to Sheila for my acupuncture once a week and still finding it the only thing that helped me relax. I read on. The article said:

West is shocked by how few women are really in tune with their bodies, especially their menstrual cycles . . . losing weight can increase your chances of conception as can detoxifying the liver. . . . West also asks women to refrain from using tampons, which can alter the mucus in the vaginal tract, and keep out of the gym and swimming pool when they are on their period—when, according to Chinese medicine, the body should rest.

I like the sound of resting, but, come on, Zita, no tampons? It's not very practical. All the same, her clients were breeding like rabbits so she must be good. I wondered how much she cost—a lot, judging by the people going to her. I was tempted, but it was unrealistic. Flying to London to see her would be a needless extravagance. Besides, I was getting fed up with conflicting advice. Everyone had an opinion and lots of them differed. It was really sweet of Sean, but I wasn't going to take him up on the offer—even though I would have enjoyed hanging out in the waiting room with Cate and the gang.

* * *

Another week of waiting, hoping and praying later—I got my period. The miracle of Lourdes was that I didn't throw myself under a bus out of frustration, disappointment and utter despondency. James had gone to London to try to persuade the London-Irish scrum half to come and play for Leinster, so I decided to call in to my mother for some sympathy and TLC.

She opened the door and as soon as I saw her, I began to wail. "Muuuuuum, I'm . . . uh-uh-uh . . . not pregnant again."

"Oh no! You poor old thing. Come on in," she said, giving me a hug. "Sit down there now and I'll get you a glass of wine."

"Thanks," I sniffled, as she poured me a goldfish bowl–size glass. "I can't bear it, Mum. It's not fair. Everyone else is getting pregnant except me. What's wrong with me? What's wrong with my stupid body?" I said, slipping easily into self-pity mode.

"Now, Emma, stop that nonsense at once. There's nothing wrong with you or your body. You're a healthy young girl and you'll have a healthy baby one of these days, but you'll have to try to calm down. Look at the state of you. It's not good for you to be so stressed out. You'll have to try to distract yourself. Take up tennis or join a folk group or something. Babies take time, you can't be impatient."

"It's been over a year and a half. I'm not being impatient. I'm sick of waiting. Why isn't it happening? It's not bloody fair. I think I'm going mad."

"Now, listen here, you'll have to get a grip. All this obsessing, drug-taking and moodiness is not good for you or your marriage. I'm sure James is finding it a strain too. I hope you're not taking your frustrations out on him. The last thing a man needs when he gets home from work is a nagging wife," she said, conveniently ignoring her behavior toward Dad for the past thirty-five years. Every time the poor man walked through the door, he was given odd jobs to do around the house, or ordered to get a haircut, polish his shoes, throw out the tie he was wearing, lose weight, help his children with their homework, feed the goldfish and—if it wasn't snowing—mow the lawn. But clearly my mother was suffering from early onset Alzheimer's as she lectured me on being a good wife.

"What you need to do is be nice and cheery when James comes in. No husband wants to be greeted by a long face. When he gets home show an interest in his life and don't be always giving him bad news. Mark my words, Emma, James is a very handsome young man and successful too. He's a good catch and I'm sure there are plenty of young ones who would be only too happy to turn his head."

"What am I? A useless old bag who no one wants? What am I supposed to do, Mum? Follow James around all day in bright pink dresses, telling him how marvelous he is? What about me? What about my life? My support? Who's going to tell me how great I am? How brave and uncomplaining I am? What if I never have kids? What if I'm barren and I just keep trying and trying and never get pregnant? I want a family, Mum. I want kids. That's what life's about. But it doesn't look like it's going to happen. That thought terrifies me. I need your support."

"You have my support, you silly girl. I'm worried sick about you. I know how much you want children. Aren't I down on my knees every night praying for you? I've even got your father to start praying too. I'm just saying that you need to calm down or you'll make yourself ill and you'll put a strain on your marriage. And everyone says that stress is a disaster when you're trying to get pregnant."

"But what if I never have a baby?"

"Of course you will."

"But what if I don't, Mum? I have to face the fact that I may never get pregnant. I have to look at my options. I'm thinking of adoption."

"Adoption? For goodness' sake, Emma, stop running before you can walk. You're thirty-four, not forty-four. Stop panicking. Now, do you want me to cook you a shepherd's pie?"

It was my favorite comfort food and she had always made it for me when I was younger—when I had the flu, or the time I broke my arm, or if I had a fight with Jess or Lucy or whatever minidrama was going on at school.

"Yes, please," I said, tears welling as happy childhood memories flooded back. Oh, to be young and carefree again.

"Okay. You pour yourself another glass of wine and I'll make the dinner. Don't worry, pet, it'll all work out. You'll see," she said, getting a bit tearful herself as she pulled a Marks & Spencer shepherd's pie out of the freezer.

THIRTY-ONE

*I*t was time to go back to see Dr. Reynolds. I had been on the fertility drugs for seven months. I had looked at numerous fuzzy screens, showing small, medium and large blobs—all useless. It was time for action. James came with me for support. I asked him to bring along some paper and a pen to take notes, so we could discuss our options afterward without forgetting anything that Dr. Reynolds had said.

Dr. Reynolds told us how sorry he was that the treatment hadn't worked. He said he was surprised as he was sure it would be effective, seeing as how we were both young and healthy. "But I think it's clear that it isn't working so we need to look at our options."

I nudged James to start taking notes.

"I mentioned the possibility of a laparoscopy before and I think at this stage it's the best thing to do. The procedure is straightforward and relatively painless as you are under general anesthetic. It takes about twenty minutes so you'll be home within a few hours."

"Okay," I said warily. Painless tests were a myth. "What exactly does it involve?"

"We'll bring you in and once you're asleep we insert a fine needle into the abdomen, then pump in gas to push away the intestine. The laparoscope—which is a fiberoptic telescope—is then inserted through a small incision under the belly button and we inspect the inside of the abdomen and pelvis, including the outside of the womb, the tubes and the ovaries."

"Incision?" I didn't want to end up with a big scar and no baby to show for it. I was all for Cesarean sections (too posh to push, and all that—it sounded very civilized to me), but I didn't want a scar for no reason.

"Don't worry, it's a tiny scar that only ever requires one small stitch. If we find any abnormalities during the procedure we deal with them there and then, thus avoiding a further operation. In your case I doubt we'll find anything dramatically wrong, as we know from your X-rays that all seems in order."

"Will it be painful when I wake up?"

"You'll need to rest for a day after the operation. I recommend taking some light painkillers and there may be some vaginal discomfort and a little bleeding, but it will be minimal."

Minimal my ass, I thought. So far nothing had been painless, despite all promises to the contrary. I sighed as I faced the thought of yet more time spent in the clinic. Still, at least this way they'd know for sure if something was wrong, and I'd be knocked out, so chances were I'd feel little pain. "Okay, what if you don't find anything that explains why I can't seem to get pregnant? What then?"

"Well, then I think we'll have to look at IVF. But let's take it a step at a time. I'll set up an appointment for the laparoscopy and we can look at our options after we've analyzed the results.

"Any more questions or concerns?" he said, looking from me to James, who was doodling on the piece of paper he was supposed to be taking notes on.

"Uhm. No, thank you, Doctor, that all seems pretty straightforward," said James, delighted the meeting was over so he didn't have to listen to any more chat about vaginas.

My appointment was made for ten days' time. James and I went for a coffee and I asked to see his notes so I could remember exactly what I was in for. He reluctantly passed over the sheet of paper.

Laparospuppy—Gas pump, No pain. No scar. Call Glen Red-grave—offer him five grand more. Need his skills. Scrum half—key position. Check budget with Eddie.

"James! Did you listen to a word he said?"

"Yes. The information is there, it's just a summary of it."

"For goodness' sake, you were supposed to be taking detailed notes."

"Well, he said it was all very straightforward so I just jotted down key points—like the name of the procedure so you can look it up later on the Internet."

"What exactly do you think a 'laparospuppy' is?" I said.

"It's when they open you up and you surprise them all by giving birth to a small dog."

A couple of days later, Lucy called me and asked me to meet her for a drink. She sounded a bit strange on the phone, but when I probed her for more information, she went all KGB on me and said she'd talk to me when she saw me. She was waiting for me when I arrived, looking a bit hot and bothered. Before I had even taken off my jacket and sat down, she blurted out, "Donal has asked me to move in with him."

"What?" I squealed. "When? How? Tell me everything."

Lucy told me that she and Donal had gone out two nights before for dinner and ended up getting pretty smashed. They stumbled back to Donal's house, and when she woke up in the morning she realized that her shirt was covered in red wine. She had an important meeting to go to and no time to wash it, so she panicked.

Donal turns around and says, "Relax, I think there are some shirts in that drawer over there." Lucy presumed he meant his shirts, but when she looked inside there were three blouses, face creams, a hair-dryer and other girly stuff. So she asked him whose they were.

"Oh, they must be Mary's," said Donal, as cool as you like.

"Mary I met at the dog coursing?" Lucy said.

"Yep," he said.

"Mary your ex-girlfriend?" she said.

"The very same," he said.

"I see," said Lucy, managing to keep calm. "What are they doing here?"

"I dunno, I suppose she left them behind."

"And you expect me to wear one of that stupid cow's shirts to work, do you?"

"Well, you said you needed a clean shirt, and sure isn't that a clean one? I was only trying to help."

"*Help!*" roared Lucy, losing her cool. "By offering me your ex-girlfriend's clothes? How am I to know she doesn't come up and stay and that's her regular drawer? I notice I don't have a drawer. Your bloody ex-girlfriend does, but I don't. I have to traipse around carrying spare knickers and a toothbrush in my bag. I'm sick of it, Donal. I'm sick of living out of a suitcase," Lucy announced dramatically.

"But we nearly always go back to your place," said Donal, looking puzzled. "You hardly ever stay here."

He had a point—they almost always ended up in Lucy's place, because she preferred it that way and he didn't care where they were. Having sex in Lucy's bed rather than his was fine with Donal.

"Well, I'm here now, and you're foisting your ex's clothes on me."

"I'm not foisting anything on you. If you want a drawer, take one. Help yourself to any drawer you like, but stop shouting—it's too early for shouting."

"Why are you keeping her stuff? If it's over, throw it out. As a matter of fact, I'm going to do it for you," said Lucy, grabbing Mary's things from the drawer and throwing them into a plastic bag.

"While you're cleaning up there, would you mind giving the place a bit of a Hoover and maybe throw on a wash if you have time?" said Donal, grinning, as he snuggled back under his duvet.

"Funny? How would you like it if you found my ex's clothes hanging in my wardrobe?"

"If he happened to be the same size as me and I needed a shirt, I'd be delighted."

"That cow is twice the size of me and I'm the furthest thing from delighted. I don't like surprises. I don't like having your past shoved in my face. I'm too old for this crap. I want my own bed and my own shower and my own bloody wardrobe. Here," said Lucy, tipping the bag upside down on Donal's bed, "clean up your own mess."

Later that afternoon Donal called Lucy for a chat. "Howrya?"

"Busy," she said coolly.

"Just wanted to check what that scene was earlier—I'm not very good at reading women's minds. Were you pissed off about Mary's shirts being in the drawer? About me thinking Mary's shirts would fit you and you thinking you're much thinner than her? Or about you not having a drawer in my wardrobe? If it's because the shirts were there, I've thrown them out. If it's because I thought they'd fit you, well, I'm not very good at women's clothes and judging sizes and if it's a drawer you want, you can have one, in fact you can have two. I just want to be clear which issue I'm dealing with. Or did I miss the point entirely, and were you doing that thing where women pick fights about something when they're actually pissed off about something completely different?"

Lucy smiled despite herself.

"Lucy? Are you there?"

"Yes. Look, I was just tired and hungover and I was annoyed to find Mary's stuff still in the drawer. It felt like I was a stranger in your house or something. All this spending the night in each other's places is becoming a drag. Not having our stuff in the same place is just a hassle, really," said Lucy, dropping large hints without actually asking him to move in.

She had been thinking about it all day. They spent almost every night together—mostly in her place—it would be so much easier to move in together. It would mean Donal wouldn't have to rush home to get changed for training and she wouldn't have to go to work in a stained shirt, and it'd be nice to wake up together every day. She really liked Donal. Truth be told, she was falling in love with him, but she wouldn't ask him to move in with her. It seemed too keen, too pushy.

"Ah, sure it's not so bad. I'll buy you a toothbrush today and if you tell me what size you are I'll get you a shirt to hang up in the wardrobe too. How about that?"

"Fine. I have to go," said Lucy, raging with him for missing the point.

An hour later, a huge package arrived at Lucy's office. It was one of the large wooden drawers from Donal's wardrobe tied in a red ribbon with an envelope taped to the inside. She opened the envelope and a key fell out. The note said, "Subtlety was never your strong point. I'd love you to live with me."

She called him. "Hi."

"You got it, then?"

"Yes."

"Well, are we moving in or what?"

"Only if you move into my place. It's much nicer."

"I can't, Lucy. Annie has her room all done up in my place. It's the only home she knows and I don't want to uproot her again."

"Of course," said Lucy. Damn, she hadn't thought of that. She couldn't force the issue: Donal's little niece needed stability. She'd have to move into Donal's house. "I understand, but I'm getting decorators in. Your place needs serious work."

"That's fine with me. I'll see you later. We'll ring Annie at school tonight to tell her. She'll be thrilled."

She's not the only one, thought Lucy, as she beamed out the window, flipping the key in her hand. Finally, a proper boyfriend, one who understood her and wanted to live with her!

When she called over to her new home later that evening, they phoned Annie at her boarding school. Donal told her the good news and Lucy could hear her screaming on the phone. But they weren't happy screams: she was screaming blue murder.

"No way," she roared. "She's not moving into my house. That's our house, Donal, it's for you and me and no one else. I don't want her moving in and changing everything. You'll never have time for me anymore. It's not fair. It's not what you promised. You said it'd just be you and me after Mum and Dad died. I'll kill myself if she moves in, I swear I will. I don't want her in my house. I hate her. I hate you. You'll get married and have babies and then I'll be ignored."

"Jesus, Annie, calm down. I'm not getting married and I'm not having any babies. Lucy is just going to move in is all. She stays almost every night anyway. It'll make no difference to you. You got on great with her when you met. I thought you'd be delighted."

"Well, you were *wrong*. I'm not. I don't want her in my house. I don't want anyone else in my house. You'll abandon me just like Mum and Dad, I know you will," screamed the hysterical Annie.

Lucy shrank back into the couch. Christ, Little Orphan Annie had a big pair of lungs for one so young. She too had thought she'd be pleased. They had got on well when they met. She'd thought the kid liked her, but now she was causing havoc.

"Come on now, Annie, calm down, nothing will change, I promise. I'll always put you first, you know that. Have I ever let you down? Well, have I?"

Put her first? Lucy didn't like the sound of that. She felt sorry for the child being orphaned and all, but she didn't want to play second fiddle to some hormonal brat who apparently hated her.

"No," admitted Annie grumpily.

"And I don't intend to start now. Lucy's going to move in for a month or two and we'll see how it goes. I'm sure we'll all get on famously. When you come home in a few weeks we'll go out and talk about it. If it doesn't work out Lucy will move out," said Donal, winking at Lucy in an effort to reassure her. "This is your home first and foremost, you know that, kiddo. Come on now, calm down, it'll all work out."

"Fine, she can move out when I come home, then. Tell her not to unpack. She's not staying, and if she dares go into my room, I'll kill her."

"Okay, I'll give you a call on Saturday," said Donal, desperately trying to get off the phone before any more damage could be done.

"That went well, I thought," said Lucy.

"She's a bit highly strung. She's terrified I'll have no time for her now I've you here. She's never had to share me with anyone before. You're my first official lodger," said Donal, smiling. "Don't worry, she'll come 'round."

He didn't sound convinced and Lucy knew how awful teenage girls could be. Suddenly their cozy cohabitation looked distinctly rocky.

Lucy finished telling me the story and took a slug of wine. She looked pretty shaken. On the one hand she was chuffed that she and Donal were getting so serious, but she hadn't planned for the sweet Annie to turn into such a monster.

"Just ignore her," I said. "She's a mixed-up kid who's scared that Donal will stop paying her attention if you move in. She doesn't mean it, she'd be jealous of anyone he loved. I'm sure it'll be fine. You'll just have to be supernice step-girlfriend/surrogate-aunt-thingy. How often does she get out of school?"

"One weekend in six."

"Well, that's not so bad. On those weekends you can come and stay with us."

"Thanks. I'm afraid I might be more Cruella de Vil than Mary Poppins. I'm not very good with kids. At least if it was you, you've had experience dealing with a younger sister."

"You can borrow Babs any time. She'd try the patience of a saint. I'll send her over to you tomorrow for some practice. Annie will seem like Pollyanna after Babs."

THIRTY-TWO

I woke up in the recovery room after the laparoscopy with Dr. Reynolds smiling down at me. I felt wonderful. If this was what class-A drugs were like, I was definitely a candidate for drug addiction. I felt as if I was floating and had the urge to laugh loudly. Dr. Reynolds said that the procedure had gone very well and that nothing unusual had been discovered. I appeared to be perfectly "normal" inside. He went off to tell James I was awake, while a nurse took my blood pressure, pulse and temperature.

Two hours later I was back home in bed with James fussing around me. He made me cups of tea and filled hot water bottles and brought me magazines and books and kept plumping my pillows. The sight of me being wheeled off in my backless gown had obviously shaken him. What might have been only a small procedure was still an operation and James was upset by it. "How do you feel now?" he asked me, for the millionth time.

"I'm fine, James, honestly. Sit down and relax. You, on the other hand, look like you could do with a drink."

He smiled. "Sorry, darling. Seeing you being carted off to theater gave me a bit of a fright. I hate you having to go through all this. It's so bloody unfair."

"Yeah, I know." I sighed. "And to be honest, I'm disappointed they didn't find anything. I wish they had—then at least they could have fixed it and we'd know why I haven't been able to get pregnant. Now we're just back to square one again. I hate the fact that it's all so vague and inconclusive. Anyway, it looks like IVF now."

"We don't have to do this, you know," said James, stroking my hair. "We could just take some time out, go on hols and try to forget about it. Give you a rest."

"No, I want to keep going," I said. "I'm on a roll now. I'm a bit scared of IVF, but loads of women go through it and have babies, so it's worth a shot."

"But what if it doesn't work?" said James. "What then? Do we just keep trying?"

"I don't know. I'm happy to give it one shot, but I'm not sure if I want to do it loads of times."

"Are you sure you want to go ahead with it?" he asked again, his face full of concern.

"Yes. It's worth trying, but if it doesn't work I think we should consider adoption. I've been thinking about it a lot lately and I think it would be a good option."

James didn't say anything.

"What do you think?" I pushed.

"I think we should take one step at a time. Adoption can be tricky."

"What do you mean?"

"Well, it's not your own flesh and blood. It's someone else's child and you don't know what those people are like. The child could be damaged in some way."

"Oh, for goodness' sake, look at Mia Farrow and all her lovely children. They always seem really happy in the pictures you see of them."

James looked at me in shock. "I hardly think Mia and her

brood are the ideal family. Didn't Woody end up having sex with his adopted daughter? It's not exactly a normal family unit."

"Okay, well, maybe that was a bad example, but look at, uhm . . ." Damn, I couldn't think of anyone—my brain was still fuzzy from the anesthetic. "I can't think of them now, but there are loads of successful people who were adopted and loved and went on to achieve great things. I'll think of them in a minute," I said, racking my brains to come up with some names.

"Look, get some rest. You've just had an operation and you need to take it easy. Call me if you need anything," said James, kissing my forehead as he switched off the light. The conversation was over. I'd think of some adoptees tomorrow, I thought, as I fell into a deep sleep.

Two weeks later we were back in Dr. Reynolds's office. He went over the findings—or lack thereof—of the laparoscopy, and told me all my bits were essentially in the right place. I had "unexplained infertility." There was no reason for me not to get pregnant, except for the small fact that, despite my best efforts and some fairly strong drugs, I couldn't seem to. I was a prime candidate for IVF, said Dr. Reynolds. My chances of success were high.

"What exactly is the rate of success?" asked my now alert and professional note-taking husband.

"The internationally accepted success rate of IVF is seventeen percent per treatment cycle," said Dr. Reynolds. "However, with youth and health on your side, your chances are much higher. I would say you have a twenty-five percent chance of conceiving first time. This can be considerably higher if you're having acupuncture in conjunction with the treatment. I hope you'll keep up the acupuncture, Emma."

I nodded. Of course I'd keep it up. It was the only part of the process I didn't dread.

"I do, however, have to warn you that it is expensive and there are risks involved."

"How expensive?" I asked.

"You're looking at about six thousand euro per treatment."

"What risks?" asked James.

"Fertility treatment can result in an increased risk of multiple pregnancies. Ectopic pregnancies are twice as common in IVF pregnancies and ovarian hyperstimulation syndrome can occur, but only in very rare cases. However, these are all very unlikely outcomes," said Dr. Reynolds, smiling at us.

James looked at me and asked me if I was sure I wanted to go ahead with it. I nodded. It was too late to back down now. I wanted to give this a go. I was going to give it my best shot. I wanted a baby.

"What exactly happens?" I asked. "Is it really painful?"

Unfortunately I had been on the Internet chat-room sites and had read some pretty dire reports about the pain and emotional trauma of IVF. I had also read of the miracle babies, but as usual had fixated on the pain and stress.

"We'll give you drugs to stimulate your ovaries into producing more eggs, not dissimilar to the drugs you've been on. These will need to be injected—which is where your husband comes in. Once the drugs kick in and the eggs mature, we'll retrieve them and fertilize the good ones in a test tube with your husband's sperm and then implant them in the womb."

"But how do you get the eggs out?" I asked, as James, on learning he had to inject me, had gone very quiet.

"Once the eggs are mature we'll begin the retrieval. We'll put you to sleep and an ultrasound probe, with a fine hollow needle attached to it, will be inserted into your vagina. Under ultrasound guidance, the needle is then advanced from the vaginal wall, punctures the back of the vagina, entering each follicle, and sucking out the fluid, which contains the egg. . . ."

My insides began to squirm at the thought of what lay ahead. Jesus Christ—puncturing? Did he actually just say "puncturing" and then follow it with "sucking"? And not even bat an eyelid? Were all doctors just sadists in white coats?

"This fluid will be given to the embryologist, Dr. Bradley, who will examine it under a microscope and count the eggs. When all the follicles are emptied, you'll be taken to the recovery room to rest. The whole procedure takes about forty minutes and you'll be out for the count so you won't feel a thing."

I was speechless. The mere description of it all had left me reeling. I glanced at James, who was looking decidedly peaky. Dr. Reynolds appeared oblivious to our discomfort and went on to describe the procedure for the embryo transfer. I had to have a full bladder; a speculum would be inserted to clean the cervix. A catheter was to be placed through the cervix into the lower segment of the uterus. A fine plastic catheter into which the embryologist had transferred the embryos would then be placed through the outer transfer catheter and advanced near the top of the uterus. Once the placement was correct, the embryos would be expelled from the catheter and inserted into the uterus.

"And then we let nature take its course," said Dr. Reynolds, having the gall to smile at us again as we sat white-faced with shock.

I tried to swallow, but my throat was dry. "Am I under general anesthetic for the embryo transfer?" I croaked.

"No, there's no need. It's very straightforward. We can offer a mild sedative if you like. Some of our patients take Valium. It's up to you."

"Put me down for the maximum dose," I said.

Dr. Reynolds then gave us a fact sheet about IVF, prescriptions for all the drugs I needed and made an appointment with the nurse to show James how to inject me with the hormones. He recommended we wait until my next cycle to give my body a rest after the laparoscopy.

Six weeks later we were in the bathroom at home, and after an hour of painstaking measuring of the vials, analyzing the needles and re-rereading of the instructions, James had finally filled the syringe and was now aiming the needle at my thigh. His hands were shaking and sweat was forming rapidly on his brow.

"Ouch. What the hell are you doing?" I snapped, as he hit me on the thigh with his free hand.

"Flicking the area to numb it before I inject," he said, pointing at the instruction leaflet on the floor to defend his actions.

"Well, it hurt. Do you have to be so rough? The bloody injection's bad enough without you bruising my leg first with all the flicking. Just stick it in and get it over with, and don't hit a nerve."

"Maybe I should get some ice to numb the area. That might help," he said, putting the needle down and heading out the door.

"James!" I roared. "Will you stop faffing around and stick the bloody needle in?"

"Okay. I was just trying to make it less painful. I think that icing the leg would be a good idea. It says here on page three—"

"STICK THE BLOODY THING IN BEFORE I KILL YOU!" I shouted, snatching up the instruction leaflet and flinging it across the bathroom.

"Fine," he said, expertly ignoring my histrionics. "Ready, then? And a one and a two and a—"

I grabbed his hand and shoved the needle into my thigh. It was James's turn to shout: "For God's sake, Emma, you'll hurt yourself."

I had expected it to be really painful. I had wound myself into a frenzy about the daily injections I was going to have to endure, but it was all right. Not painless, but not too bad. I looked down at my thigh where the red mark was. Well, let's face it, there was plenty of flesh available to soften the blow. James, breathing deeply to stay calm, inserted the drug into my leg, gently pulled out the needle and stuck a Band-Aid over the mark. "Sorry," I said, "you were making too much of a production of it. I don't want it to take longer than absolutely necessary."

"Fine. Tomorrow I'll just stab you," he said, picking up the torn leaflet.

"That would be lovely, thanks."

For the next two weeks James injected me, and as the level of hormones in my body increased I became ever more volatile and my mood swings had to be seen to be believed. On the fifth day when James arrived five minutes late to give me my injection because he'd got stuck in traffic, I accused him of having an affair and told him I wanted a divorce. Then I locked him in the bathroom and refused to let him out until he swore on his mother's life that he wouldn't divorce me because I couldn't bear him children. On the eighth day we went grocery shopping but had to leave the supermarket when I saw an old woman shopping alone and began to sob hysterically about the sadness of loneliness.

On day eleven I was back in the clinic having my fourth ultrasound and blood test in ten days. The waiting room was full of hopeful, desperate women like me. I felt right at home. I preferred these women to the pregnant ones. At least we were all in the same barren boat. We nodded and smiled at each other. I was surrounded by kindred spirits. The room was full of unspoken empathy. A small blonde woman to my left turned to me and asked me how my follicles were coming along. I said they seemed to be doing okay, they weren't A students, but they certainly couldn't be admonished for lack of effort.

"I've got twenty beautiful ones," gushed the blonde. "I think it's partly to do with the fact that my husband is so good at giving me the injections. Mind you, I have fantastic veins, which helps. The nurses said my follicles are the best they've seen. I meditate and use visualization techniques daily, it's very effective. . . ."

Suddenly I felt wretched again. I had seven measly follicles and Fertility Barbie had twenty. Obviously Ken was doing a better job at injecting Barbie than James was doing with me, or maybe it was my veins. I'd never really thought about my veins before. I looked down at my arms as Barbie rattled on. What made a good vein? Were bulgy ones good? I looked at hers; they seemed pretty normal to me. Before I could throttle her, the nurse called me in for my tests. I had ten follicles and my estradiol was two thousand. This, judging by the smiles and nods from the nurse, was good news. She told me to sit by the phone, as I'd be ready for my hCG injection soon.

HCG (human chorionic gonadotropin) is a crucial part of the IVF cycle and is given about 35 hours before egg retrieval.

So said my IVF guidelines book. While it was all good news, I was dreading the egg retrieval, so I wasn't exactly dancing around the room when Nurse Nancy called the next day to tell me exactly when I needed to have the hCG shot. James injected me at the exact time indicated and we went into the clinic two days later for the procedure. While I was being punctured by giant needles and sucked free of eggs, James was going to be masturbating at his leisure in a nice room the clinic provided, with wall-to-wall porn to help him along the way.

I don't remember much about the retrieval, as I happily wafted off into a deep sleep for the duration of the process. I woke up in the recovery room feeling groggy and sore and glad it was over. I was sent home with a goody bag that included antibiotics to prevent yeast infection, steroids to protect the prospective embryo from attack by white blood cells and—just in case I thought I was getting off lightly—vaginal progesterone suppositories.

The embryologist called me the following morning to discuss how many eggs to transfer. He suggested that we let eight of the embryos grow for a few days before choosing the best ones. He reckoned we'd be able to transfer three in three days' time. I was hoping he'd shove all of them in for good measure, but he assured me that three embryos was the standard number and would give me an excellent chance of getting pregnant.

Three days later I was back in for the embryo transfer, full bladder, gown and hat on, legs in the air. I had been given the Valium I had requested and Dr. Reynolds allowed James to come in with me to hold my hand—and, I suspect, to take any abuse I might dish out. When I saw the speculum coming toward me, I lay back and closed my eyes, willing the Valium to kick in. It was sore and uncomfortable and I wept with relief when it was over: I was finished with extractions and insertions. I was told to go home and rest for two days, then continue as normal.

"Normal." How easily the word slips off the medical profession's tongue. After weeks of injections, puncturing, steroids, suppositories, sucking of eggs out and pumping of eggs-plus-sperm back in, I was supposed to go home and be normal. I went home and was very abnormal. Although abnormal was now my normal.

For the next two weeks I cried a lot, slept little and tried not to obsess over anything that could be construed as a symptom, limiting myself to poking my boobs six times a day. I shouted at my mother for getting my hopes up when she told me about some friend of a friend's daughter who had given birth to beautiful twin girls after her first IVF treatment. I shouted at James when he said he had a good feeling about the treatment. I chased a magpie for two miles in desperation for it to find a friend—one for sorrow, two for joy—but the bastard bird was a one-man show. Then I cried because I felt sorry for it being alone in the world. I even began speaking to the embryos, begging them to cling on and hang in there.

But as the two weeks drew to a close, I thought seriously about the possibilities of failure. Could I go through this again? What about surrogacy? No, I didn't want another woman giving birth to my egg and James's sperm. It'd be like he'd had sex with her or something. Besides, any of the surrogacy women you saw on TV were rough as old boots and the thought of having to hold some dodgy bird's hand while she pushed my baby out was way too weird. Adoption was the only solution I could imagine going through with. Still, I thought, maybe this time we'll get lucky. Maybe this time we'll be celebrating.

THIRTY-THREE

Two weeks after the embryo transfer, I went for a blood test to see if I was pregnant. The result was negative. There were no tears. I felt nothing. I was numb. Numb to pain, numb to being upset, numb to bad results. It had been nearly two years of disappointment. I had no tears left.

Dr. Reynolds told me not to worry. He said my chances were excellent of getting pregnant during the next session of IVF. He told me not to be despondent. He said I was healthy and young and had time on my side. He came out with the same platitudes that I had been listening to for months. I sat in his office listening but not hearing. I looked over his shoulder out the window.

"Approximately three out of four embryos don't survive the period of early implantation long enough to become viable pregnancies, so don't be too discouraged by this first failure. I can assure you it will happen. We just need to be patient. . . ."

Patient! I thought wearily. Be patient. Relax. Stop worrying. Chill out. I couldn't listen to it anymore. I stood up while Dr. Reynolds was in midsentence. "I don't think I can do this anymore. Thank you for your time and for being so nice, but I don't think I'll be seeing you again," I said. My voice sounded as if it were coming from somewhere behind me, like an echo.

"I understand that you're disappointed, but please sleep on it.

Don't make any rash decisions yet. Call me in a few days and let me know how you feel then," he said kindly.

"Yes, fine."

I left the clinic and walked slowly to the car. I noticed things I had never noticed before. Details. The pictures on the walls, the plant pot, the color of the receptionist's nails as she bade me good-bye . . . I sat in the car for a long time, my mind a blank. I had no energy. I felt completely lifeless. Even breathing was an effort. Eventually I summoned the strength to drive home, where I lay on the couch and stared at the ceiling. The phone rang.

"Hi, Emma, it's me," said Lucy, to my answering machine. "Just ringing to say I've got a booking for nine at Chez Gérard. Did you get Jess a present or will we just pay for her dinner? I suppose thirty-five is a bit of a milestone. Anyway, I'll see you in the bar for drinks at eight."

I had forgotten Jess's birthday. I used to be really good at re-membering birthdays and special dates. I had been a thoughtful person before I had become an obsessive psychotic. I looked at the clock. It was six. We were meeting in two hours. Two hours is one hundred and twenty minutes, I thought. One hundred and twenty minutes is seventy-two hundred seconds. In the time it took me to calculate that, twenty seconds had elapsed. I sighed and closed my eyes. Maybe I could sleep now.

I couldn't. I was too tired to sleep. My bones were tired. I felt one hundred years old. Weary of everything. Lifeless. I wondered if I was having a nervous breakdown. Was this what it felt like? Did you just lie down and never get up? I thought about ringing James to tell him about the IVF failure, but I couldn't summon the en-ergy. Besides, all I did was tell him bad news or shout at him these days. I used to entertain him with funny stories about my day. I used to be witty and full of life. I used to make him laugh all the time. Now all I did was cry, shout or rant about the injustice of infertility. In fact, I couldn't remember the last time I had made him laugh with one of my stories or impressions. It was always him trying to cheer me up and I could see that the novelty was wearing off.

I wouldn't blame him if he left me. He had married a fun-loving, energetic, sassy fireball—a girl who loved to go out and have a good time, someone who lived every moment—and he had ended up after three short years with a certifiable, moan-a-minute drip. Something had to give. I couldn't go on like this. I couldn't put myself or my marriage through any more strain, not to mention my poor family. My mother bore the brunt of a lot of my anger and frustration, as did Babs. Although I wasn't so worried about Babs—she just ignored me or roared back. But my mother had suffered enough of my mood swings. It was time to make a decision. Did I really want to continue pumping myself full of drugs that made me utterly miserable? Did I want to spend the next God-knew-how-long hoping and praying every month for a miracle? Did I want to know exactly what day I was at in my cycle for another two years? It had to stop, and I was the only one who could control it.

But then what? If I stopped my treatment I'd be back to square one and I knew that if I did that and went back to "nature," no matter how much I pretended to myself that I wasn't trying to get pregnant I would still obsess about it. But if I decided to adopt, I would be involved in a process that would guarantee me a baby at the end. Unless, of course, the social worker thought I was an unfit parent. There was no use waiting for Imogen and Henry to die in a car crash and leave me the twins (actually I always saved Henry, but left him able to cope only with Thomas). No matter how much I fantasized about it, the likelihood of it happening was slim to none. So we'd adopt a baby from China or Cambodia like Angelina Jolie. It wouldn't be our flesh and blood. It wouldn't be a mini-me or a mini-James, but it would be a baby and we'd be helping the world. The problem was that when I had brought up the possibility of adoption with James, he had got a bit shifty and said we should keep trying ourselves. He hadn't seemed to like the idea. He'd not said as much, but he hadn't been very enthusiastic. What to do? I lay there and tried in vain to weigh up my options, but I was too weary to decide anything.

I looked at the clock—it was half seven. I had spent an hour and a half procrastinating on the couch and now I was going to be late. I hauled myself up and sat listlessly under the shower, sighing as if the cross of Calvary was welded to my back. I had to snap out of it. I tried to give myself a pep talk. "Come on, Emma, it's not that bad. You could have AIDS or no legs. Come on now." Fuck AIDS and fuck leglessness. I was sick of feeling guilty about being miserable. I'd allow myself to wallow for a few more minutes.

The shower perked me up enough to get dressed—albeit at the pace of a snail. I drove myself into town: I wanted to be able to leave early. I'd have a quick bite to eat, then crawl back into bed.

Lucy and Jess were there when I arrived. They were drinking champagne.

"There she is. Hi, Emma," said Lucy. "Hey, are you okay?"

"Uhm . . . yeah, why?"

"Your hair is soaking wet."

"What?" I said, feeling my hair, which had been dripping down my back, soaking my shirt. I had forgotten to dry it.

Lucy and Jess looked at me with concern.

"Sit down and have a drink, you look like you need one," said Lucy gently, leading me to my chair.

"Emma sweetheart," said Jess, holding my hand, "did you get bad news on the IVF?"

I nodded. They both welled up.

"Oh, Emma," said Lucy, hugging me.

"I'm so sorry," said Jess. "Look, I've been thinking, why don't I give you some of my eggs? I'd like to help. Honestly. The only thing I'm good at is making babies, so let me help."

I shook my head. "Thanks, Jess, but I'm not going to do it anymore. I don't know what I'm going to do, but no more IVF. It's horrible."

"Drink?" said Lucy.

I nodded. What the hell? I needed a drink. I needed to blot out the day. I downed the glass of champagne they put in front of me and held it out for a refill.

"What happened?" asked Lucy.

"Let's not talk about it. I'm not going to ruin Jess's birthday with my boring infertility. I'm sick of it myself. Tell me funny stories. Tell me gossip. I don't feel like talking. I want to listen to fluff tonight. Is that okay?"

"Absolutely fine," they said, and they proceeded to entertain me with all the stories they could think of. I drank and drank and drank. I nodded and I laughed and occasionally I spoke—but it was all a blur. I felt as if I were hovering above the table, looking down on the scene. Now and then I'd catch Jess and Lucy glancing at each other. They looked worried. I continued to drink—my hair eventually dried and my shirt did too.

Four hours later we stumbled into the pub next to the restaurant and sat up at the bar to order cocktails. It was my idea. I didn't want to go home until I knew I'd fall into a dreamless sleep. Tonight I wanted to forget who I was. But no matter how drunk I got, I still kept thinking, What am I going to do? How am I going to face tomorrow? I decided to order shots. As I was throwing a tequila slammer down my throat, I lost my balance and fell off the bar stool onto the marble floor, landing on my head. Finally, I thought—

Silence.

THIRTY-FOUR

I woke up three hours later in hospital with James by my side and a large white bandage 'round my head. We were in Accident and Emergency, and the smell of urine and vomit was nauseating. Drunks shouted at each other and a fight broke out in the corridor. We were behind a curtain in a tiny cubicle. I looked at James: he was a deathly shade of pale.

"You're all right, darling," he said, holding my hand. "You had a slight concussion and you cut your head so they had to bring you in for observation. How are you feeling?"

"I'm not pregnant, James. It didn't work," I said. The tears—missing earlier—were free-flowing now.

"I know. Lucy told me. Why didn't you call me?"

"I'm going to be thirty-five in six weeks. I am a thirty-four-and-three-quarter-year-old woman in hospital because I got so drunk that I fell off a bar stool and bashed my head. I'm such a loser. How did I end up here? What happened to me, James? I want to be old Emma. I want to be fun Emma. I want my life back. I want to be me again. I hate myself. I hate what I'm turning into," I said, sobbing.

"But you are you. You've just had a really difficult time lately. We're going to stop the IVF. You need a break, darling. It's been really tough on you."

"I'm sick of it, James. I'm sick of it and sick of me. It's so boring. I'm so boring. I'm sick of feeling like shit. I'm sick of being grumpy and mean. Don't you want us to be back to normal?"

"Of course I do. That's why I think you need to stop all the treatment. I hate seeing you upset. Let's just forget about children for a while."

"But I can't," I wailed. "I've tried to, I really have, but I can't stop obsessing. It just takes over, you can't control it. James, I think the only way to get my life back and still have children is to adopt."

James looked away. "Come on, darling, let's get you home. We'll talk about this tomorrow. Put your arm 'round my neck. There you go."

I was too tired to argue. I leaned against him as he gently lifted me off the bed and helped me out to the car.

The next morning, Mum called over to check up on me. "How are you, pet?" she asked.

"Not great."

"You've had a bad run. I'm sorry about the IVF."

"Thanks, me too."

"Well, Emma, getting drunk and falling over are not the solution."

"I'm aware of that."

"Your uncle Eddie's a drinker, so it's in the family. You need to be careful of that. These things can be hereditary, you know."

"I'm not an alcoholic."

"It creeps up on you and before you know it you're hooked. It's a slippery slope, Emma. It's especially easy to get addicted when you're down in the dumps. That's the worst time of all to be drinking. You're far better off out in the fresh air going for a nice walk."

"I'm not an alcoholic."

"Mark my words, young women your age are very susceptible to alcoholism. It's a dangerous age you're at. The best thing to do is keep away from it altogether."

"I'm not an alcoholic. I had a few drinks last night that went straight to my head because I'm an emotional wreck. I'm sitting here with a throbbing head, feeling really bad about everything, and I don't need you to rub it in."

"Snapping at people and aggressive behavior in general are some of the first symptoms of a problem drinker."

"Mum!"

"I'm not saying you are one, I'm just saying be careful. Anyway, how's James after last night?"

"He's fine. He's not the one who split his head open. In case you hadn't noticed that was me, your daughter, the person sitting opposite you right now."

"There's no need to be smart. The poor boy is worried sick about you. He's finding it hard too, Emma. Remember that."

"I know. I'm sorry for shouting at you. I just need some time to figure out what I'm going to do next, and having you telling me I'm on the cusp of being a wino isn't helping."

"I'm just worried about you. I think you need to stop taking all these hormones and get back to a normal life. Let nature take its course."

Over the next few days, I kept a low profile and thought long and hard about the future. What were we going to do? What was I going to do? I wanted to enjoy life again, not spend every hour of every day wondering where I was in my cycle, or silently praying that this time I'd be pregnant, and constantly feeling let down and depressed when I wasn't. It was time for a change. I had to move on to the next stage in my life.

The more I thought about adoption, the more it seemed like the perfect solution. I wouldn't have to take any more drugs, go for any more tests or endure any more horrible procedures. We'd just put our names down on a list, fill out a few forms and in a couple of months have a baby. I wouldn't have to go through pregnancy or labor. It was perfect. Why on earth hadn't I thought of this earlier? Not only would we have a baby, but I wouldn't have to spend nine months going to the loo every five minutes, swelling up like a balloon and then spend thirty-six hours huffing and puffing in a labor ward. My vagina would remain a normal size and I wouldn't have to hang out with other mothers from my antenatal classes and lie about having sex with my husband. And, speaking of sex, James and I would be able to get back to having a normal sex life! Oh my God, this was perfect. And on top of that we could adopt a baby from a war-torn country and save its life. The more I thought about it the better it got. Adoption was the solution to everything. Fantastic.

When James arrived home that night, I met him at the door with a bottle of champagne. "Welcome home, darling. I've got great news. We're going to adopt a poor baby from an orphanage in China or Brazil and give it a wonderful life. It's all going to be okay. Everything's going to be perfect. We're going to be great parents."

James sat down. He spoke slowly and deliberately. "It's certainly an option, but not as straightforward as you may think. There are lots of things to consider with adoption."

"Like what?" I asked, fully confident that I would be able to allay his every concern.

"What if the baby has AIDS or some hereditary disease we know nothing about? These orphanages don't give you a proper medical history. We could be biting off more than we can chew. You don't know anything about their families. The mother could have been a heroin addict and the baby might be too. It could be autistic . . . there are so many things that can go wrong. It's a very big leap of faith."

"Of course it is, but so is having a baby of your own. I'm sure Charles Manson's parents didn't think he'd turn into a savage killer, but he did. If we have a baby of our own it could get AIDS from a blood transfusion or become a drug addict when it's a teenager. You can never know what's going to happen. Adopting a child is a risk—a really scary risk—but if we love the child and give it a happy home, well, then, chances are they'll turn out all right. Your environment is what forms the person you turn into, not genetics."

"Not necessarily. You can inherit some pretty bad genes."

"Well, look at your mad uncle Harry, all his kids all turned out to be totally normal—humiliated by their father, but normal." I had an answer for everything. James's Uncle Harry, his father's elder brother, was a certifiable loon, who walked around his local village flashing at people. Mr. Hamilton had constantly to bail him out of the local police station. But Harry had three sons who were all totally normal and well balanced.

"True," said James, softening.

"Look, James, I know it's scary, but we'll just have to deal with problems as they arise. And we could go back to having a normal sex life. No more handstands. No more coming down to your office and sexually assaulting you in front of your boss. No more green tea. And you can masturbate as often and for as long as you like. Come on, James, it'll be great. I'll be me again."

He looked down at his hands. "It's not a decision to be taken lightly. We need to look into it properly before making up our minds. It's a big commitment. Let's just sleep on it."

"Fine, sleep on it all you like, but my mind is made up. This is the right thing for us. I have never been so sure of anything before in my life," I said, smiling at him as I put the champagne back into the fridge for a later date. Nothing was going to ruin my buzz. I hadn't felt this alive in months. I knew James would come 'round. I just needed to do some research and dazzle him with facts and figures. I'd do a power-point presentation if I had to. I went upstairs to log on to the Internet and gather my evidence.

While I was bouncing from adoption website to adoption website, I heard James on the phone.

"Hi, are you free for a pint? I need to pick your brain . . . yes, there's a first time for everything . . . say half an hour in Hogan's? . . . see you, then."

James came up and told me he was going to meet Donal for a drink. While he was in the shower, I called Lucy. "Hi, it's me," I whispered.

"Why are you whispering? Are you okay?"

"Fine, thanks. Look, James is meeting Donal for a pint to talk to him about adoption."

"Really?"

"Yeah. I want to adopt and James is a bit reticent so I think he's going to ask Donal about Annie and what it's like bringing up a child that isn't yours, blah-blah-blah. So you have to make sure he says all the right things. It's the perfect solution for us, Lucy. If we adopt we can get back to having a normal life again. But I want James to be as enthusiastic as I am."

"Okay, what do you want Donal to say? I'll have him word perfect for you."

"He has to say that it's great, and that although bringing up someone else's child is difficult, so is bringing up your own child. That things can go just as wrong for biological children as they can for adopted children. That after a while you forget the child is adopted and think of it as your own. That it's a great idea because it means I won't have to have any more horrible operations and tests and will be back to myself again. That James would be an amazing father and the adopted child would be blessed to come into our home. That it's a no-brainer and he has to go for it."

"No problem, I've jotted them all down."

"Gotta go, James is coming. Thanks, Lucy."

"Don't worry about a thing."

Two hours later James came in from the pub and pulled the bottle of champagne out of the fridge. Swaying slightly, he said, "Darling, I've just been talking to Donal about adoption. He said it's great, that although bringing up someone else's child is tough, so is bringing up your own child. He said things can go wrong for biological children as well as adopted children. That after a while you forget the child is adopted and think of it as your own. That it's a great idea because it means you won't have to go through any more nasty operations and tests and will be back to your jolly old self again. That I will be a great father and the adopted child would be lucky to come into our home . . . and what was the other thing Donal said Lucy wrote down for him to say?" He fished a crumpled piece of paper out of his coat pocket. "Oh, yes, that it's basically a no-brainer and we should go for it," he said, winking at me.

"Well, was he persuasive at least?" I asked sheepishly.

"Yes, very."

"You see?" I said, beaming at him. "I told you it was the right thing to do. I knew you just needed a little extra persuasion. And wait till I tell you about the fantastic website I found called 'Famous and Remarkable Adoptees,' which lists all the amazing people who've been adopted. Ella Fitzgerald and Richard Burton and Marilyn Monroe—and, oh, yeah, Moses. He was adopted by the Princess of Egypt and look how well he turned out. And other people like, uhm . . ."

James came over and kissed me. He was smiling. "Well, if it was good enough for the Princess of Egypt, it's good enough for me."

The Baby Trail

Sinead Moriarty

Readers Club Guide

Questions for Discussion

1. Why do you think Emma wants to have a baby? She resolves to get pregnant at New Years, saying, "It was high time I had a baby. I was thirty-three and although I may have felt—and, truth be told, behaved—like I was twenty-five, it was time to knuckle down and get up the duff" (3). It sounds as though she wants to have a baby because she feels as though she should, and that's not hard to believe, given the incredible amount of pressure she picks up from her social circle to have kids. Still, there are other moments, holding her goddaughter, for instance, when even observers can tell she's feeling "broody." What compels her to undergo all the painful medical treatments and devote her life to baby-making?

2. How does Emma's character change over the course of the novel? She says of herself, "I had been a thoughtful person before I had become an obsessive psychotic" (296). Do you think Emma's appraisal of her behavior is fair? While her mum thinks she's been tough to take, James doesn't seem to think she's lost her character. He says, "But you are you. You've just had a really difficult time lately" (301). Do you think Emma's behavior crosses the line during her treatments, or would any woman who wants a baby that badly act similarly?

3. Were you surprised when Emma decided not to continue with IVF? What do you think the final straw was? Had she lost her faith in modern medicine? Was she tired of waiting? Did she feel that the treatments were unhealthy?

4. Adoption seems like the perfect solution for Emma, who desperately wants a child but can no longer handle the invasive medical procedures. James, however, has some qualms. He's afraid that their adopted child might bring unforeseen complications

into their lives. Do you think James has valid concerns? Were Emma's counterarguments convincing? Can an adopted child be a true substitute for a biological one?

5. In Emma's world, it is almost universally assumed that a woman will want to have children. Emma says this even of Lucy, her exceptionally career-oriented friend: "She wants to meet a guy, settle down and have a family" (44). The lone hold-out is Amanda Nolan, who regularly tries to persuade Emma not to have kids. Emma says, "I liked her for being different: it made a nice change from hearing and reading that you're not complete as a person until you have a child" (146). Do you think this attitude is as uncommon in general as it seems to be in Emma's world? Do you think there are more Amandas out there than there used to be? Or more Lucys? Does it surprise you that "modern" women, such as we see in this novel, have such traditional desires?

6. Emma isn't shy about sharing her opinions, and she is clearly her mother's daughter in this regard. On many topics, Emma and her mother hold polar opposite positions. Emma's mom thinks Emma rushed to the doctor when she had trouble getting pregnant; Emma thinks having more information can only help. Emma's mother thinks Babs will shame the family name with her use of "hard" drugs; Emma accepts Ecstasy from her younger sibling and dances the night away. Do you think their differences in opinion can be attributed to the generation they grew up in? Are either Emma or her mother right or wrong about any of the topics they disagree on?

7. According to Emma's version of events, James has very little to do with deciding whether they will try for having a family. When Emma tells him she is ready to try for a baby, "He seemed pleased—if a little surprised that I was feeling broody as I'd rough-handled his nephew over the Christmas holidays" (3). The two of them agree that Emma will be a good mother, but neither of them

comment on whether James will make a good father. Do you think James is as invested in having a family as Emma is? Does she expect him to be, or is it assumed that the family is her domain?

8. After Emma plans their anniversary trip to Lourdes, she tells the unenthusiastic James, "I'll go on my own. Just like I go to all my appointments on my own. Just like I take the drugs on my own. Just like I get the bad results on my own" (260). Do you think James is unsupportive of Emma? Does he grow more or less supportive over the course of Emma's treatments? Is there any way he could have shared the stress of her experiences more fully or can he, as a man, never really understand?

9. During a night out to celebrate Lucy's recent promotion, Jess reveals that she is pregnant with her second child. Instead of being excited, as Emma would be if she discovered she was pregnant, Jess is depressed. Being a mom isn't all she thought it would be. Jess and Lucy argue over who has it worse: the new mom or the single girl. Do you think either of them won this argument? Why do each of them assume that the other has it so good? Emma is reluctant to believe new motherhood can be all that bad—why do you think she assumes that she'll fare better than Jess?

10. Emma goes through a frightening array of medical treatments over the course of the novel. Were you surprised by the amount of pain, expense, and stress she has to undergo in order to get help for infertility? By the end of the novel, she has very little faith in her doctors, who tend to assume that she'll have little trouble getting pregnant and that the treatments will not be painful. How do these assumptions make things more difficult for Emma? How could medical staff be more considerate of women struggling with infertility?

11. During her treatments, Emma rarely discusses her troubles with friends and family, like Imogen, who tend to assume that since she is not pregnant she must not be trying. How do these

assumptions weigh on Emma's mind? When people assume that she hasn't been trying to get pregnant, why doesn't she correct them and share her story? What would it mean for her to admit that she's had trouble getting pregnant? How might people's assumptions on this topic demonstrate the way culture holds women responsible for all aspects of pregnancy and child bearing?

12. Late in the story, Emma talks to a couple of people who can empathize with her. Mrs. Curran and Policeman Mooney both know what it is like to have trouble with child bearing. What do you think these conversations mean to Emma? How do they help her come to terms with her troubles?

13. Throughout the hard times, as Emma tries to keep everything in perspective, her chief support is her sense of humor. What did you think were the funniest scenes in the book? How does Emma's sense of humor reveal the absurdity in her own behavior, her relationship with James, and the medical treatment she received?